PRAISE FOR *PURPOSEFUL EMPATHY: TAPPING OUR HIDDEN SUPERPOWER FOR PERSONAL, ORGANIZATIONAL, AND SOCIAL CHANGE*

"Anita Nowak has achieved something rare: she inspires soul-searching and action without sounding preachy. *Purposeful Empathy* should be on every socially conscious leader's reading list."

—John Wood, founder of Room to Read and U-Go, and author of *Purpose, Incorporated*

"I've been saying for decades that humanity is on a collision course and must become more empathic to save our civilization. In this splendid book, Anita Nowak explains why each of us stands to benefit by flexing our empathy muscles. What are we waiting for?"

—Paul R. Ehrlich, PhD, Bing Professor of Population Studies, emeritus, and president of the Center for Conservation Biology at Stanford University, and author of *Humanity on a Tightrope*

"Whether you're an artist, educator, activist, or entrepreneur, if you care about the well-being of others—and achieving great results at the same time—you must read this book."

—Maria Ross, brand strategist and author of *The Empathy Edge*

"Reading *Purposeful Empathy* is like attending a wellness retreat and leadership masterclass at the same time. Do yourself a favor and read it."

—Derek Sivers, founder of CD Baby and author of *Anything You Want*

"*Purposeful Empathy* is a necessary book for our time."

—Edwin Rutsch, founding director of the Center for Building a Culture of Empathy

"*Purposeful Empathy* debunks the myth that empathy is a soft skill. Anita Nowak has written a definitive guide to empathic leadership and culture. I recommend this book with a five-star approval."

—Paul L. Gunn Jr., founder and CEO of KUOG and author of *Success the Right Way*

"Anita Nowak's work is thoughtfully designed to help guide readers toward true, action-oriented changemaking. If you want to contribute to a better, brighter future, *Purposeful Empathy* is required reading."

—Michael Ventura, advisor and author of *Applied Empathy*

"Anita Nowak's passion and relentless work toward building empathy in our world is inspiring. Her book *Purposeful Empathy* is a great example."

—Elif M. Gokcigdem, PhD, founder of Organization of Networks for Empathy and author of *Designing for Empathy*

"For the latest on empathy research and why every child, adult, family, teacher, business, and community can benefit from improved social-emotional skills, look no further than Anita Nowak's *Purposeful Empathy*."

—Lynne Azarchi, director of Kidsbridge Youth Center and author of *The Empathy Advantage*

"*Purposeful Empathy* is beautifully written. Through compelling stories and thought-provoking exercises, Anita Nowak makes practicing empathy accessible, inviting, and rewarding."

—Katharine Manning, president of Blackbird DC and author of *The Empathetic Workplace*

"In *Purposeful Empathy*, Anita Nowak has done a masterful job bringing the reader on a journey that makes the complex seem easy, the intangible feel real, and delivers a dose of courage to make the world a better place."

—Rob Volpe, CEO of Ignite 360 and author of *Tell Me More About That*

"Anita Nowak offers a blueprint for business leaders hoping to create a thriving workplace culture, a how-to for parents hoping to be positive role models for their children, and a call to arms for anyone seeking to make the world a better place."

—Minter Dial, speaker, podcaster, and
author of *Heartificial Empathy*

"*Purposeful Empathy* validates our fears about what's going wrong in our lives and in the world, but then shows us how to be part of the solution—without burning out."

—Kaitlin Ugolik Phillips, author of *The Future of Feeling*

"One of the most important books of our time on the vital role that empathy plays in leading with purpose."

—April Adams-Redmond, chief marketing officer,
Unilever / Pepsi Joint Venture

"Changemaking is tough work that requires grit, collaboration, and, above (and beneath it) all, empathy. *Purposeful Empathy* is the unambiguous call to action we need to bring about a more just and sustainable world."

—Barb Steele, executive director, Ashoka Canada

PURPOSEFUL EMPATHY

PURPOSEFUL EMPATHY

Tapping Our Hidden Superpower
for Personal, Organizational, and
Social Change

ANITA NOWAK, PhD

Broadleaf Books
Minneapolis

PURPOSEFUL EMPATHY
Tapping Our Hidden Superpower for Personal, Organizational, and Social Change

Cover design by Jay Smith—Juicebox Designs

Print ISBN: 978-1-5064-8505-8
eBook ISBN: 978-1-5064-8510-2

As an educator, I dedicate this book
to all those who have taught me to be a better human being:
my mom, who taught me about kindness,
my dad, who taught me about courage,
my sisters, who taught me about resilience,
Juls, Deb, Sue, and Care, who taught me about friendship,
Tullio, who taught me about generosity,
Bruno, who taught me about self-awareness,
Jim, who taught me to believe in myself,
all my students, who taught me about co-creation,
Giorgi, who taught me that dreams come true,
and Annika, who taught me that miracles happen.

CONTENTS

CONTENTS

FOREWORD

by Nobel Laureate Dr. Muhammad Yunus

In May 2016, I held my friend Anita's ten-day-old baby in my arms. Very few experiences surpass the feeling of gazing at an infant, knowing you're holding the future in your hands. It reminded me how I felt cradling my grandson for the first time. From that moment onward, it was impossible to think about tomorrow without imagining him in it.

Collectively, we face enormous social and environmental threats. Challenges that all our grandchildren will inherit. That's why it's our responsibility as citizens and leaders to consider these two crucial questions: How did we get into this mess? And more importantly, how do we get out?

It's clear that our bedrock systems are failing. For example, the market economy, which unleashed unprecedented prosperity across the globe, is now in direct conflict with sustainability and social good, serving the interests of the privileged few at the expense of the disenfranchised many. That's why we need to redesign economics as a social science.

Thankfully, transformation is already underway, driven by a different set of human values. And innovations like social business give expression to our inherent altruism.

In the same spirit, *Purposeful Empathy* is a timely and inspiring read that carries an important message—one that aligns with my vision for a better world, animated by mutual care, respect, cooperation, and solidarity.

I urge you to read Anita Nowak's debut book *Purposeful Empathy*. It will swing you from cynicism to hope, from selfishness to selflessness, and from apathy to action.

PREFACE

I've written this book to satisfy five goals. The teacher in me wants to share what I have learned about empathy over the past fifteen years. The coach in me wants to inspire you to live your best life. The rebel in me wants to shatter systems of oppression and injustice. The spiritual seeker in me wants to align with my calling. And the mother in me wants to protect and nurture our children. Here's the backstory.

In college, I dreamed of being a hotshot advertising executive, but after watching one particular documentary at a film festival, the earth began rotating on a new axis for me. In 1995, the United Nations hosted a five-day human rights conference, one day of which was devoted to women's human rights. Delegates from across the globe gathered to testify about the plight of women in their countries. The film, *The Vienna Tribunal,* was a compilation of excerpts from those testimonials. I remember sitting in the theater gobsmacked. I'd never heard of female genital cutting before. Or women being stoned to death. Or prepubescent girls being trafficked as sex slaves. I left the theater in rage about gender-based violence, and the idea of ascending to a C-suite job instantly lost its allure.

Pre-film, I was a bona fide material girl. Post-film, I was a nascent social justice warrior. I plunged into women's studies, made my way through the canon of feminist texts, and shed an uninformed worldview the way a snake loses its skin. I trained as a volunteer for a crisis line, taking anonymous calls from survivors of rape and sexual abuse. I even completed a master's thesis devoted to deconstructing the representation of women in advertising from a critical feminist perspective.

To be clear, it was painful to learn about the real-life consequences of misogyny in our world, but I was lit up by the idea we could smash the patriarchy. That's why I sincerely believe that film was a nudge from the universe to help me align with my truth.

A decade later, my ears were on fire. A woman on stage had just issued a call to action to seven hundred people in the audience, but I felt she was talking directly to me. Esther Mujawayo, a Rwandan genocide survivor, had been invited to speak at the *Global Conference on the Prevention of Genocide* at McGill, the university where I teach. At the beginning of her talk, she projected a photograph onto a jumbotron. "You see these forty members of my extended family gathered for a celebration?" she asked. "Only my three daughters and I survived." Silence filled the auditorium. "I hear all the time you're sorry for having failed us with your collective inaction. And I want to forgive you. But it's not easy because you continue to fail us. Everywhere on the planet people are suffering. Surely you can do more."

Martin Luther King Jr. asked, "Life's most persistent and urgent question is, what are you doing for others?" Yes, I worked in the nonprofit sector. Yes, I volunteered. And yes, I donated to good causes. But could I dig a little deeper and do a little more? Of course I could. That's why I believe that Esther's rebuke was my second nudge from the universe.

Two years later, I landed in the country of a thousand hills. The vista was breathtakingly beautiful, but the bursts of colorful wildflowers made it nearly impossible to reconcile the scale of evil that had taken place amid those peaks and valleys. It was especially surreal to drive past the hotel that acted as the UN headquarters during the so-called peacekeeping efforts, which saw nearly one million people slaughtered within a matter of weeks.

My sister Helen and I worked in the capital city of Kigali as volunteers with Tubahumerize, an NGO dedicated to providing trauma counseling and vocational training to approximately four hundred women. All had lost family members, many had contracted AIDS through *genocidaire* rape, few had formal education, and most lived in absolute poverty. They were among the most vulnerable women on the planet—and the most resilient.

Helen and I hadn't planned on shooting video testimonials, but it quickly became clear that survivors wanted to share their stories and have their experiences documented. This included a man who had taken refuge with his family in a church and watched in horror as his wife and seven children were massacred by machete. Miraculously, he'd managed to escape the same fate by running thirty miles barefoot to a friend's home. He hid under their kitchen floorboards for three months, surviving without eating, drinking, or moving, sometimes for days at a stretch—tormented relentlessly by nightmares.

After hearing his account, neither of us could eat, sleep, or talk for more than a day. His anguish was inconceivable. I kept asking myself, *How could neighbors and friends turn against one another with such cold-blooded inhumanity?*

Two nights before my departure, I had a breakdown. I'd desperately wanted to heed Esther's call to action. Instead, I felt like a genocide tourist, mortified by my hubris that I would somehow make a difference. I was also incensed by the magnitude of injustice and agonized about going home and carrying on with life, knowing that so many would continue to suffer. By then I knew I would never become a humanitarian, but I couldn't shake the feeling that I needed to do *something*.

A few months earlier while preparing for my trip, Michael, my thesis adviser had requested a meeting. After exchanging pleasantries and telling him about my summer plans, he said, "Anita, we've known each other four years, so I'll be straight with you. I don't think you'll graduate unless you change your topic." I was speechless. "I bet you have a box or drawer that you use to stash random stuff," he continued. "Go home and explore what's there. That's how you'll discover your passion." I left his office livid.

Two weeks later, I discovered a legal-size folder in my filing cabinet marked "miscellaneous." I emptied the contents across my dining room table; they included ticket stubs from speaking events and yellowed newspaper clippings. That's when it clicked. Without conscious awareness, I was naturally drawn to people trying to change the world.

Michael was right about discovering my true passion, and the focus of my PhD thesis pivoted accordingly. My obsession became: how can I inspire the next generation of changemakers? To that end, I interviewed dozens of social entrepreneurs to learn what they had in common. My data revealed a simple and elegant answer: empathy inspired them into action. That insight continues to animate all the work I do.

For more than a decade, I have been singularly focused on how to leverage empathy on purpose. I've developed courses and programming at McGill to teach and mentor the next generation of social innovators. And as a certified coach, I help organizations and leadership teams create cultures of empathy; I also advise high-net-worth families how to translate their philanthropic goals into social impact.

As with my experiences with *The Vienna Tribunal* and Esther Mujawayo, I believe Michael was put on my path on purpose—and for that I'll always be grateful. Back in the day when I was gunning for the C-suite, I was seeking something outside of myself. Had I followed that route I might have been better off materially, but spiritually, there is no comparison. Today, I'm a happier, healthier, and kinder person thanks to the choices I've been nudged by the universe to make.

Over the years, I have learned to center empathy in my life. I've become a pescatarian, I steer away from fast fashion, I take my daughter to protest marches, and I vote for political parties that put a premium on women, children, peace, and the environment.

It hasn't been easy going against the grain. I'm a middle-aged woman who still doesn't own a home. I have often lived from paycheck to paycheck and I'm sure many of my life choices have been judged by some family members and friends. That's never an easy pill to swallow. Perhaps toughest of all is knowing that I rub some good people the wrong way by unintentionally triggering some cognitive dissonance. My guess is that they may be ignoring their nudges, perhaps afraid of what change might entail or what other people will think.

But here's what I know for sure: Those nudges from the universe are sacred clues. Sometimes they come in the form of a movie. Other times, a global pandemic. It's only by paying close attention to what they're trying to tell us that can we discover our true path of purpose. So the next time you hear the universe whisper, give yourself permission to listen. You might even consider *asking* for a nudge.

If you want to know what I hope you'll get from reading this book, the answer is simple: an a-ha moment when you realize that *this* is the sign you've been waiting for.

INTRODUCTION

Empathy is the only human superpower—it can shrink distance, cut through social and power hierarchies, transcend differences, and provoke political and social change.

—Elizabeth Thomas

Empathy is the most powerful emotional force in the world, second only to love—especially when it's wielded on purpose. When our natural capacity to empathize is summoned into action on behalf of others, two things happen: the recipient benefits and so does the empathic actor. To our brains, empathy in action is as rewarding as good sex and the high of psychedelic drugs. It increases our dopamine, reduces our stress, boosts our self-esteem, heightens our immune system, enriches our relationships, and even improves our key performance indicators at work.

Did you know:
- The top-ten most empathic companies generated 50 percent more earnings.
- You're less likely to have a heart attack if you regularly help others.
- Children are more likely to succeed in life if they volunteer.

That's why empathy is our superpower. And it is finally getting the recognition it deserves. In fact, lately empathy has become a business buzzword. Nearly

1

every week, a new study affirms that empathic leadership, cultures, and workplaces help organizations overcome crises, facilitate equity, diversity, and inclusion (EDI) strategies, provide psychological safety, bolster mental health, and drive recruitment, engagement, and retention. Empathy is central to design thinking. And according to Forbes, sometimes the acronym CEO now refers to "chief empathy officer." Artificial empathy is driving affective computing, tele-empathy is disrupting healthcare, and videogames using virtual empathy are expected to help grow the metaverse. Given all its applications, it's a mystery that it took corporate America so long to catch on.

According to research, most employees would work longer hours and even take a pay cut if they felt their employer cared about them. In addition, they believe organizational empathy decreases turnover and drives productivity. Despite this, under half of workers rate their workplaces as empathic. Many CEOs believe empathy drives better business outcomes too, but nearly seven in ten fear they'd be less respected if they showed it at work.

The good news is we can practice empathy to help our organizations succeed and humanity thrive—all while simultaneously reaping personal rewards. That's what *Purposeful Empathy* is about. Instead of bogeyman tales of "otherness" that sow division and hatred, this book celebrates our innate goodness and interdependence. Through inspiring stories; interviews with experts including neuroscientists, social entrepreneurs, and spiritual and business leaders; the introduction of a new self-development tool rooted in positive psychology and coaching; and purposeful empathy practices at the end of each chapter, this book offers wisdom and practical advice to foster personal, organizational, and social transformation.

It's also an invitation to join the biggest social movement humanity has ever known: a revolution aimed at raising global empathic consciousness and then converting it into collective empathic action. Skeptical? Let me explain.

OUR MASSIVE EMPATHY DEFICIT

Liberal democracies are splintering as political polarization grows. Predatory capitalism is on a collision course with life on the planet. And inequality between the rich and poor is getting worse every day. It's so overwhelming and anxiety-provoking that sometimes we feel we may as well hoist a white flag and call it a day. Which is what plenty of us do—but not everyone. Today, an inclusive, intersectional, global coalition of empathy warriors is forming, transcending generations and geography, demanding positive change in the world. Millions are railing against systemic racism and poverty while also fighting for sustainability, food security, and accessible housing, healthcare, and education. That said, until purposeful empathy has become more of a global priority, there's still plenty of work to do.

According to the World Food Program, one in nine people on the planet is hungry or undernourished—despite one-third of food produced for humans going to waste. A few years ago, experts calculated that an extra eleven billion dollars per year of public spending until 2030 could end world hunger. Sadly, no such public spending occurred because of the 2008 economic crisis, during which over one trillion taxpayer dollars were used by the twenty richest nations to stabilize the global financial system.

The World Health Organization reports that nearly two billion people have no basic sanitation facilities like toilets or latrines, and at least ten percent of humanity consumes food irrigated by wastewater. Meanwhile, one in three people lack access to safe drinking water, partially explaining why 1.6 million people die from diarrheal disease every year, one-third of whom are children under five years. Finally, as the planet's population grows by eighty million per year, so, too, does the demand for freshwater—at the mindboggling rate of sixty-four billion cubic meters per year, equivalent to nearly three thousand Olympic-size swimming pools *per hour*.

Tragically, enslavement is not a thing of the past. It's estimated that twenty-five million people are living as modern-day slaves. That's more than the population of Australia. Hundreds of thousands of kids also serve as child soldiers. According to the International Labour Organization, bonded labor and human trafficking is the world's third-biggest organized crime and has one of the biggest profit margins of any industry in the world.

Oxfam International reports that today's ten richest billionaires have six times more wealth than the poorest 3.1 billion people on the planet. "If these ten men were to lose 99.999 percent of their wealth tomorrow," says their executive director Gabriela Bucher, "they would still be richer than 99 percent of all the people on this planet." The thousand richest people in the world recouped their pandemic losses within nine months, while experts calculate it could take more than a decade for the world's poorest to recover from the economic impacts of the virus—hurting women disproportionately.

Even those who benefit most from our economic system are suffering. Consider this: the rate of depression in industrialized countries is doubling each generation. Thirty years ago, the average age for the onset of depression was thirty. Today, it's fourteen. Lest we forget all the other afflictions normalized by "advanced nations," including homelessness, mass shootings, drug overdoses, and eco-anxiety, the last being so widespread among young adults that the idea of having kids is increasingly considered reckless.

But who could blame them? Global temperatures are on track to rise 10°F over the next century, one million plant and animal species face extinction, and millions of people are expected to become climate refugees. What kind of species destroys its own habitat and jeopardizes the lives of its progeny? A species that has forgotten to practice empathy.

EMPATHIC BY NATURE

Some argue we got here thanks to our selfish human nature. Is that true? In Darwin's *Descent of Man*, he mentions "survival of the fittest" only twice but speaks of love ninety-five times. Meanwhile, Adam Smith, famous for having popularized the merits of self-interest, also extolled the virtues of "others-interest" in *The Theory of Moral Sentiments*, a work lauded as one of the most comprehensive empathy-based moral theories in the Western canon. Still, our society treats altruism as exceptional or suspect.

According to Dutch primatologist Frans de Waal, author of *The Age of Empathy: Nature's Lessons for a Kinder Society*, our understanding of human nature is fundamentally flawed because research has focused almost exclusively on chimpanzees, who are known to be aggressive, hostile to outgroups, and prone to egregious acts of violence, including cannibalism and infanticide. De Waal believes our concept of what it means to be human would be entirely different if we had spent the last fifty years studying bonobos instead. Unlike their primate cousins, bonobos are naturally nurturing, playful, cooperative, and egalitarian. They even use sex to promote social bonding—they literally make love, not war.

Homo sapiens share 98.7 percent DNA in common with bonobos. We also share a similar amount of DNA with chimpanzees. In fact, we share more DNA in common with chimps *and* bonobos than they share with each other. So while humans have quite a few chimp-like tendencies, we're also remarkably like bonobos. This means we can't blame our selfish genes for the mess we're in. Instead, we must take a long, hard look in the mirror and hold ourselves to greater account.

We must also flex our empathy muscles, but that's becoming increasingly difficult to do in a world that primes us *not* to care. Once upon a time, we lived our entire lives in small clans with close relationships. That's how our proclivity for empathy grew. According to Stanford research psychologist Jamil Zaki, humans developed larger eye whites than other primates (among other physiological traits) to easily track one another's gaze, and intricate facial muscles to better express our emotions. Back then, if we didn't empathize, we were ousted by our clan and left to die alone.

Today, we live solo lives *by design*. Even pre-COVID-19, social isolation was baked into our culture. Nearly a third of US households are inhabited by just one person, which comes at a very high personal cost. Research tells us that people who experience long periods of loneliness develop serious health problems including cardiovascular disease and dementia at much higher rates than people who don't feel isolated.

To make matters worse, our sympathetic nervous system is perpetually exposed to a diet of 24/7 stimuli with the dictum "When it bleeds, it leads." Seeing so much pain and suffering every day can cause apathy, depression, and anxiety. No wonder psychologist John F. Schumaker concluded, "Never before has a cultural system inculcated its followers to suppress so much of their humanity."

CALLING 911

Are you concerned about the direction the world is heading and that we're running out of time to get things right? Does anxiety about global geopolitics and the next election cycle keep you up at night? Has presenteeism invaded your workplace, abducted your colleagues and direct reports, and dragged down productivity, innovation, and engagement? Have you started to notice the common thread among racism, climate change, wealth inequality, mental illness, addiction, and loneliness? Are you beginning to connect the dots between the shitstorm happening *out there* and the one going on *in here*? If so, this book is for you.

Seven issues require our urgent attention.

Predatory capitalism has created abhorrent wealth inequality and is fundamentally at odds with planetary boundaries. It's hard to fathom, but of the top hundred global economic entities, sixty-nine are now corporations. A system once celebrated for "lifting all boats" has become degenerate in its asymmetry. If we care about humanity and life on our planet, we must seek alternative economic approaches animated by a new set of values, including empathy.

Our social fabric is in tatters thanks to crippling polarization. A robust democracy always includes discord, but today's divisions run dangerously deep. In a zero-sum game, voters loathe their opponents, fomenting the potential for violence. To avoid that outcome, we must exercise empathy to restore mutual respect and common ground.

Our mental health is also under siege. Five years ago, the world's first *minister of loneliness* was appointed by the United Kingdom. Now, in the aftermath of COVID-19 and mass social distancing, the rates of chronic anxiety, addiction, depression, self-harm, mental illness, domestic violence, and suicide have risen everywhere. Despite our 24/7 digital connectivity, we are desperate for human connection and a sense of belonging and we need more empathy to transcend the era of social isolation.

Our ethos of materialism and consumerism worsened by our addiction to social media and hollow celebrity culture is making us more selfish, eroding our self-worth and harming our mental health. We human beings suffer without meaning in our lives. In response, we must turn inward to reflect deeply on our values and purpose and ignite a cultural renaissance of brotherly and sisterly love rooted in empathy.

Our Western bias toward science, objectivity and linear thinking is limiting our capacity to problem-solve. Neuroscience has revealed that our brains have an analytical network for critical thinking *and* a social network for empathy and moral reasoning. To address our wicked problems, we must engage both sides of our brains holistically and embrace alternative ways of knowing. This includes tapping into embodied, metaphysical and spiritual wisdom. Indigenous cultures have much to teach us in this regard.

Society's dated model of leadership fails to grasp that organizations are living systems. Most corporate leaders are hopelessly out of touch with their workforces, and the "old, stale, male" paradigm of command and control must be replaced by conscious leadership that's inclusive, generative, and empathic.

Finally, sexism, systemic racism, and other forms of discrimination continue to run rampant. To be clear, misogyny and white supremacy harm women and people of color the most, but wherever oppression lives, so, too, does an insidious form of social cancer. Humans cannot flourish at the expense of one another. Only unjust systems make that so. We must decolonize our hearts and minds. That's why empathy, which unites us in our shared humanity, holds so much promise.

I don't pretend to have solutions to the biggest problems we face today, but thanks to my doctoral research and a couple of decades doing impact work, here's what I know for sure: The world needs more empathy. Humans need empathy to thrive. Everyone is capable of empathy. And sustained purposeful empathy can elevate our lives as we change the world.

IN THIS BOOK

This is a hopeful book that argues that a better future lies ahead providing that we flex our empathy muscles.

Chapter 1 celebrates the power and potential of empathy. It also addresses its limits, which sets the stage for an emphasis on *purposeful* empathy.

Chapter 2 is dedicated to the fascinating and cutting-edge neuroscience of empathy, research into which has proven that humans are wired for altruism.

In chapter 3, I introduce my purposeful empathy diagram and describe how it offers a path beyond self-actualization to self-transcendence.

Chapter 4 showcases seven empathy-training initiatives that demonstrate we can all become more empathic with practice.

Chapter 5 celebrates five businesses and one nonprofit organization that exemplify empathic leadership and/or culture in the workplace.

Chapter 6 considers if and how new technology is affecting our natural capacity to empathize, and what we can do about tech's negative impacts.

In chapter 7, I argue that purposeful empathy is a profoundly spiritual *and* political undertaking and that coupling empathic consciousness with social action is the best way to achieve social change.

Chapter 8 explores families and groups as sites for empathic action and explores the benefits and advantages of communities of empathic practice.

Chapter 9 highlights the Herculean empathy efforts undertaken by healthcare providers, educators, humanitarians, and other caring professionals.

And in chapter 10, I explain why practicing self-empathy is so important and I offer six pathways to sustainable purposeful empathy that simultaneously allow us to flourish.

Perhaps you want to repair a relationship with a neighbor, become a more conscious consumer, or just *do something* in the face of dark and dispiriting days. Perhaps you want your company to take environmental, social, and governance (ESG) issues more seriously to feel a heightened alignment with your personal values. Maybe you're already a seasoned environmentalist or a devoted political activist. It doesn't matter. If you can envision a world of peace, justice, sustainability, and shared prosperity, you are welcome to the empathy revolution.

PART I

1

I EMPATHIZE, THEREFORE I AM

Empathy makes us human.

—Daniel Pink

At one of Montreal's finest hospitals, there's a special team of volunteers trained to cuddle newborn babies when their mothers are recovering from a complication at birth. Nevine Fateen, who was responsible for recruiting and training those volunteers, believed they were all minor saints. After hearing some of their stories, I understand why.

One day, a twentysomething-year-old woman went into cardiac arrest during labor and miraculously survived. A few hours later, she had a second arrest. Again, she made it through. Sadly, a third arrest took her life, and her beautiful baby was born brain-dead. Normally, under those circumstances, the newborn would have been placed in an incubator to die. Instead, a volunteer cuddler was summoned to rock the baby until its final breath.

"It was a tall order," Nadine admits. "But I found a volunteer as tough as nails who cuddled the infant tenderly in her arms for over two hours until it passed. Then she had a long, hard cry. A week later, she told me, 'If you ever need a cuddler for a situation like that again, you can always count on me.' Her compassion and resilience still give me goosebumps. Not long after, she was diagnosed with terminal cancer and asked me to find a couple of volunteers to sit with her in silence once in a while. With tears welling up in her eyes, she whispered, 'Now I'm the one who doesn't want to die alone.'"

If that story pulled at your heartstrings, you were touched by empathy—the innate trait that unites us in our shared humanity. Nearly four centuries ago, Descartes declared, "I think, therefore I am." It's a compelling notion that has endured to the present day. But humans don't experience the world as thinkers only. We feel a kaleidoscope of sensations and emotions throughout our lives. Those common feelings are the glue that binds us. In other words, it's our capacity to empathize that best characterizes the human condition. When we imagine or sense what someone else is feeling, we transcend "otherness." That's what makes empathy our superpower.

I'm not alone in having reached this conclusion. Philosophers, mystics, and sages have been saying it for millennia. Psychologists and social scientists have concurred for decades. And most recently, neuroscientists have been celebrating its power. When I ask my students or an audience to tell me what empathy means to them, they typically say one of three things: stepping into someone else's shoes, seeing through someone else's eyes, or feeling what someone else is feeling. All of these are perfectly reasonable responses, but they miss something significant. As President Obama put it, "Empathy is a quality of character that can change the world." With that in mind, this chapter explores seven important things to know about empathy.

THE CONCEPT OF EMPATHY HAS A LONG HISTORY

The word *empathy* made its English debut in 1908, but the notion has been contemplated by thinkers throughout the ages. More than two thousand years ago, Confucian scholar Mengzi wrote, "No man is devoid of a heart sensitive to the suffering of others." Similarly, in the thirteenth century, Italian theologian Thomas Aquinas affirmed, "The compassion we feel in our hearts for another person's misery . . . drives us to do what we can to help him."

By the mid-1800s, the concept of empathy took on a new meaning. It began with Friedrich Vischer, a German poet and political activist who rejected the idea that art could be critiqued objectively—the dominant belief at the time. Instead, he saw art interpretation as entirely subjective. His son

Robert agreed and introduced the German word *einfühlung* ("feeling into") in his 1873 doctoral thesis to describe the emotional response we have to works of art. The concept quickly found favor among psychologists exploring the phenomenological impact of art on observers at the time. Three decades later, American psychologist Edward Titchener translated *einfühlung* into the English word *empathy*, derived from the Ancient Greek ἐμπάθεια (*empatheia*). The word has stuck ever since.

EMPATHY AS *FEELING* AND EMPATHY AS *KNOWING* ARE BOTH IMPORTANT

By the late 1940s, empathy was a *cause célèbre* within psychology circles—albeit across two distinct research tracks. Some argued that empathy meant cognitive awareness of another person's internal states. Others viewed empathy as a natural emotional response to stimuli. This bifurcation became known as the affective-cognitive axis.

Today, cognitive empathy refers to our intellectual capacity to imagine what someone else is feeling or projecting how we would feel in their place. In a nutshell, it involves perspective-taking and is under our control. When we listen to a friend share a poignant story and draw inferences about what they're saying, we're engaged in cognitive empathy. Scientists believe this is an advanced neural skill because it requires both conscious effort and the capacity to understand one's inherently separate self.

Affective empathy, on the other hand, refers to emotional resonance, triggered spontaneously by our network of mirror neurons. Think of laughter or fear spreading quickly through a group of people. When I give public talks about empathy, I usually do an experiment with my audience to bring this to life. I project an image of a child beaming with joy and share what I see: a bunch of smiling faces looking back at the screen. That's because it's nearly impossible to see an image of a kid blissing out and not feel a little warmth wash over. In stark juxtaposition, I project a second image of a child in despair, like the haunting image of a Syrian boy sitting in an ambulance covered in dust and blood. Inevitably, everyone's smiles disappear. That's affective empathy at work.

Today, thanks to pioneering neuroscience, we know that empathy is a meta-concept with cognitive *and* affective attributes, both of which are important. In *Against Empathy*, Yale psychologist Paul Bloom writes, "I see a child crying because she's afraid of a barking dog. I might rush over to pick her up and calm her, and I might really care for her, but there's no empathy there. I don't feel her fear, not in the slightest." I disagree, because Bloom fails to consider our ability to imagine what someone else is feeling. Surely, anyone who's ever been afraid of a spider or spooked by a scary sound can empathize with a child staring down an intimidating dog. Bottom line: there's a difference between affective and cognitive empathy, but they're both important.

EMPATHY HAS AN EVOLUTIONARY PURPOSE

Our capacity to empathize can be traced back to neural circuits that emerged in response to our primordial need for safety as we evolved over millions of years. At the heart of mammalian survival is the ability of our nervous systems to distinguish whether an environment is safe and whether someone is friend or foe. Our brain's evaluation of risk, known as neuroception, is swift and occurs without conscious awareness. Over millennia, that safety-versus-threat detection system became a rudimentary form of empathy.

According to Jamil Zaki, author of *The War for Kindness: Building Empathy in a Fractured World*, around thirty thousand years ago, there were at least five large-brained human species that roamed the earth. Over time, the testosterone levels of homo sapiens dropped, and we became less aggressive. We also acquired a slew of facial muscles that allowed us to better express emotion. All of this allowed us to forge strong social bonds and learn to care for one another. In fact, our brain has tripled in size over the past three million years because our neural connections are continually being shaped by increasingly complex social interactions. This means humans have always leveraged empathy to thrive as a species.

OUR CAPACITY TO EMPATHIZE IS A MATTER OF NATURE *AND* NURTURE

While pregnant, I was fascinated to learn that babies engage in "proto-conversations" and can identify the cries of other infants and will often cry in return. Sure enough, when my daughter was three months old, I took her out for a stroll. She was in a perfectly good mood until we passed a little boy sobbing in his stroller, and she burst spontaneously into tears. Please don't judge me, but as an empathy researcher, I was delighted to witness her emotional mimicry kick in right on time!

By eighteen to thirty months, children develop a sense of self, realize that others exist as separate beings, and begin to respond empathically. For example, a two-year-old will typically wince at the sight of another kid in pain and offer to share a toy or bring the child in distress over to its mother or father for soothing. Additional empathy milestones occur over time.

All told, we have the neural capacity and genetic predisposition to empathize. Does that mean nature is the winner? Not exactly. Research shows that the combination of cognitive maturation *and* environmental influences determines the degree to which empathy manifests in one's life. Lived experience and interactions with caregivers and the wider community also help forge empathic pathways in the brain.

Early childhood is a particularly critical time for empathy because the most intense neural growth occurs between the ages of one and seven. Healthy neurotypical babies are born with a hundred billion neurons that weave synaptic connections into a complex network of nerve pathways. The brain strengthens the synaptic connections that are used often and drops those used less frequently. This process is known as pruning and underscores the importance of a healthy and loving parent-child relationship. Consider the reassuring cooing sounds or warm smiles that caretakers make. According to psychoanalyst Heinz Kahut, those nonverbal cues are "psychological oxygen" and give kids raised in nurturing environments an empathy advantage. That said, despite a disadvantaged upbringing, anyone can become a super-empathizer with effort.

AFTER LOVE, EMPATHY IS THE MOST POWERFUL ALTRUISTIC EMOTION

"Like a snowball rolling down a hill, the term *empathy* has taken on association with a rather heterogeneous class of phenomena," writes behavioral change researcher Rick van Baaren. That's why the words *pity, compassion, sympathy,* and *empathy* often get conflated—which is a mistake. To decipher one from the other, I like to situate them on a continuum. On one side, there's pity. On the other, empathy. In between, sympathy and compassion.

Pity is an emotional response to another's perceived pain, distress, or misfortune. It might motivate a response, but only one that's predicated on power asymmetry. That's because pity regards its object as inferior and often with contempt. When you pity someone, you look down on them and can almost hear "Oh, you poor person." By comparison, when you sympathize, you feel bad for someone. There's much less disdain but still a degree of distance in the relationship. A typical refrain sounds like "I'm sorry this is happening to you." Compassion—which derives from the Latin verb *pati* (to suffer, to endure) and the prefix *cum* (with)—is more heartfelt and typically involves wanting to alleviate another's suffering. It sounds something like, "It pains me to hear what you're going through. How can I help?"

What makes empathy unique is the recognition that we all share a common humanity and have intrinsic worth. In *The Empathic Civilization: The Race to Global Consciousness in a World in Crisis*, Jeremy Rifkin writes, "Empathic extension is the only human expression that creates true equality between people. . . . That doesn't mean that empathetic moments erase status and distinctions. It only means that in the moment one extends the empathic embrace, the other social barriers—wealth, education, and professional status—are temporarily suspended in the act of experiencing, comforting, and supporting another's struggle as if their life were one's own." When you empathize with someone, there's an implicit awareness that we're essentially the same. That's what gives empathy its edge.

I describe the word as follows: Empathy is the innate trait that unites us in our shared humanity—with one important caveat. It does not deny, negate or ignore lived experience. This means we can never *fully* know what someone else is going through, so we must be careful not to make assumptions or projections. As historian Susan Lanzoni puts it in *Empathy: A History*, "Empathy marks a relation between the self and other that draws a border but also builds a bridge."

THE BENEFITS OF EMPATHY ARE WORTH CELEBRATING

Arguably, the best part about empathy is that it's good for us. Research shows that extending empathy improves our relationships and makes us healthier and happier. When we empathize, we produce oxytocin, a neurotransmitter that increases trust and cooperation. We also release serotonin, a feel-good hormone, as well as endorphins that activate the opiate receptors in our brains to boost pleasure and diminish pain. On the flipside, empathy also reduces stress and anxiety by decreasing cortisol and inflammation, which helps prevent illnesses and other health problems, including diabetes, cancer, chronic pain, obesity, and migraines.

Emotional contagion also makes us more prosocial. In fact, as people become more emotionally interdependent, they regulate each other's physiology. And fortunately for us, as we offer an empathic embrace, it's nearly impossible not to receive a reciprocal psychic gift of inner peace and joy.

SOME IMPORTANT LIMITS TO EMPATHY

If humans evolved to be empathic, and we're all born with the capacity to empathize, why are we suffering from a massive empathy deficit? And why are there so many examples of egregious empathy lapses littered across history? Well, despite the hype, empathy is not a cure-all. There are significant barriers and risks associated with empathy, all of which we must strive to overcome.

First is our tendency to "other," which means assigning people to ingroups and outgroups. Think of the unconscious biases we have toward people who are different from us. This empathy inhibitor can be traced back to our primal aversion to risk and manifests across many categories such as gender, race, religion, and political and national identity, as well as smaller categories like sports team affiliations, alma maters, and neighborhoods. That said, there's promising research that demonstrates how proximal interaction and intentional perspective-taking with "others" helps to foster feelings of connection and increase empathy across difference. Nonetheless, our propensity toward "us versus them" speaks to the need for purposeful empathy.

Next is a phenomenon known as psychic numbing, which, according to science reporter Brian Resnick, explains "how tragedies turn into abstractions in our minds, and how abstractions are easily attenuated and even ignored." As the number of victims in a tragedy increases, our capacity to empathize and willingness to do something in response decrease. Think of the three-year-old Syrian boy whose body lay lifeless on the shore of the

Mediterranean Sea. That image had a greater impact on how much attention we paid to the refugee crisis than did statistics detailing the scale of the humanitarian tragedy. Similarly, the first time something terrible happens, we feel it acutely. Remember when time stood still after hearing that two teenagers killed twelve classmates and a teacher in Columbine? Fast forward two decades and we've become increasingly numb to mass shootings, despite their shocking prevalence.

University of Oregon psychologist Paul Slovic is the leading expert on psychic numbing. He says one of the key reasons this happens is due to a sense of helplessness. According to his research, our capacity to empathize decreases even when the number of victims in a tragedy goes up from one to two. This matters when we think of injustices like domestic violence or police brutality as well as environmental catastrophes. Again, this speaks to the need for purposeful empathy.

Third is compassion fatigue, coined in 1992 by registered nurse Carla Johnson to describe the mental toll of caring for people who are suffering. The condition is characterized by physical and emotional exhaustion that inhibits one's baseline capacity to empathize. Millions of professionals in healthcare, service provision, social work, education, humanitarian aid, and counselling carry the cumulative trauma of their patients, clients, students, and beneficiaries. In the United States alone, the pre-COVID cost of compassion fatigue to employers was estimated at $200 billion annually. To combat this epidemic, self-directed purposeful empathy is necessary.

Finally, is the inverse relationship between empathy and power or privilege. Several studies have determined that those with power have a diminished capacity to perspective-take, a key aspect of empathy. A mitigating factor, however, is if they already had a prosocial orientation. In addition, people from wealthy backgrounds have lower levels of empathy than those from lower-income backgrounds, even when controlling for gender, ethnicity, and religious background. Finally, individuals in the upper-middle and upper classes are less able to detect and respond to the distress signals of others.

On the flip side, according to Elizabeth Segal, professor of social work and author of *Assessing Empathy*, "It seems that with a lack of resources and control those who identify as lower-class are more used to focusing on external events and the social context to help them understand a given situation." This means that power and socioeconomic status matter in terms of the degree to which empathy is felt and expressed. Again, this points to the need for purposeful empathy.

EMPATHY IS GREAT, BUT ON ITS OWN, IT'S NOT ENOUGH

This chapter has been an empathy primer. I've covered the origins of the word and have unpacked how empathy has both cognitive and affective dimensions. I've described its evolutionary antecedents, how it develops thanks to nature *and* nurture, and how it differs from other altruistic emotions. I've also covered its health benefits while highlighting four important limits. The good news is that by intentionally wielding our superpower, we can overcome our flawed reflexes and impulses and change our lives, organizations, and the world for the better. That's what this book is all about.

PURPOSEFUL EMPATHY PRACTICES

The following exercises explore some barriers to empathy and will give you opportunities to flex your purposeful empathy muscles. You can download a free workbook from my website.

1. Participate in the following thought experiments, from easy to more difficult. The goal is to practice perspective-taking, a demonstrated way to develop empathy. Don't rush through any of the four scenarios. Instead, bring them vividly to life in your mind by adding details about the people, places, and circumstances involved. Also think about what you might be wearing, what mood you are in, and so on. After each, ask yourself: What are the conditions under which these scenarios would likely take place? And what would inhibit you from acting on empathy?

   • Imagine an elderly woman carrying grocery bags approaching the exit doors of a shopping mall. Now imagine yourself rushing over to push the door open for her.

- Imagine a couple of tourists on the street holding a map or staring at their phones trying to figure out which way to go. Now imagine yourself offering them help.

- Imagine being at the drive-through of your local coffee house and paying for your order at the window. Now imagine paying for the customer behind you and driving off without seeing their reaction when they get to the counter and have nothing to pay.

- Imagine learning about a cousin with three kids who needs a kidney transplant. Now imagine taking tests to determine if you could be an organ donor, discovering that you're a perfect candidate, and making the decision to go for it.

2. Engage in an active listening exercise, followed by a debrief. In most contexts, the capacity to listen is a prerequisite to empathy. This simple exercise will demonstrate how unskilled we are as listeners and ideally inspire you to become a better one.

   - Find a partner and sit facing opposite directions but not back to back. Instead, sit with your shoulders aligned. Be sure you are sitting close together but are unable to see each other's faces.

   - Set a timer for one minute and decide who will speak and listen first.

   - The first speaker will talk about a favorite day or an ideal day from the past or in the theoretical.

   - When the minute has elapsed, switch roles. Now the listener becomes the speaker (same topic), and the speaker becomes the listener.

- The goal of the speaker is to notice how it felt to be uninterrupted. The goal of the listener is to notice when their mind is hijacked by thoughts and to bring their attention back to the speaker.

- After the two minutes are up, discuss the experience using these prompt questions:

  ◦ How did it feel to speak without seeing the listener, and what does this suggest about nonverbal communication?

  ◦ How did it feel to listen while bringing your conscious attention back to the speaker when thoughts entered your mind, and what does this reveal about the effort active listening requires?

  ◦ How would listening have been different if the topic were emotionally charged? What does that mean for our closest relationships and for those with whom we don't share our moral, political, or ideological views?

3. Take one or more *Implicit Association Tests* made available by Project Implicit, a nonprofit organization committed to advancing scientific knowledge about stereotypes, prejudice, and other group-based biases. A willingness to examine your unconscious biases is an important step toward disrupting discrimination. Even the most progressive social justice warriors uncover hidden and internalized biases, so don't judge yourself too harshly. After taking one or more tests, journal about what you discovered.

Over the next few days, look for proactive ways to engage in purposeful empathy. Be sure to pay attention to how those experiences make you feel in the moment and the impact they have on you throughout the day.

2

YOUR BRAIN ON EMPATHY

The old view that we are essentially self-interested creatures is being nudged firmly to one side by evidence that we are also homo empathicus, wired for empathy, social cooperation, and mutual aid.

—Roman Krznaric

Chandra Groves knew she was driving precisely sixty-six miles per hour seconds before a head-on collision nearly took her life. She'd been carefully monitoring her cruising speed to avoid upsetting a friend seated in the passenger seat, who, four weeks prior, had tragically lost her best friend and three godchildren in a separate car crash. In an unspeakable twist of fate, she and Chandra were on a road trip intended to help her heal from that ordeal.

Months after the accident, Chandra learned that her car had left forty feet of skid marks, and based on the distance between the hoods of both vehicles after impact, the cumulative speed at the time of the crash was estimated at 125 miles per hour. Incredibly, the occupants of the other vehicle walked away from the wreck. Unfortunately, Chandra suffered a traumatic brain injury (TBI).

TBI is considered a silent epidemic, and its victims are often called "the walking wounded." They appear physically normal but have hidden disabilities, including cognitive deficits; memory loss; and difficulties with attention, perception, reasoning, and language, and they grapple with a host of personality and behavioral changes such as increased aggression, problems recognizing others' emotions, and the inability to share another's feelings. In other words, a loss of empathy.

In an interview nearly four years after the accident, I asked Chandra if she could relate to any of the common outcomes of TBI. "Totally," she replied. "I was frustrated, anxious, angry, and sad, but I couldn't tell you why. Every single relationship in my life was impacted. I felt isolated, misunderstood, and lonely. It was the darkest experience I've ever had, and the interpersonal suffering lasted nearly two years."

A meta-analysis conducted by the American Psychological Association found that an astonishing 60 percent of people with moderate to severe brain injuries experience a condition known as alexithymia, which impedes the ability to identify, describe, and process one's own emotions and those of others. Again, a decreased capacity to empathize. For the 1.5 million Americans who suffer from TBIs each year, this poses a serious problem because their ability to respond in a socially appropriate manner is significantly diminished.

When I asked Chandra how she managed to transcend her brain injury, she shared a heartfelt story about her husband: "Lyle had faith I'd return to the woman he'd fallen in love with. So, he was patient and incredibly supportive. All I can say is bless his heart." She also credits her recovery to a team of healthcare professionals, including an occupational therapist who first identified some cognitive problems and then recommended getting tested by a neuropsychologist, who then advocated on her behalf to get insurance coverage for regular treatment and assistance.

Today, Chandra continues to receive support to help her cope with anxiety, a common mental health challenge for people with TBIs, but is otherwise a happily married elementary school teacher. Not everyone is so lucky. For too many, TBIs lead to long-term psychosocial impairment, as well as a higher rate of unemployment, separation or divorce, and suicide. A desire to help patients fully recover from TBI is one of the many reasons researchers have sought to understand the neural basis of empathy.

THE NEUROSCIENCE OF EMPATHY

The human brain, which contains about a hundred billion neurons (1 with 11 zeros behind it) and connected by 10^{15} synapses, is considered by many to be the most complex entity in the known universe. Its size alone is an evolutionary puzzle. According to Allan Young, a professor of anthropology, psychiatry, and the social studies of medicine, "Our ancestors split from the great apes six million years ago. During this period the ancestral brain quadrupled in volume. The metabolic costs of the brain are enormous: It constitutes 2% of total body weight and consumes 15% of cardiac output and 20% of body oxygen, and these demands are ceaseless and inflexible." Because the cost-benefit ratio of having a larger brain is not in our biological favor, it's natural to wonder why ours continued to grow in size and power. To Young, the answer is simple: Our brains adapted to other brains. And that capacity to relate to another through the mechanism of empathy is what led to our successful evolution.

If empathy unites us in our shared humanity, what neural processes are responsible? To answer this question, two schools of thought have emerged based on parallel tracks of scientific inquiry, reminiscent of the affective-cognitive axis discussed in the previous chapter. The first focused on mirror neurons, the mechanisms by which we vicariously experience the internal states of others. The second explored our cognitive capacity to draw inferences about other peoples' beliefs, intentions, and thoughts—what psychologists refer to as *theory of mind*.

Mirror Neurons and Theory of Mind

Throughout the 1980s and '90s, a team of neurophysiologists was busy conducting experiments with macaque monkeys in a laboratory in Parma, Italy. One of their studies investigated how a special group of neurons controlled hand and mouth actions. According to legend, a graduate student licking an ice cream cone walked into the lab, where a group of monkeys was hooked up to electrodes connected to neurons in the frontal lobe of their brains. As the student lifted the cone to his mouth, the monkeys' neurons began to fire. Quite by chance, the researchers discovered that their neurons responded to the *execution* of an action and the *observation* of an action in the same way. Four years later, the term *mirror neurons* was coined.

Neuroscientist Vilayanur Ramachandran compared their discovery to that of the double helix and famously said, "I predict that mirror neurons will do for psychology what DNA did for biology."

As might be expected, this accidental breakthrough triggered an eruption of research with other primates, birds, and eventually humans—all of which confirmed the existence of a mirror neuron system. Next, a number of human experiments, using fMRI and other advanced technology, revealed how certain regions of the brain are triggered not only when individuals *experience* an emotion firsthand but also when they *witness* someone else's emotion. Think of how you wince when you see someone stub their toe.

Today, there's an abundance of neurophysiological evidence confirming *affect sharing* across all sorts of human emotions, including happiness, sadness, anger, disgust, and surprise. This research has led some to conclude that mirror neurons are the roots of empathy, and we are biologically wired and evolutionarily designed for interdependence. Another group of researchers barked up a different tree.

It's well established that humans are inherently social. Just think about how tough it was for everyone to endure social isolation and distancing during the pandemic. Being able to successfully navigate the complex web of social relations that we encounter in normal daily life requires social cognition. One of the most important social-cognitive skills we have is called Theory of Mind (ToM). ToM allows us to contemplate not only our own mental states (thoughts, intentions, desires, and beliefs) but, importantly, also those of others. This includes the ability to interpret emotional experiences and to empathize. Over many years, brain studies have confirmed that ToM and empathy stimuli have overlapping neuronal networks. For example, when cognitive empathic responses are generated in the brain, the ToM networks (i.e., medial prefrontal cortex, superior temporal sulcus, temporal poles) also typically engage. And when only paralinguistic cues are available, such as facial expressions, vocal intonation, and gestures, viewers tend to rely on cognitive empathy to make accurate inferences. To some neuroscientists, *this* points to the neural basis of empathy.

Despite these two historically distinct research tracks, either/or theories about the neural bases of empathy are now passé. Recent neuroanatomical evidence supports the existence of two possible systems. As such, empathy is viewed as a flexible process with both cognitive and affective components. Looking ahead, an exciting new frontier in neuroscience is beginning to emerge, with an even wider and integrated frame for empathy.

Shared Circuits

In *The Empathic Brain*, Christian Keysers, head of the Social Brain Lab at the Netherlands Institute for Neuroscience, and member of the Parma research team that discovered mirror neurons, describes that prior to their discovery, scientists mistakenly believed human brains processed information in a rational, a logical, and an abstract way just like a computer. Debunking this fallacy, he writes, "Both leopards and Ferraris are fast, but should we therefore assume that a combustion engine must be hidden somewhere in the leopard?" According to him, scientists had no choice but to rethink the paradigm and acknowledge that our brains are "almost magically connected to each other."

Since then, he's been centering his research on "shared circuits," which suggest that we are not strictly separate from others. He explains, "The motor cortices in which we program what to do next, the theatres of free will and individual responsibility, turn out to mix our own will with the actions and intentions of others." This means, "a little bit of you becomes me, and a little bit of me becomes you." In an interview for my podcast, he elaborated, "The fact that we're so deeply connected, it's almost as if we had a thousand eyes and a thousand bodies, and together, like a swarm, we are more than a single individual . . . and more like an organism."

I was surprised to hear a neuroscientist describe our brains in almost spiritual terms. At the same time, I was heartened by the idea that our shared circuits could be harnessed for purposeful empathy. Therein, however, lies the problem. Our ability to recognize emotions in others transcends race, culture, nationality, social class, and age. When photographs of human faces are shown to people of various ages around the world, they can readily identify anger, disgust, contempt, sadness, grief, happiness, and so on. And incredibly, our facial muscles are affected within a couple of hundred milliseconds by the observation of other people's expressions. Nonetheless, studies have shown that we have less empathy for people who appear different from us and more for those who appear similar. This means our neural capacity for empathy does not translate automatically into empathic equity. Some neuroscientists are studying how to change that.

Donald Pfaff, retired head of the Laboratory of Neuroscience and Behavior at Rockefeller University and author of *The Altruistic Brain*, describes how our brains naturally "propel us toward empathic behavior and feelings leading to altruistic behaviors." Since he sees this as fundamental to the maintenance of civilized society, his goal is to translate his altruistic brain theory into behavioral change at scale for society's benefit. He writes, "After all, if it is natural and desirable to support one another, then shouldn't the economic, political, and legal culture promote—and not discourage—this result?" Certainly. But how?

Neuroplasticity

Neuroplasticity is an umbrella term used to refer to our brain's capacity to change itself—both in structure and function. More specifically, it's the ability of synaptic connections and neural networks to reorganize themselves in response to daily stimuli and environmental influences. Initially, according to Norman Doidge in *The Brain That Changes Itself*, scientists didn't dare use the word *neuroplasticity*, and those who did were belittled by their peers for promoting what they perceived as a fanciful notion. Yet the pioneers persisted and slowly overturned the doctrine of the unchanging brain. Today, thanks to numerous MRI studies, it's well accepted that our experiences, choices, and habits do indeed change our brains.

You've likely heard the saying "neurons that fire together wire together." This catchphrase was first used in 1949 by neuropsychologist Donald Hebb to describe how pathways in the brain are formed and reinforced through repetition. Practice makes perfect, right? More recently, it's been discovered that unlearning is equally important. This involves breaking down old neural connections through "synaptic pruning," thus creating space for new and stronger ones. Once believed to occur only during childhood, we now know—thanks to the pioneering work of neuroscientist Michael Merzenich—that cortical remapping happens throughout our lives. This means we can train our brains to think and behave differently through intentional rewiring. That's precisely how we can become more empathic with practice.

Jamil Zaki, director of the Stanford Social Neuroscience Laboratory, has recently made major contributions to this discourse by proposing a "motivated account of empathy" that focuses on encouraging people to *want* to empathize. His research demonstrates that people who believe empathy can be developed apply greater empathic effort than do folks who think it's static. This finding has significant implications because it means people's mindset about empathy influences how much empathy they ultimately extend—and speaks once again directly to the importance of *purposeful* empathy.

EMPATHOGENS AND THE PSYCHEDELICS REVOLUTION

Readers of a certain age will surely remember the advertisement featuring an egg sizzling on a frying pan. Considered one of the best ads of all time, *"This Is Your Brain on Drugs"* was part of a large-scale campaign by the Partnership for a Drug-Free America. The thirty-second spot was not just iconic; it was highly effective at perpetuating the war on drugs, launched by President Nixon in 1971 when he declared substance abuse and addiction "public enemy No. 1."

The consequence of his offensive, which continued unabated for five decades regardless of the party in power, is now well documented. The number of Americans sent to prison for drug offenses skyrocketed from 40,900 in 1980 to 430,926 in 2019 at an estimated cost of one trillion dollars. And close to 80 percent of federal and 60 percent of state inmates incarcerated for overwhelmingly nonviolent drug offenses have been Black or Latino. A lesser-known fact is the antinarcotics campaign also had a devastating impact on mental health research using psychoactive drugs to treat posttraumatic stress disorder, depression, social anxiety, alcoholism, and even suicide.

Today, a renaissance of scientific research is currently underway exploring the therapeutic use of psychedelics. Among the drugs being studied are 3,4-methylenedioxymethamphetamine (aka MDMA, ecstasy, Molly) and 3,4-methylenedioxyamphetamine (aka MDA, sassafras, Sally), both of which release the neurotransmitters serotonin, dopamine, and noradrenaline, known to increase feelings of empathy, benevolence, and emotional connection to others.

MDMA was created by Merck Pharmaceuticals in Germany in 1912 as a base compound for synthesizing other drugs. Never used in clinical practice, it was forgotten until 1976, when American chemist and Mensa member Alexander Shulgin noticed its chemical similarity to compounds like mescaline and amphetamine. After testing the drug on himself—something he'd been doing with other drugs for many years—he confided in a small group of psychotherapists and physicians about its effects.

Because the most salient feature of MDMA is empathy, which happens to be one of the strongest positive predictive outcome measures between patients and therapists, his discovery inspired a small group of research practitioners to study its psychotherapeutic potential. According to Ralph Metzner, an early psychedelic research pioneer at Harvard, who later coined the term *empathogen*, MDMA gained a reputation among psychotherapists for being "one of the most effective, fast and safe ways of helping people heal from severe trauma, as well as opening up interpersonal communication in couples."

No surprise, word got out, and by the early 1980s, MDMA was being used recreationally at nightclubs. That's when a clever member of a distribution network in Los Angeles decided a rebrand was needed. Instead of calling the drug *empathy* to signal its primary effect, he decided *ecstasy* would help grow the market faster. An aggressive marketing campaign followed, complete with pyramid sales structures, 800 numbers, and credit card purchase options. The popularity of MDMA grew so quickly that it swiftly faced a Schedule 1 ban by the US Drug Enforcement Agency. In hindsight, we know criminalization didn't deter recreational use, but it certainly thwarted high-potential therapeutic research.

Looking forward, however, the future for empathogens is bright. A randomized, double-blind, placebo-controlled Phase 3 study conducted by the Multidisciplinary Association for Psychedelic Studies (MAPS) revealed that MDMA-assisted therapy is highly efficacious for individuals with PTSD. "After decades of demonization and criminalization," MAPS founder and executive director, Rick Doblin, says, "psychedelic drugs are on the cusp of entering mainstream psychiatry, with profound implications for a field that in recent decades has seen few pharmacological advancements for the treatment of mental disorders and addiction."

Many think it's just a matter of time before the Food and Drug Administration approves psychoactive compounds for therapeutic use—a development that has investors and research centers paying close attention. Once upon a time, funding was nearly impossible to secure. Today, psychedelic research is awash in money as venture capitalists invest in startups and philanthropists donate to research, including podcaster and lifestyle guru Tim Ferriss, who launched a ten-million-dollar matching grant on behalf of MAPS. World-class institutions like Johns Hopkins, Stanford, Yale, UC Berkeley, Massachusetts General Hospital, and New York's Mount Sinai Hospital have also established psychedelic research divisions. The psychedelic drugs market is expected to reach nearly eleven billion dollars by 2027.

Of course, the pharmaceutical industry is expected to fight back since their profits are tied to conventional psychopharmacology treatments that people ingest for weeks, months, or even years at a stretch. But thanks to new scientific evidence, the case for empathogens and other psychedelic and hallucinogenic drugs, including Psilocybin mushrooms and Lysergic acid diethylamide (LSD), is growing stronger by the day.

Users of MDMA, for example, have been found to be more empathic than those taking other drugs like cannabis, cocaine, and ketamine— even when they're not high. New research also shows that MDMA might enhance long-term prosocial processes. Finally, MDMA may help researchers determine more precisely the neural mechanisms of empathy. Because the drug's breakdown in the body is highly predictable, changes in the brain that occur in the hours after ingestion can be directly linked to the substance. Consequently, research may reveal a new set of neurons being activated when people experience empathy. This is exciting. "At a time of great hostility and mistrust both nationally in the United States and internationally," Stanford research colleagues Boris Heifets and Robert Malenka ask, "what is more important than elucidating the mechanisms in our brains that generate empathy, openness, and the most positive of social experiences?" I completely agree, so let's take this one step further.

Metzner shared that prior to empathogens becoming contraband, he completed a single MDMA therapy session with a traumatized vet from Vietnam who then went on to found Veterans for Peace, an organization that educates high school students about the devastating personal costs of war. Of course, that's just one anecdote from someone with skin in the game, but one has to wonder how different the world would be today if early psychotherapeutic research had been allowed to flourish.

According to Metzner, the presence of MDMA in the body triggers the release of prolactin, the same hormone needed for breastfeeding and associated with mother-infant bonding. He argues this is "perhaps the paradigmatic example of empathic, non-striving, relaxed empathic mergence of two beings." Makes you wonder: what if our brains on empathy could change the world?

SIGNIFICANT IMPLICATIONS FOR SOCIETY

Understanding the neural mechanisms that underpin empathy is important. To that end, a torrent of research studies has been conducted over the past couple of decades, and stacks of books dedicated to empathy and the brain have been published to translate findings into digestible knowledge for public consumption. Summarizing all that work goes well beyond the scope of this chapter. Instead, since this book is about tapping our hidden superpower for personal, organizational, and social change, I've highlighted brain research that has practical implications for this important project.

Specifically, I hope you'll take away three things: Neuroscience has proven we have the innate capacity to empathize. By leveraging our brain plasticity and motivation for more empathy, we can become more empathic on purpose. Finally, empathogens may have the potential to elevate our empathic consciousness for more sustainable empathic action. Consider the implications of this trifecta at an aggregate level!

There's never been a better time to integrate science-based empathy interventions into schools, workplaces, and communities, as well as our political and economic systems. Now it's up to us to cocreate the more empathic society we all know is possible.

PURPOSEFUL EMPATHY PRACTICES

The following exercises will help you gauge your current level of empathy, activate it in your brain and body, and learn how to optimize it for greater joy and wellbeing in your life. You can download a free workbook from my website.

1. Take these three empathy tests to learn how empathic you are, and afterward, take some time to journal about your results:

    a. *The Empathy Quiz* developed by the Greater Good Science Center at the University of California, Berkeley

   b. *The Empathy Quotient* questionnaire developed by
       Dr. Simon Baron-Cohen at the Autism Research Centre
       at the University of Cambridge

   c. *The Interpersonal Reactivity* Index developed by Mark H.
       Davis, a professor of psychology at Eckerd College

2. Participate in these two exercises to activate empathy on purpose:

   a. A visual experiment to elicit affective empathy and
       demonstrate the speed by which our mirror neurons are
       spontaneously aroused. Instructions:

       • Look at image 1 and notice what happens to your face.
          Next, look at image 2 and notice if and how your facial
          expression shifts. Go back and forth between images, pay-
          ing attention to any emotional resonance you feel.

© Getty Images 2022; iStock / Getty Images Plus

- Going forward, test out what happens when you smile at random people. First, you'll likely notice how their facial expression changes. Second, you might be surprised by how this small gesture changes your mood too. Strangers may not respond favorably 100 percent of the time, but the positive impact of succeeding most of the time will undoubtedly leave you with a warm glow.

- Try also to notice when you're feeling affective empathy throughout the day and pay attention to what triggers your emotions the most.

b. An eye-gazing exercise to reveal how we oscillate between affective and cognitive empathy. Instructions:

- Find a partner (family member, neighbor, colleague, friend) and sit facing one another, ideally with uncrossed legs and palms facing upward on your laps.

- Acknowledge (to yourself and partner) that this exercise will take courage and vulnerability. It's not easy to sit quietly with someone, eye gazing.

- Set a timer for thirty seconds and begin looking into each other's eyes. Be sure not to stare or speak. The only rule is no talking throughout the exercise.

- Once the alarm rings, shake off any feelings of discomfort or self-consciousness and exchange a few words with your partner.

- Set the timer again—this time for ninety seconds—and continue eye gazing. It's possible that one or both of you may start to giggle or chuckle. Contagious laughter is quite common.

- As you look into your partner's eyes and they do the same, pay attention to your thoughts as well as any sensations arising in your body. Be sure to observe what happens without judgment.

- After the alarm rings again, discuss your experience with your partner using these prompt questions:

  - How did it feel to sit together without speaking? Could you sense a different kind of communication? If yes, how would you describe it?

  - What bodily sensations did you notice?

  - What thoughts did you have?

  - Did you feel more connected to your partner and/or a heightened sense of empathy? If yes, why do you suppose?

  - Did you feel affective *and* cognitive empathy? If so, how were they different?

- Finally, thank your partner for holding space with you.

3. Adapted from the *Wheel of Life*, a popular coaching assessment tool, complete the Wheel of Purposeful Empathy. This exercise will illuminate degrees of empathic engagement across different domains of life and where there is room for improvement.

   Instructions:
   - Draw a big circle on a sheet of paper and divide it into six even pieces.

   - Along the perimeter of the circle, name each of the six parts as follows: self-empathy, empathy for kin and clan, empathy for others, empathy at work, empathic consciousness, and empathic action.

- Trace nine concentric circles inside the perimeter of the main circle, starting from the epicenter. Give the epicenter a value of 0, the next circle a value of 1, the next circle a value of 2, and repeat until the outer circle is given a value of 10.

- Color in each of the six parts. No shading means that aspect of empathy is entirely untapped, and complete shading means that aspect of empathy is fully maximized.

Wheel of Purposeful Empathy Legend

- Self-empathy: Being kind to yourself, able to say yes and no according to your boundaries, respecting your time and energy, being able to forgive yourself for making mistakes and being flawed, having the capacity to exercise self-care as needed.

- Empathy for kin and clan: Having empathy for members of your ingroups, including family, friends, neighbors, teammates, book club, classmates, and so on.

- Empathy for others: Having empathy for people who are part of your outgroups, including strangers and people you'll never meet or who have different lived experiences; gender identities; political, religious, national, and cultural affiliation; and so on.

- Empathy at work: Feeling a sense of belonging at work, coupled with emotional safety to be authentic and vulnerable; knowing your employer values you as a whole person and not simply as a human resource; having workplace policies, practices, and KPIs that incentivize and reward empathic behavior; seeing your employer engage with the wider community in empathic ways.

- Empathic consciousness: Feeling that all of humanity is interdependent and that each of us is inherently worthy of dignity, respect, and basic human rights.

- Empathic action: Feeling a sense of personal responsibility to strive toward greater peace, justice, and sustainability, especially on behalf of future generations, and being actively engaged in the struggle for a better world.

PART II

3

LEANING INTO PURPOSE

The two most important days in life are the day you were born and the day you discover the reason why.

—Mark Twain

After eight years at Microsoft, John Wood quit his job as director of business development in China to launch a nonprofit dedicated to global literacy. Taught to set BHAGs (big hairy audacious goals) by Steve Ballmer, John aspired to reach ten million children by 2020. "If I was going to give up millions in stock options, I wasn't going to play small," he says.

The approach worked. By leveraging his corporate playbook, Room to Read surpassed its target five years early and outpaced Starbucks for a decade, building more libraries year over year than the coffee giant opened stores. Today, the NGO has impacted more than twenty-eight million children from Bangladesh to Zambia by partnering with over forty thousand schools and training ten thousand teachers every year. Those are impressive results by any standard, but to John, they're just a good start. "We've reached only a small percentage of children who need us," he says. "And the idea that a child can be told she was born in the wrong place at the wrong time and that's why she can't get an education belongs on the scrap heap of human history."

What prompted John to leave his thriving corporate gig to bootstrap a charity? Here's a hint: purpose. John admits he's always been a bookworm. When his parents wanted to reward him for something, he didn't ask for toys or treats. Instead, he begged them to stay up late to read. Rather than respect the eight-book limit at his local library, he negotiated a secret agreement with the librarian to borrow a dozen at a time. Reading remains his lifelong passion.

After a major burnout at Microsoft, John needed to tend to his mental health and figured a hiking trip in Nepal would do the trick. One afternoon while sipping chai, he met a local education department official who invited him to a school in the village of Bahundanda. He accepted and, the next day, visited a ramshackle building. He was devastated to see that it had no age-appropriate children's books, only two backpacker castoffs: a Danielle Steele paperback and a *Lonely Planet Guide to Mongolia*—both under lock and key. The headmaster said, "We're too poor to afford an education, but until we have an education, we'll always be poor." Then he uttered nine words that would forever change John's life: "Perhaps, sir, you will someday come back with books."

Back in Beijing, despite being ridiculously busy preparing for a high-profile visit by Bill Gates, John was more focused on emailing friends around the world, asking them to donate kids' books for Bahundanda's first library. Within two months, he'd collected over three thousand, all warehoused in his parents' garage. The following year, he and his seventy-three-year-old father returned to the Nepalese village, accompanied by six book-bearing donkeys.

Anticipating their visit, the community had built wall-to-wall bookshelves in the schoolhouse. The morning of the ribbon-cutting ceremony, John was delighted to learn that two boys had snuck in overnight, unable to resist the wait. "At the official opening, I watched kids erupt with joy. They were literally falling over themselves enraptured by images of sharks, rollercoasters, and the solar system," John recalls. "It reminded me of the reverie I felt in my hometown library." In the words of Simon Sinek, John had found his why.

When he first announced his departure from Microsoft to start an NGO, people told him he was having a midlife crisis. "I thought the real crisis would have been for me not to follow my calling," he says. These days, when asked about his decision to quit his job, he replies, "Did I want my tombstone to read that I had cranked out twenty-nine consecutive quarters of earnings growth for some big company? No. I respect those who go that route. But that wasn't for me."

After twenty years of championing global literacy, John stepped off Room to Read's board to launch a new venture that tackles the "logical next challenge." U-Go helps ambitious and promising young women in low-income countries pursue higher education. And in his spare time, John coaches executives and organizations on how to turn purpose into a competitive advantage. His website reads, "I believe we were put on this earth to do more than just make money. Our careers can and should stand for something bigger than just ourselves."

CORPORATE REFUGEES AND THE GREAT RESIGNATION

John jumped ship to pursue a path of purpose, despite the financial benefits and social capital afforded by his C-suite job. He's not alone, especially among highly educated workers. Pre-COVID-19, corporate refugees would typically have a day of reckoning, often on the heels of a catalyzing event, when they would realize they've worked too hard, made too many personal sacrifices, and aren't happy with their lives regardless of outward signs of success. Radical change would usually follow.

Post-pandemic data shows that professionals are flat-out exhausted from the crushing workload and digital overload they endured, all of which took a grave toll on workers' mental health. Not to mention the disruptive burdens of working remotely and keeping their families intact. That's why so many workers have been in sober reflection about their jobs, especially if they work for an organization that wasn't particularly empathic throughout the pandemic.

According to a 2021 WorkLab study, 41 percent of the global workforce was expected to leave their current employer within the following year. This corresponds with the Job Openings and Labor Turnover Statistics (JOLTS) data from the US Bureau of Labor Statistics, which showed quit rates above prepandemic levels and continuing to rise. Inspired by a surge of pandemic-related epiphanies about family time, remote work, commuting, passion projects, mortality, and one's life purpose, workers are fed up with the current work paradigm.

Millennials and Gen Zers are especially unapologetic about wanting to change the rules of the game. Not only are two-thirds to three-quarters, respectively, willing to switch jobs to get more control of their schedule, but according to Deloitte, nine out of ten millennial workers are willing to earn less money to do more meaningful work. Plus, the vast majority believe that making a positive difference in the world is more important than professional recognition.

All told, the Great Resignation coupled with a new set of generational values means that organizations are facing a dearth of talent, which poses serious risks to their business. That's why "trust and empathy are the foundations of success for long-term reinvention strategies," concludes a recent Global Talent Trends report by Mercer. Empathic workplaces are becoming the new cultural and strategic goal.

Gallup has been measuring employee satisfaction in the United States for more than two decades, and their findings are disconcerting: A little over half of the country's hundred million full-time employees say they're "not engaged" at work, meaning they feel disconnected from their jobs. Worse, 17.5 percent are "actively disengaged." This means two out of three employees are unhappy at work, which translates into 37 percent higher absenteeism and 18 percent lower output.

Disengaged workers also cost the economy $350 billion in lost productivity each year, and their employers $3,400 for every $10K paid out in annual salary. Economically, that's no joke. But the underlying issue of compromised wellbeing is even worse. We know from a growing body of evidence that having a sense of purpose fosters optimism, good relationships, and life satisfaction. But recent studies reveal that a critical mass of employees feel dissatisfied by midcareer, largely because they aren't pursuing work with existential value.

A few years ago, the *New York Times* article "*Why You Hate Work*," by Tony Schwartz and Jerry Porath, went viral because the core message resonated with so many. In partnership with *Harvard Business Review*, they surveyed more than twelve thousand mostly white-collar employees across a broad range of companies and industries to find out why they hated their jobs. Lack of purpose was one of the key reasons cited, the consequences of which are dire. According to a report commissioned by the John Templeton Foundation that reviewed six decades of research, individuals without a sense of purpose are less healthy and more likely to suffer from depression, loneliness, anxiety, and drug abuse. Take Jennifer Lonergan, for example.

PURPOSE MATTERS

Jennifer admits she's always held her middle finger up to authority. As editor of her school paper, she published many controversial pieces despite regular shutdowns by the administration. Censorship emboldened her, even prompting a solo trip to the USSR during the Cold War. "I wanted to see autocracy up close and evaluate it with my own eyes," she says.

As a grad student, Jennifer explored what helps and hinders social and political change, focusing on women's roles in accelerating shifts in social norms. Armed with a PhD in public history, she became an expert on women's roles in society and why their collective experiences and contributions have been largely ignored across the globe.

Early in her career, while working as a curator for Canada's Museum of Civilization, Jennifer went to India with a high school bestie. Over the years, she'd heard many stories about her friend's dad and his humble beginnings. What she didn't know was that later in life, he built a school in his birth village. Standing in the one-room structure with him, Jennifer was struck by four back-to-back thoughts: how much poverty there is in the world, how arbitrary it was that she had so many advantages in life, that one person *can* make a difference, and, finally, how little *she* was doing with her privilege to contribute to meaningful change.

Back home, those insights weighed heavily on her—until a eureka moment when she realized how much she hated her life. "I had a dream job with great benefits. I drove a new car and owned a three-bedroom house," she said. "But I also had chronic back pain and was taking medicine for ulcers. I couldn't sleep at night. I cried for no reason, sometimes three or four times a day. I was living on alcohol and antidepressants and even had suicidal thoughts. I just couldn't figure out how to hang myself from the wooden rafters in my living room without distressing my dog."

Thanks to a good therapist, Jennifer reflected upon what made her genuinely happy, and she discovered a deceptively simple answer. She felt joy helping others. Drawn to the idea of a boutique specializing in women's handmade crafts from the Global South, she took a small business course, wrote a business plan, found a location, and, without a stitch of retail experience, signed a lease. What mattered most was that she'd found a sense of purpose.

Having a north star, however, didn't guarantee sales, and after two years in business, she was forced to close her shop. But she didn't give up. She liquidated her inventory and pivoted to entrepreneurship training for skilled artisans. Jennifer knew that if given the opportunity, women could grow their own small businesses and lift themselves out of poverty.

Known as the multiplier effect, once women generate their own revenue, they prioritize their children's education, health, and nutritional needs. They assume new roles in their households and communities. Life expectancy increases while infant and maternal mortality rates drop. HIV transmission decreases, and the GDPs of entire countries go up. Women's empowerment is even credited for mitigating climate change!

Jennifer is now executive director of Artistri Sud, a nonprofit organization that offers virtual and on-location micro-entrepreneurship training to women in low-income countries, from Bolivia to Vietnam. When asked how her life has changed since leaving her cushy government job, she says, "I used to be materially comfortable but miserable. Now I live modestly but with a great deal of abundance. Seeing women embrace what's possible for themselves has been the biggest blessing of my life."

Ray Zahab, who ran an 111-day marathon across the North African desert, captured in a documentary film narrated by Matt Damon, is also grateful to have found his calling. Born in 1969 and raised on a horse farm, Ray led a life that consisted of coffee, booze, and cigarettes. Unhealthy and awash in self-pity, he drifted aimlessly in and out of odd jobs for years. On New Year's Day of the new millennium, Ray woke up hungover on his brother's living room couch. He spotted an ashtray overflowing with cigarette butts and remembered that he'd smoked his last one of the night all the way down to the filter. Disgusted with himself, he reached for a magazine on the coffee table and started skimming the pages. He came across an article about the *Yukon Arctic Ultra Marathon*, considered the toughest foot race in the world because it requires competitors to drag their supplies ninety-nine miles by sled across a frozen abyss. The story's cover photo featured a man who had just crossed the finish line, radiating triumph and bliss. In that moment, Ray vowed to compete in the next race.

After three months of training as a long-distance runner, the incredible happened. Ray ran the race and finished first. Nearly overnight, he had become an ultra-marathon champion. Hooked on the sport, he began to train in earnest and competed in many other races around the world, winning several more. In 2016, he set out on his biggest challenge yet: to run across the Sahara Desert to draw attention to H20 Africa, an NGO devoted to clean drinking water.

Accompanied by two ultra-marathon friends, he ran from Senegal to Egypt, covering an average of thirty-nine miles per day. The trio ran through sandstorms, injury, illness, and 100+°F for nearly four months straight without missing a single day. Awake by 5:00 a.m., they'd eat for an hour and run until noon. They'd break for a few hours to eat and rest and then run some more. Short days ended at 6:00 p.m., long ones at 11:00 p.m., depending on the running conditions. In Niger, the sand was so soft that Ray and his buddies sank up to their ankles with each step. They consumed at least six thousand calories per day, foregoing water because it has none, and took just two showers the entire journey. By the time the trio reached Egypt, they could taste the finish line. They ran more than sixty miles per day for an entire week and completed the final 186 miles to the Red Sea in a mindboggling sixty-hour sprint on just two hours of sleep.

Ray celebrated with an ice-cold beer and a juicy cheeseburger at a five-star hotel. His meal was delicious, but the lasting taste in his mouth was an epiphany: "I used to be a pack-a-day smoker, but I just ran across the African continent. We underestimate ourselves but are all capable of extraordinary things."

That's when Ray made three important life decisions. He cofounded *impossible2Possible*, a nonprofit organization dedicated to encouraging youth to reach beyond their limits. He committed to competing in races only if they could be leveraged for social good. Finally, he decided to step up as a role model. While his feet did the busy work of running across the Sahara to draw attention to the water crisis, his eyes bore witness to what water scarcity meant for real people, families, and communities. This cemented his resolve to engage in a lifetime of purposeful empathy. To Ray, sitting on the sidelines while others suffer is simply not an option, and he rejects all excuses to the contrary. "Limitations are ninety percent mental," he says. "And the other ten percent is all in our head." What a great mantra for this empathy manifesto!

JAPANESE *IKIGAI*

John, Jennifer and Ray are all aligned with their purpose. As a result, they are flourishing as human beings. This doesn't mean they're immune to challenges, disappointments, or heartbreak. But it does mean they wake up every day with a sense of direction that makes their lives meaningful and satisfying. In Japan, this is known as *ikigai*.

Originating from the island of Okinawa, which is home to the largest per capita population of centenarians in the world, *ikigai* (pronounced *ee-kee-guy*) translates into English as "reason for being." The word is formed by combining *iki* (生き), meaning "life," with *gai* (甲斐), which means "value or worth." Visually, the concept is often depicted at the point of intersection of a four-circle Venn diagram and addresses four questions: What do I love? What am I good at? What does the world need? What can I be paid for?

In *The Little Book of Ikigai*, Tokyo-based neuroscientist Ken Mogi argues that it doesn't matter whether "you are a cleaner of the famous Shinkansen bullet train, the mother of a newborn child or a Michelin-starred sushi chef—if you can find pleasure and satisfaction in what you do and you're good at it, congratulations, you have found your Ikigai."

ECHOES OF MASLOW

If the concept of *ikigai* sounds familiar, that's because the path to a meaningful life has been contemplated throughout human history. Roman Emperor Marcus Aurelius believed we each have a unique purpose, and Italian philosopher Thomas Aquinas evangelized about human flourishing long before the term was coined. More recently, the positive psychology movement has mainstreamed the significance of fulfilling one's potential, starting with Abraham Maslow's concept of self-actualization.

His original theory of human motivation included a hierarchy of needs, typically depicted in a five-level pyramid that you probably remember from an *Intro to Psych* class. From bottom to top are physiological needs (air, water, food, shelter), safety needs (personal security, employment), belonging needs (friendship, intimacy, family), esteem needs (respect, recognition), and, finally, self-actualization (the realization of one's potential). In *Transcend: The New Science of Self-Actualization*, psychologist Scott Barry Kaufman writes that Maslow identified several characteristics of self-actualizing people, including greater life satisfaction, curiosity, positive relationships, personal growth, and purpose in life.

Toward the end of his life, however, Maslow realized his theory was misguided. Self-actualization was not the apex of personal achievement and fulfillment. Instead, most of his late and unpublished work explored the notion of self-transcendence, which he viewed as reaching "the very highest and most inclusive or holistic levels of human consciousness." This is congruent with holocaust survivor Viktor Frankl's overriding message in *Man's Search for Meaning*: "Only to the extent that someone is living out this self-transcendence of human existence, is he truly human or does he become his true self. He becomes so, not by concerning himself with his self-actualization, but by forgetting himself and giving himself, overlooking himself and focusing outward."

That said, self-actualized people do not forsake their potential in order to serve others. Instead, they apply their talents and gifts in service. Ultimately, it's the combination of self-actualization and self-transcendence that brings our lives the greatest degree of fulfillment.

INTRODUCING A NEW SELF-DEVELOPMENT TOOL

With that in mind, I'd like to introduce a diagram to represent the five key elements and seven virtues of purposeful empathy. It's meant to provoke introspection and provide clues for creating positive change across all areas of your life, including your family, community, and organization—as well as the world at large. As a certified personal and professional coach, I know how transformational frameworks can be, especially if presented at the right time. That's why I hope this tool resonates with you. The diagram's five elements correspond with five questions for reflection. Starting at the top, let's consider them one at a time.

Issues You Care About

When it comes to engaging in purposeful empathy, start with one issue (or a couple) you care deeply about, like John's love of reading, Jennifer's passion for women's empowerment or Ray's commitment to youth. Perhaps you've lost a loved one to cancer, you hate animal cruelty, or you believe green energy is the key to a sustainable future. Starting with one (or two) issue(s)

you're already passionate about will activate your intrinsic motivation. Alternative frames include issues you're curious about or issues that concern you. For example, I became a pescatarian because I'm anxious about climate change and know that livestock production is responsible for 18 percent of greenhouse gases.

Ask Yourself: What Issue(s) Do I Most Care About?

Global Challenges
It's equally important to align the issue(s) you care about with challenges facing the world. This matters in terms of meeting likeminded allies who care about the same issue(s) for mutual inspiration and support. It's also helpful to secure partners and resources and to build momentum. Of course, the number of issues facing the world is overwhelming, so one helpful way to narrow the list is to refer to the United Nations Sustainable Development Goals (SDGs). The SDG framework includes seventeen goals set in 2015 by the UN General Assembly as a "blueprint to achieve a better world and a

more sustainable future for all." Don't be surprised if your issue overlaps with several goals. Given their interconnected nature, that's perfectly normal.

The SDGs are: (1) no poverty, (2) zero hunger, (3) good health and wellbeing, (4) quality education, (5) gender equality, (6) clean water and sanitation, (7) affordable and clean energy, (8) decent work and economic growth, (9) industry, innovation, and infrastructure, (10) reducing inequality, (11) sustainable cities and communities, (12) responsible consumption and production, (13) climate action, (14) life below water, (15) life on land, (16) peace, justice, and strong institutions, and (17) partnerships for the goals.

Ask yourself: How does the issue(s) you care about align with the most pressing challenges facing the world?

Personal Growth

Decades ago, Freudian psychology held that human behavior was driven by two impulses: the fear of death and the desire for sex. More recently, positive psychologists who study human flourishing have determined that we're motivated by two entirely different drives: the desire to learn and grow and the need to be of service to others or a cause greater than ourselves.

During one summer I spent volunteering in Rwanda, I was conscious of white saviorism but still wanted to make a contribution. What I hadn't anticipated was leaving the country with a different worldview. It's a misconception that social impact work is unidirectional. When it comes to engaging in purposeful empathy, it's not only appropriate to want to experience personal growth; it's also a predictable outcome.

Ask yourself: What do you want to learn, and how do you want to grow?

Social Progress

Social progress does not happen on its own. Across history, most social movements have been inspired by the desire for meaningful changes to laws, public policies, and social norms. But that's only half the story. Any attempt to promote peace, justice, and human rights is also animated by the human need for goodness, fairness, and kindness. We are, after all, empathic by nature, and waves of collective empathy have been part of our successful evolution as a species. Modern history has shown that when we practice empathy on purpose, we can move mountains.

Ask yourself: What system(s) need(s) to change, and what is my role?

Ongoing Self-Empathy

Because social progress is fiercely contested and moves at glacial speed, the final element of the diagram is ongoing self-empathy. Many novice and seasoned activists experience burnout and compassion fatigue, both of which diminish their capacity to empathize. Without tending to our personal needs and limits, there's little chance to integrate purposeful empathy into our lives, especially on a sustainable basis.

On the heels of my summer in Rwanda, I had trouble sleeping and felt angry most of the time. Thanks to a good therapist, I was diagnosed with a mild case of PTSD. I followed a treatment plan to help me integrate everything I'd experienced overseas, and in time, I was grateful to find my footing. Ongoing self-empathy is essential to social change work—at both the individual and collective levels.

Ask yourself: How can I be kind to myself while practicing purposeful empathy?

Seven Virtues

In addition to those five elements of the diagram, there are seven virtues that animate purposeful empathy. They are:

1. Elevated consciousness: Learning about social and environmental issues challenges our worldviews and engenders introspection. And as people experience personal growth, their perspectives tend to broaden too. Together, this leads to elevated consciousness.
2. Moral courage: Social progress only happens when values that honor peace, justice, equity, and sustainability are present. That's why making a commitment to social change, especially in the face of pushback, judgment, or critique, requires moral courage.

3. Collective action: As people make connections between issues they care about and challenges facing the world, it's easier for them to find a community of likeminded people. Empowered by strength in numbers, groups can then engage in collective action.

4. Humility: Purposeful empathy is allergic to power and privilege. It's also practiced between people, not bestowed upon anyone. Remaining humble is paramount, as is listening to and centering others.

5. Reflexivity: Being conscious of how we show up in the world is key to purposeful empathy. It requires us to question taken-for-granted assumptions and examine our feelings, motives, and behaviors through a critical lens. We don't need to be perfect, but we can't circumvent doing the important work of self-reflection.

6. Tenacity: Purposeful empathy can be exhausting because changing the world isn't easy. For all the steps forward we take, there are plenty of steps back—not only in the external environment but also within. If you want to "be the change," dogged determination is necessary.

7. Mutuality: Purposeful empathy is not a solo sport; it's entirely relational. Cooperation and reciprocity always trump hierarchical, transactional, win-lose relationships and organizing systems. Much like solidarity, mutuality reminds us that we're all in this together.

In short, purposeful empathy requires intentionally committing ourselves to improving our communities, organizations, and society at large *while* becoming a better version of ourselves. It is the essence of self-transcendence and living our life on purpose. Let me bring this to life through another story.

A GATEWAY TO SELF-TRANSCENDENCE

As a child, Elsa-Marie D'Silva had been exposed to domestic violence in her home but had a fiercely independent mother, who walked away from the abuse. Adamant about securing her own financial freedom, Elsa started working in her late teens. And with determination, she fast-tracked her way to the senior ranks of an Indian airline. Twenty years later, in recognition of her own privilege as a fully emancipated woman, she began fighting for gender equality in India, prompted by an incident that took place in a yoga class.

One morning during sun salutations, a regular practitioner created a stir. He bolted into the studio and announced, "In the middle of the night, a young woman called my son begging him to pick her up. Apparently, after a wedding, she and some friends went out to a bar and were being physically and verbally harassed." In short succession, three women next to Elsa replied, "That's what happens when young women go bar hopping"; "Girls who drink are known to be cheap"; "They must have been wearing something provocative." Elsa was incensed. A group of well-educated women in the progressive city of Mumbai was judging the girls at the pub. Jyoti Singh had died only days earlier. Did these women believe she was also to blame for her infamous gang rape and murder?

According to the National Crime Records Bureau of India, approximately one hundred sexual assaults are reported daily to the police. Experts say the real number is much higher. Some assert a rape occurs in the country every fifteen minutes. Elsa stormed out of the studio and called a friend: "I must do something to end sexual violence in India once and for all."

Within two weeks of Jyoti's death, Elsa launched Safecity, an award-winning online platform that anonymously crowdsources personal stories of sexual harassment and violence in public spaces. Shortly thereafter, she also cofounded the Red Dot Foundation, a nonprofit organization that works at the intersection of gender, technology, and urban planning. Elsa's goal is to keep girls and women safe and push local administrators and law enforcement agencies to identify factors that lead to violence and develop time-sensitive interventions as well as long-term solutions. To date, the organization has reached one million beneficiaries through its various programs, workshops, campaigns, and public conversations.

When asked about her work, Elsa says she was meant to be in that yoga class, convinced the upsetting exchange was a sign from the universe. "I liked my job in aviation, but I suffered from the Sunday blues," she admits. "Now I have no idea what day of the week it is, and I've never been happier. My friends tell me I look younger and have a glow. That's nice to hear, but what I appreciate most is living with purpose. These last few years have felt like a spiritual journey."

Living in alignment with purpose is one of life's greatest gifts—not just to ourselves personally but to all of humanity. In our culture, we're constantly reminded of our deficiencies and where we fall short. It's time to reject those messages and center our unique talents and gifts. As poet laureate Amanda Gorman put it on President Biden's inauguration day, "For there is always light, if only we're brave enough to see it. If only we're brave enough to be it."

PURPOSEFUL EMPATHY PRACTICES

The following tools and exercises are intended to help you identify your priority values and make decisions and plans in service of your purpose. For maximum benefit, dedicate a couple of hours of quiet time to work through them and avoid rushing, distractions, and interruptions. Consider this time a gift to yourself. You can download a free workbook from my website.

1. Take the following assessments:

   - *Personal Values Assessment* by Barrett Values Centre. It's only possible to live by your values when you know what they are, and doing this assessment may surprise you. For example, fairness and compassion are two values that are highly regarded. Yet in your personal life, you may value fairness over compassion (or the other way around). No value is objectively superior, but knowing which ones matter most to you will help you make better decisions, including how to prioritize your time, talents, and treasures.

   - *Meaning in Life Questionnaire (MLQ)* by Michael F. Steger. This ten-item questionnaire is designed to measure your *presence of meaning* (how much your life has meaning) and your *search for meaning* (how much you strive to find meaning in your life). Ideally, gaining insight into your present state will inspire changes for the future.

- *Self-Actualization Scale* by Dr. Scott Barry Kaufman. Based on Maslow's original writings on the characteristics of self-actualizing people, this test measures ten facets of self-actualization. Seeing where you stand with each of these characteristics will also shed light on opportunities for growth.

Once you've completed these assessments, take thirty minutes to reflect on what's come up for you. Here are a few prompt questions to help you get started:

- What did the results reveal that was otherwise not obvious to me before?

- What do the results suggest in terms of how I'm currently living my life?

- What stands out to me and begs further attention?

- How have the results inspired me to make some changes in my life?

2. Discover your *ikigai*. Download and print a blank copy or hand draw four big circles that intersect as a Venn diagram on a blank piece of paper. Each circle represents a question: What do you love? What are you good at? What does the world need? What can you be paid to do? If the same answer repeats for all four questions, you have identified your *ikigai*. If you don't have an existing *ikigai*, consider reengineering parts of your life to live with greater purpose.

3. Answer the five questions for reflection prompted by my purposeful empathy diagram:

- What issue(s) do you most care about: climate change, systemic racism, global poverty, human trafficking? Consider what compels you to read a feature article online, make a donation, or sign a petition. Identify one or two issues that you're inherently passionate, concerned, or at least curious about.

- How does that issue (those issues) align with the most pressing challenges facing the world? For inspiration, look at the *UN SDGs framework*.

- What do you want to learn? And how do you want to grow to become a better version of yourself? Ignore or resist social expectations and projections. Also, keep in mind that, regardless of your accomplishments, there's always room for improvement.

- What system(s) need(s) to change, and what is my role? Let's be real. Systems of oppression such as white supremacy and neocolonialism, misogyny, and neoliberalism are worth toppling. It's up to each of us to reflect on how we are part of the problem.

- How can I be kind to myself while practicing purposeful empathy? Think of all the ways you can recharge your batteries, heal, integrate, and grow. Mindfulness practices, leisure activities, communing with nature—even occasionally binge-watching a Netflix series. It's not selfish to take care of yourself.

After answering these questions, take some time to journal about what's come up for you and consider sharing what you wrote with a good friend, partner, therapist, or coach. Your journey of leaning into purpose has begun.

4

EMBRACING A CULTURE OF EMPATHY

Empathy is a muscle, so it needs to be exercised.

—Satya Nadella, CEO of Microsoft

Nestled in the Caucasus Mountains, at the intersection of Eastern Europe and Western Asia, is a small country that punches above its weight. Inhabited by *Homo erectus* since the Paleolithic era, Georgia may have fewer than four million inhabitants but welcomed over seven million tourists in 2019. Archeological evidence reveals that the country has been producing wine since 6000 BC—long before Italy or France. And despite a tiny population, its national rugby team plays in the big leagues, living up to its country's motto: "Strength in Unity."

In 2021, I spent six months living in Georgia's capital city and worked with the Petre Shotadze Tbilisi Medical Academy (TMA). Initially, they wanted me to integrate empathy into their curriculum, but during my first meeting with their leadership team, the dean spoke passionately about their commitment to graduating physicians dedicated to the health of their patients *and* to social and planetary wellness. Impressed by their holistic view of medical education, I shared my reservations about incorporating empathy so far downstream. If the goal was to have it in their organizational DNA, gaining top-to-bottom support seemed like a better approach. I was delighted they agreed.

Over four half-day sessions, I facilitated workshops for twenty-five managers and administrators. The team laughed and cried together through a series of exercises, including eye gazing, storytelling, active listening, and empathy circles. They mapped out measurable ways to operationalize empathy using a design thinking process. They even had a couple of eureka moments working through my purposeful empathy diagram. Not only did they discover a common desire to do more for their local community, but one senior member shared with me in confidence that she had an epiphany and finally understood her life's purpose. It was magical.

No matter the size or industry of an organization—be it a major financial institution or a small humanitarian NGO—I always look forward to the a-ha moment when my clients realize the enormous value of empathy as a strategic opportunity and cultural norm. Contrary to popular belief, having empathy at work is not a sentimental, feel-good nice-to-have. It's become a hallmark of great companies. It's also the number-one leadership skill to help fuel business growth, build strong teams, and contribute to career success.

In a study with fifteen thousand leaders, those who master listening and respond with empathy outperform their peers by 40 percent in coaching, planning, and decision making. Empirical evidence also shows that empathy in the workplace positively affects communication, productivity, performance, talent acquisition, retention, innovation, resilience, growth, and, yes, even profit. In 2015, the Global Empathy Index found that the ten most empathy-focused companies had generated 50 percent more earnings per employee than did the bottom ten. Even *Harvard Business Review* has reported on the direct link between empathy and commercial success.

In 2019, the Society for Human Resource Management calculated that toxic workplace cultures had cost US employers $223 billion over the previous five years. In 2020, it reported that nearly half the employees it surveyed had considered leaving their job given the company culture. And that's before COVID-19 put things into overdrive.

The Great Resignation happened for good reason. Low-wage earners called it quits because the personal costs and risks of working were too high. Meanwhile, professionals could no longer justify or tolerate their working conditions either. Feeling chronically overworked, underappreciated, or both, millions of workers hit a tipping point. It appears to have taken a global pandemic to fully appreciate the significance of an empathic culture at work.

Sadly, many companies learned the hard way, and the fallout continues to be consequential. According to a Deloitte study published in 2021, three-quarters of CEOs anticipated work shortages would disrupt their businesses over the subsequent twelve months, and nearly six in ten believed that attracting talent would be among their company's biggest challenges. In addition, over the next decade, sixty million members of Gen Z—the most diverse generation the United States has ever known—will begin their careers. And they're expected to transform the workforce by bringing a new set of values, expectations, and goals.

This will have major implications for corporate America. For example, according to recent research, more than two-thirds of Gen Z respondents say they'd be "absolutely" more likely to apply for a job with a company that reflects racial and ethnic diversity through its recruitment and marketing materials. In addition, given their comfort with gender fluidity and nonbinary identity, 88 percent say it's important for employers to ask about gender pronouns. All told, leaders and organizations must become more inclusive and empathic. The question is: *how?*

LEARNING TO BE (MORE) EMPATHIC

I'm often asked, "Can empathy be taught?" The short answer is yes but not overnight and not in the same way other skills are developed. According to Julie Battilana and Tiziana Casciaro, coauthors of *Power, for All*, "Deep and lasting development of empathy requires more than temporarily seeing the world through someone else's eyes. It entails sustainably shifting from a focus on the self to an awareness and appreciation of interdependence." Cultivating empathy takes practice, not a one-off webinar. Some pioneering organizations already get this, but the critical mass is just starting to clue in.

At the time of this writing, I have uploaded more than twenty-five hundred consecutive "Daily Empathy Posts" covering a wide variety of empathy-related content. Over the past couple of years, I have watched the volume of articles about empathy, leadership, and culture skyrocket, especially in unlikely business publications like *Forbes*, *Inc.*, and *Fast Company*. As a long-time empathy enthusiast, I'm thrilled by its newfound rock-star status, but I'm also weary of *empathy-washing*, a term coined by Belinda Parmer, founder of The Empathy Index, to describe corporate virtue signaling. After all, "for companies to live out empathy in real and meaningful ways, it must become the fabric of organizational culture," writes Maria Ross in *The Empathy Edge*. That's why empathy-training programs must be carefully evaluated to weed out the phonies and fakes.

With that in mind, below are seven examples that span early childhood to executive education. Some were ahead of the curve, with long track records of impact. Others were created more recently, using research into human consciousness, trauma, or neuroscience to inform their approach. Regardless of their theory of change, each example is relevant to leaders and organizations seeking to foster a culture of empathy. And despite their different approaches, they share a core belief in common: empathy is not a fixed trait, and we can all become more empathic with practice.

Roots of Empathy

Founded in 1996 by Mary Gordon, Roots of Empathy (ROE) is an award-winning, evidence-based program that has taught social and emotional learning to over one million schoolchildren worldwide by bringing babies into classrooms. Once a month throughout the academic year, a baby and their parent or guardian visit a designated class. Schools with twelve grade levels engage twelve different babies and their families, and each trained facilitator uses age-appropriate curricula. On a typical visit, students sit in a circle around a green blanket, and the baby is placed in the middle. The facilitator asks the kids to describe how the baby has changed since their last encounter and how it appears to be feeling that day.

Throughout the visit, they reflect on the baby's needs, witness tenderness between the infant and their caregiver, and come to appreciate the importance of kindness and empathy in the world. Ultimately, the program helps kids develop "emotional literacy" and learn that, as Gordon says, "heartwork is as vital as brainwork." After decades of independent research, ROE has been found to reduce aggression; increase sharing, caring, and inclusion; and promote resilience, wellbeing, and mental health. Who knew that babies could be such powerful teachers?

Culture of empathy takeaway: When a workplace feels unsafe, anxiety goes up, conflicts emerge, and people are afraid to speak up and take risks, all of which have negative consequences for organizational success. Ensuring psychological safety at work has never been more important, especially to the younger generation of talent. Encouraging people to express their feelings reminds us that we have complex lives, identities, roles, and responsibilities and gives us permission to be more authentic. This, in turn, increases belonging, trust, and wellbeing.

Dialogue Social Enterprise (DSE)

Andreas Heinecke was a teenager when he learned that some of his family members had been Nazis and others had been killed in gas chambers. He spent the next decade studying humanity's capacity for good and evil. In 1988, he launched an experiment to challenge biases and mindsets about diversity and counteract "othering." Informed by transformative learning theory, Dialogue in the Dark involves participants being guided by the visually impaired through specially constructed pitch-black rooms to experience familiar environments in unfamiliar ways.

Since its debut in Germany, nearly eight million people have participated in DSE's highly experiential exhibitions in seventy-eight cities around the world. They now include Dialogue in Silence, an interactive experience in which the hearing-impaired guide participants to discover a repertoire of nonverbal expression, and Dialogue with Time, an encounter that fosters intergenerational understanding and helps participants overcome stereotypes about aging. Through their public exhibitions, and more recently their corporate training, the overarching goal of DSE's programming is to facilitate mutual understanding and build social cohesion.

Culture of empathy takeaway: It's widely understood that diversity of thought has a positive impact on innovation and workplace productivity, but we all have an unconscious preference for people who are like us. At a time when identity politics dominate public discourse, it's important for organizations to help their staff develop awareness about implicit bias and deploy strategies that promote diversity, equity, and inclusion in the workplace. Embodied practices and experiential learning help foster empathy and a sense of belonging.

In Your Shoes

In Your Shoes is a collaborative project between Georgetown University (in Washington, DC) and Patrick Henry College (in rural Virginia) that uses theatrical performance to bring diverse students together to engage in "deep, challenging, and mutually respectful dialogue with one another to promote mutual understanding and empathy." Led by Derek Goldman, codirector of Georgetown's Laboratory of Global Performance and Politics, the program has developed a signature methodology called Performing One Another.

Students are put into pairs and given a prompt question or topic for discussion. They record their conversation, and once it's complete, both students transcribe verbatim what their partner said. After rehearsing their partner's words, they reunite to recreate their dialogue, each from the other's perspective. The process is transformative to participants because it engenders empathy while respecting different viewpoints.

Culture of empathy takeaway: The office used to provide opportunities to fraternize across party lines. Today, political polarization in corporate America extends all the way to the C-suite. Hostile us-versus-them environments burden businesses with additional costs related to mediating internal conflicts, additional security, leadership turnover, employee attrition, and expensive recruitment activities. Acrimonious workplaces are also unpleasant and unhealthy for everyone. As ideological divides continue to seep into the workplace, it's essential for organizations to find ways to build bridges and encourage connection.

Radical Empathy

Terri Givens is a world-renowned political scientist with expertise on the radical right, the politics of immigration, and antidiscrimination policy. As a Black woman, she also has lived experience navigating America's racial divides and overcoming internalized oppression. Her book *Radical Empathy* was published in the aftermath of George Floyd's murder as white supremacy was once again on full display. Meanwhile, Black Lives Matter (BLM) marches were taking place across the globe. Within the context of a deepening racial divide, she wrote, "Empathy allows us to see the humanity in others, and radical empathy moves us to work towards social justice and change that will benefit us all."

In her professional development training, she invites leaders to embrace radical empathy through the following six-step process: a willingness to be vulnerable; becoming grounded in who you are; opening yourself to the experience of others; practicing empathy; taking action; and creating change and building trust. Her goal is to help create inclusive workplaces that value diversity and train inclusive leaders to espouse authenticity as an organizational norm.

Culture of empathy takeaway: The social reckoning of BLM continues to reverberate as organizations navigate important EDI conversations and decisions. Leaders can no longer pay lip service to advancing racial equity. Meanwhile, private sector businesses are rightfully being called upon to leverage their assets, power, and influence to contribute to systemic change. Strategies and practices that foster racial repair and reconciliation are needed more than ever. And in the face of growing diversity-training backlash, psychologically safe listening sessions and other forms of empathy-based interventions provide alternative pathways.

LASER Method

Workers everywhere are still recovering from the past few years of heightened stress, anxiety, and brain fog. That's why Katharine Manning writes in *The Empathetic Workplace*, "If we work with people, we are working with people in trauma." She would know, after having spent fifteen years as a senior attorney adviser with the Justice Department, working to protect victim rights after tragic and high-profile events, including the Boston Marathon bombing, the Pulse nightclub mass shooting, and the Unite the Right rally violence in Charlottesville. Today, she trains leaders and managers how to respond empathically to employees and members of the public experiencing trauma using what she calls the LASER method.

"L" refers to "listening" and is considered the most important step. When someone shares a distressing story, being fully present is a healing balm to the speaker. "A" stands for "acknowledge." Often, a simple "thank you for telling me" helps a speaker feel validated. "S" refers to sharing information or resources. Many victims of trauma feel a loss of control. Asking for permission to share information may help them regain a sense of agency. "E" stands for "empower." Despite the concern a listener may have when hearing a traumatic story, only victims themselves are responsible for moving forward. That said, offering choices about next steps can be empowering to them. Finally, "R" refers to "return" and has two components. Returning to the victim at some point for a check-in, and returning to oneself. Supporting victims often leads to secondary trauma or compassion fatigue. Self-care is key to completing the LASER method.

Culture of empathy takeaway: Throughout the pandemic, nearly one in three American adults reported having symptoms of anxiety and/or depression, up from 11 percent pre-COVID-19. Many studies also found that women and racialized people were disproportionately impacted. Marriages suffered, substance abuse skyrocketed, and the burnout rates shot to all-time highs across professions. This means for one reason or another, nearly the entire American workforce is traumatized. Given these extenuating circumstances, empathic leadership is required to restore a baseline of wellness at work.

Empathic Intervision

Group dynamics are complex at the best of times. Misunderstandings, misaligned intentions or expectations, lack of trust, tunnel vision, and groupthink can all inhibit or derail group cohesion. Cue Empathic Intervision, a process codesigned by Dr. Lidewij Niezink from the Netherlands and Dr. Katherine Train from South Africa. Unlike *super*vision, which is inherently hierarchical, *inter*vision involves a facilitated exchange between colleagues that tosses the organizational chart out of the window. Grounded in a multilayered empathy approach, the process helps overcome the inherent flaws of groupwork, and is intended to produce better organizational outcomes.

To optimize this peer-to-peer practice, Empathic Intervision uses the following five empathy-building capacities: self-empathy—becoming aware of our own inner state at any given time to differentiate our feelings and emotions from those of others; kinesthetic empathy—the ability to sense movement to improve interpersonal connection; reflective empathy—the capacity to reflect what one hears to facilitate mutual understanding; imaginative empathy—gaining insight into the experiences and worldviews of others through embodied imagination by stepping in and out of perspectives to lessen polarization; and empathic creativity—moving from hierarchical to horizontal power dynamics to encourage actionable solutions and innovations.

Culture of empathy takeaway: Locked into a purely logical or Cartesian way of problem solving, leaders and managers often miss opportunities for different kinds of collective intelligence to emerge. Meanwhile, "power over" dynamics still remain more commonplace in today's workforce than "power with." As self-organizing systems continue to gain momentum, and a new generation of talent enters the workforce, organizations that adopt co-creative processes for problem solving and innovation will have a competitive advantage. Empathy can be harnessed as a generative force to that end.

Moral Courage Network

Irshad Manji was four years old when she and her family arrived in Canada as refugees from Uganda. During the week, she went to secular public school near Vancouver, and on Saturdays, she attended a madrasa. She grew up in a violent household, and by the age of 14, she was expelled from the Islamic school for asking too many questions and challenging religious dogma. As a vocal lesbian and reformist Muslim, she's received numerous death threats and had the windows of her home fitted with bullet-proof glass.

Today, she is the founder of the Moral Courage network, an initiative that empowers people to hear, not fear, different perspectives and recognizes that "empathy is a smarter and more constructive emotion than feeling offended." The organization offers a unique training program called Diversity Without Division, which teaches participants how to think clearly by lowering their emotional defenses and pivot from an either/or to a both/and mindset.

Culture of empathy takeaway: "Call-out culture" aims to publicly call attention to someone's wrongdoing and "cancel culture" involves swarm-like public shaming. They are different by degree, but both tend to banish the accused rather than engage with them as complex and fallible individuals, capable of redemption. Given the high stakes involved in being called-out or cancelled, many individuals are choosing to stay silent, which compromises freedom of expression. And since businesses are not immune to the financial consequences of taking a stand—one way or the other— there's an urgent need to deploy mechanisms that help lower the discursive temperature between people who don't share the same point of view.

EMBRACING A CULTURE OF EMPATHY ON PURPOSE AND BY DESIGN

As an empathy evangelist, I believe all efforts that help people become more empathic are important. But I've highlighted these seven programs because they do more than develop a skill. They invite participants to deepen their self-awareness, gain new perspectives, build bridges across differences, and become more wholehearted. At its best, empathy training provides an onramp to a kinder and more just world for everyone.

Practically speaking, however, and based on my professional experience, empathy-building programs should include the following ten features:

1. An overview of what empathy is and isn't, as well as its power, potential, and pitfalls
2. Embodied practices to *feel* empathy
3. Invitations into safe and brave conversations that require authenticity and vulnerability
4. Exercises to improve listening skills
5. Opportunities to practice perspective-taking
6. Storytelling
7. Rituals for mindfulness and self-empathy
8. A human-centered design process to operationalize empathy
9. A commitment from leadership to track and reward empathic behavior
10. An acknowledgment that values-based culture change work is a marathon, not a sprint

If culture eats strategy for breakfast, empathy is the tray upon which it is served. In other words, organizations with empathic cultures win big, especially if they're empathic by design. That's why I want to highlight the eighth item on my list. First, let me share a story from Michael Ventura's *Applied Empathy* to illustrate the power of human-centered design. It's about his former company, Sub Rosa, being asked by the chief marketing officer at General Electric (GE) to help the latter's medical imaging business become the market leader.

The specific mandate was to increase the volume of mammogram machine sales without changing the unit specs. As a strategy and design company, Sub Rosa knew user experience was key, which meant talking to doctors, technicians, and most importantly, patients. They quickly discovered that most women find mammograms painful, but they couldn't address that issue without changing the machine specifications. Next, they learned that most women don't like the exam waiting rooms because they tend to be sterile, uncomfortably cold, and intimidating. Armed with that insight, they turned to an infamous brand that works hard to mitigate against anxiety-provoking shopping experiences for women (lingerie, anyone?) and began looking at the entire mammography process from a holistic lens. This led to their breakthrough idea: Having GE sell physical environments *with* its machines to elevate the comfort and wellbeing of patients prior to their breast exams. Think of a spa-like waiting room with comfortable sofas, relaxing music, scented candles, and mint tea.

To its credit, GE accepted the recommendation and watched its market share grow. But that's not all. One of the unintended consequences of this design innovation was that cancer was detected earlier in some women because their breast tissue was less dense during their exam—a direct result of less anxiety after sitting in a warm and cozy GE waiting room! The use of human-centered design not only gave GE a sales edge; it saved lives.

Now let's circle back to the work I did with the medical school in Tbilisi to illustrate how design thinking can help an organization create a culture of empathy. After a couple of half-day sessions, in which all the participants engaged in embodied empathy exercises, shared stories, and felt a growing sense of group cohesion, I invited them to partake in a collaborative process aimed at operationalizing empathy at TMA. Quick aside: I know that "operationalizing empathy" sounds like an oxymoron, but creating a culture of empathy does not happen through wishful thinking. Organizations must establish behavioral norms that affirm how much empathy is valued, and policies that reward its practice—ideally by engaging users in their design.

First, I went over the afternoon's agenda and underscored how each individual engagement would contribute to the outcome and overall success of the day. Then I split the group into small clusters. Depending on the size of the cohort, this number will fluctuate, but five to eight per group is usually ideal to optimize participation and inclusion. Next, I primed everyone to ignore practical limitations and withhold judgment about their own ideas and those of their colleagues. In the early stages of design thinking, unrealistic (even outlandish) ideas are welcome. Finally, I revealed the three questions they would explore and walked them through the six-step process that would be repeated for each question.

The questions were:
- In a perfect world, how would you experience self-empathy at work?
- In a perfect world, how would empathy for others manifest at work?
- In a perfect world, how would TMA demonstrate organizational empathy?

The six-step process included:
- Asking each participant to answer the question on their own using sticky notes.
- After 5–10 minutes of brainstorming, asking each participant to share their ideas with their group and affix their respective sticky notes to a big sheet of paper.
- Asking the group to continue brainstorming new ideas together for another 5–10 minutes and adding new sticky notes to the big sheet of paper.
- Asking the group to organize their ideas thematically.
- Asking the group to select their three favorite ideas.

- Asking the group to write those top three ideas on a new sheet of paper and affixing it to the wall for the entire room to see.

After completing this process for each question, every group had three sheets of paper hanging on the wall. Then came time for sharing in a plenary. One representative from each group was invited to describe the top three ideas generated per question. This was repeated for each group. The final step involved giving each participant in the room ten new sticky notes to "vote" for the ideas they found most compelling. By the end, everyone could see which ideas were most popular, providing a road map for the leadership team to follow.

In TMA's case, one idea caught everyone's imagination: having a staff room in the building to chill out and socialize. Imagine how valued everyone felt when the school's rector had a big stock room emptied and painted with stylish colors and outfitted with comfortable sofas, a big-screen TV, and shelves full of books and board games. I was there to witness the big reveal, and I can tell you the excitement was palpable. The organization had responded empathically, and a new culture of empathy was spawned.

WORKPLACES WITH AUTHENTICITY, VULNERABILITY, AND SOUL

I'm a big fan of Brené Brown, the self-described Texan researcher and storyteller who spent years studying vulnerability and shame and then broke the internet with two unforgettable TED Talks. I girl crush on her for lots of reasons, but here are the two most important: Her work is empirical *and* intuitive, meaning she has a mountain of research to back up whatever she says but is also trustworthy on a gut level. And whenever I'm feeling emotionally lousy, she always helps me find my center of gravity.

Her book *Daring Greatly* helped me realize I was letting an insecure boss make me feel small, and thanks to an interview she did on Russell Brand's *Under the Skin* podcast (available on YouTube), I felt empowered to share my truth with a group of students after being triggered by feelings of shame. My meta-takeaway from her formidable body of work is this: to live a courageous life—one that's aligned with your values and purpose—we must let ourselves be seen, warts, wounds, wisdom, and all.

In *Dare to Lead*, she writes, "Vulnerability is the birthplace of love, belonging, and joy . . . [and] empathy is the rocket fuel for building trust and increasing connection." This means vulnerability and empathy go hand in hand, and the best empathy training in the world will only go so far if people can't be vulnerable or feel fully expressed—in all their colors and complexity. Yet how many leaders or organizations encourage their talent to bring their whole messy selves to work? That's why embracing a culture of empathy requires a paradigm shift.

Reinventing Organizations: A Guide to Creating Organizations Inspired by the Next Stage of Human Consciousness, by Frederic Laloux, is considered one of the most influential management books of the past decade. In it, he explains why the tired model of command and control leadership (beholden to a fear and scarcity-based mindset) no longer serves us, and describes the emergence of a new organizational model that honors human evolution. He writes: "In *Evolutionary Teal*, we seek wholeness beyond ego and see the inner lives—the emotional, intuitive, and spiritual—as valuable domains of learning. We define a life well-lived by inner, not outer standards . . . Such a worldview is bound to produce news ways of working. Many of us sense that the current way we run organizations is deeply limiting. We will come up with better ways—because there is simply too much life, and too much human potential, waiting to express itself." Indeed, and embracing a culture of empathy is certainly a better way.

PURPOSEFUL EMPATHY PRACTICES

The following exercises illustrate how empathy can be developed and nurtured. You can download a free workbook from my website.

1. Encourage your team at work (or in your organization as a whole) to participate in a *Human Library* event. This involves volunteers typically from a marginalized or stigmatized group acting as "books" in which they share their life stories with "readers." According to its website, the Human Library is a global, innovative, and hands-on learning platform that works with companies, institutions, and organizations "committed

to incorporating social understanding and cultural awareness as a part of their business model in relation to their workforce, partnerships, clients and customers."

2. Set aside an afternoon with a group of colleagues to watch the award-winning documentary *HUMAN*, available on YouTube. The description reads, "What is it that makes us human? Is it that we love, that we fight? That we laugh? Cry? Our curiosity? The quest for discovery? Driven by these questions, filmmaker and artist Yann Arthus-Bertrand spent three years collecting real-life stories from 2,000 women and men in 60 countries. Working with a dedicated team of translators, journalists and cameramen, Yann captures deeply personal and emotional accounts of topics that unite us all; struggles with poverty, war, homophobia, and the future of our planet mixed with moments of love and happiness."

    After watching the film together, respond to the following prompt questions:

    *   How do you *feel* after watching this film?

    *   Which story(ies) did you find most compelling, fascinating, surprising, or upsetting, and why?

    *   Which story(ies) filled you with hope, appreciation, or love, and why?

    *   Why and how does storytelling increase empathy and diminish "othering"?

    *   What is the overarching message of this film?

    *   In light of that message, what can we as individuals and as a group do differently?

Consider hosting a monthly film screening with colleagues about different social issues, followed by a conversation using the Empathetic Reaction Discussion Questions provided by *Teach with Movies*.

3. Commit to listening to one episode of *This is Civity* per month. The podcast "features people who are building relationships to dismantle inequities and strengthen communities grounded in respect and empathy." It's produced by Civity, a national nonprofit organization that seeks to "build the relational infrastructure necessary for communities in which everyone has what they need to thrive." Again, consider hosting a monthly podcast club with colleagues to discuss each episode.

5

PUTTING EMPATHY TO WORK

Empathy helps transform jobs into careers and careers into callings.

—Dev Patnaik

Award-winning author Annie Dillard once said, "How we spend our days is of course how we spend our lives." Since we work on average ninety thousand hours over our lifetime, she's not kidding—and that was before COVID-19 obliterated any modicum of work-life balance that we had. For a long time, burnout was considered a personal stress-related syndrome. But in 2019, the World Health Organization redefined it as "chronic workplace stress that has not been successfully managed." Now that it's seen as an occupational hazard, employers are beginning to recognize their responsibility for the overall wellbeing of their talent.

Seen from a glass-half-empty perspective, that's a huge burden for organizations to bear. But the flip side offers a tremendous opportunity for empathic leadership to shine. Imagine how 210,000 Citigroup employees felt reading a memo from CEO Jane Fraser in spring 2021 announcing "Zoom-free" Fridays and imploring them to take their vacation days and avoid scheduling calls outside traditional office hours. To a worn-out workforce, empathic cultures and practices are game-changing. Sometimes even life-saving. And what's becoming increasingly clear is that all this matters to consumers too. Research shows that 42 percent refuse to buy something from a company they perceive to lack empathy. No wonder the World Economic Forum believes it's "a must-have business strategy."

To demonstrate the power of empathy at work, this chapter highlights six organizations that have it baked into their purpose, mission, or corporate culture. I also explore a new type of corporation that puts people and planet before profits. Of course, no business is perfect—and let me make that explicitly clear. But in their own unique ways, these five companies plus one nonprofit are purposeful empathy champions. I hope they provoke introspection about your place of work that leads to empathic transformation. The need has never been greater and return on investment never more assured.

UNILEVER

The truest and highest form of enlightened self-interest requires that we pay the fullest regard to the interest and welfare of those around us, whose wellbeing we must bind up with our own and with whom we must share our prosperity.

—William Hesketh Lever, cofounder of Unilever

Vaseline. Lipton. Ben & Jerry's. Dove. Knorr. The list of household names in Unilever's four hundred-plus product portfolio is impressive, but the degree to which empathy animates the consumer goods company is extraordinary. As a giant multinational with over sixty billion dollars in annual sales, products used by 2.5 billion people every day, approximately 150,000 employees, and operations in 190 countries across the globe, Unilever could easily be the poster child for business as usual.

Instead, by decoupling its environmental footprint from its growth and being adamant about increasing its positive social impact, the company seeks to be an agent of change. As CEO Alan Jope framed it in an open letter to the public, "It's up to businesses like us—working with NGOs, government organisations, academics, suppliers, customers and other partners—to drive a new model of capitalism and build a better future." To that end, in 2019, the company launched a bold fifteen-year corporate strategy called the

Unilever Compass, with three ambitious goals: improve the health of the planet; improve people's health, confidence, and wellbeing; and contribute to a fairer, more socially inclusive world.

The specific environmental targets they announced include investing $1.5 billion in a new climate fund; achieving zero-deforestation by 2023; making all their plastic reusable, recyclable, or compostable by 2025; and reaching carbon neutrality by 2039. Skeptics may roll their eyes, but the company's track record speaks for itself. It has reduced its waste footprint per consumer by 32 percent, achieved zero waste across all its factories worldwide, and reached 100 percent renewable grid electricity on five continents. These bold efforts to mitigate against climate change demonstrate empathy for humanity, especially future generations, as well as all other living species.

Unilever is also bullish about social and economic inclusion. As former C-suite leader Leena Nair said, "There are 660 billionaires in the U.S. who added $1.4 trillion to their wealth [in 2020], as 20 million Americans lost their jobs. The divide between rich and poor got wider. After two decades of progress, we have gone backwards on world poverty." In response, the company pledged that anyone who provides goods and services directly to them—estimated at ten million people—will earn a living wage by 2030. Unlike minimum wage, living wage is meant to lift workers, their families, and communities out of sustenance living. Unilever's antipoverty commitment is another example of its empathy ethos.

The company also launched #Unstereotype to liberate genders from restricting social norms in advertising. This quickly scaled to Act 2 Unstereotype, which introduced structural changes to its entire marketing process. In a study commissioned by the company, nearly one in two individuals from marginalized communities, namely BIPOC, LGBTQ+ and those with disabilities, said they felt stereotyped by advertising. In response, Unilever introduced a 100 percent ban on digital alterations to models' body shape, size, proportion, or skin color and now works with more diverse and underrepresented groups, both onscreen and behind the camera. By celebrating diversity and normalizing difference, the company's deliberate inclusion strategies show empathy for people who have been historically excluded.

Finally, the company prioritizes employee wellbeing. A few years ago, it launched a program called Develop Your Purpose to encourage its staff "to bring their passions, their causes, and the things they really care about to the workplace and their work." As of June 2021, sixty thousand employees had participated in the workshops, and according to the chief human resources officer, engagement metrics "have gone through the roof," with workers reporting higher intrinsic motivation and overall life satisfaction. No wonder two million people apply for jobs with Unilever every year, making it the third most searched-for company on LinkedIn, after Google and Apple. Unilever has mad empathy street cred, and its efforts are paying off in spades.

GOALCAST

Letting people be themselves is the most empathic thing we can do.

—Cyrus Gorjipour, CEO of Goalcast

Goalcast is a digital media company that attracts half a billion unique video views per month. It produces and distributes transformative content including speeches, documentaries, and original short films to help people realize their potential. The company was cofounded by two first-generation Canadians who share the belief that every person on the planet has the power to live a life of purpose. But that wasn't always the case.

As a teenager, Cyrus Gorjipour suffered through years of depression and low self-esteem, blaming everyone around him for his unhappiness, until one day, while mindlessly watching TV, he reached out for a book on the coffee table in front of him. It was an *Intro to Psych* textbook for a class his sister was taking at college. While flipping through the pages, he landed on a concept called *locus of control*, which holds that each of us is responsible for our own success, regardless of circumstances. Cyrus was taken by the idea and immediately put the theory into action. The results spoke for themselves. Today, he is CEO of one of the fastest-growing startups in Canada and married to the high school crush he didn't have the courage to speak to as a young man.

Cofounder Salim Sader was once a passionate physics teacher who refused to see his students though the metrics of test results and grades. One evening, he and some fellow educators were copied on an email sent by a student to the school's guidance counselor. The message described the overwhelming pressure he felt to become a pharmacist and hinted at suicide. The next morning, Salim caught up with the student and learned that he was already a successful entrepreneur who had earned $30K the prior summer booking bands for weddings and shows around the city. The student felt better for having offloaded some of his angst the night before, but Salim left the conversation wondering why schools don't do a better job of empowering kids to pursue their dreams, while helping them develop their innate gifts and talents.

Salim and Cyrus met at a dinner party and spoke passionately about their frustration with the school system. That's when the idea for a new learning platform was seeded. Soon enough, they became partners and failed forward a couple of times before landing on Goalcast's winning formula. Today, they co-lead the company by embracing a growth mindset and continually stretching beyond their respective comfort zones. Rooted in empathy, they want others to feel a sense of agency.

When I asked Cyrus to describe his company's organizational culture, he initially dismissed the idea that they're a gold standard of Zenlike workplaces. "But if wellness means coming to work as your authentic self, making mistakes without fear of retribution, and feeling that personal growth is encouraged, then Goalcast fits the bill," he said. Staff members are also invited to participate in weekly "mastermind" sessions with experts who facilitate self-care and competency-building workshops. Plus, they receive a generous benefits package, including an annual fitness and personal development stipend.

What makes Goalcast an empathic place to work is that both co-founders want their staff to feel psychologically safe and empowered in their roles and in their lives. According to a typical employee review I found online, "Goalcast is an environment where you continuously learn, grow, innovate, and work on meaningful projects, leaving you inspired and driven every day. It's fast-paced, challenging, and competitive, yet exciting and motivating. The entire team works hard together to ensure we all show up as our best selves and use our strengths. It's a space where I feel supported."

Goalcast is a good example of an empathic organization for another reason. The company's DNA is all about connecting empathically with viewers. Cyrus explains, "Fear of rejection, the complex relationship with our parents, heartbreak, and self-doubt are universal themes we can all relate to, regardless of age, gender or race. Our goal is to create relatable stories to empower people. As a digital media company, we could jump on all sorts of trends to increase our views, but we don't. That's because thousands of people comment on our stories on a daily basis and share how our videos have changed—and even sometimes saved—their lives. That positive impact is the currency we're looking for with every video we put out into the world."

FROG

When it comes to making things people love, empathy is core to the process.

—frog Insights

Despite his mother's disapproval (she even burned his sketchbooks), industrial designer Hartmut Esslinger launched Frog Design at the age of twenty-five. Before long, his agency was revolutionizing industries, with a portfolio that boasts the Sony Walkman and the first design language for the original Macintosh computers. Today, frog—stylized in lowercase to signal a democratic workplace—is a global creative powerhouse that strives to "shape a regenerative future that is both sustainable and inclusive for businesses, people and planet."

Design thinking, also known as human-centered design, prioritizes the user experience throughout its iterative, problem-solving process. That's why empathy is considered the point of departure for any design project, be it for a product (from a toothbrush to a spaceship) or a service (from legal representation to an all-inclusive vacation). This means all design companies deploy empathy by de facto. What sets frog apart as an empathic organization is how far it goes above and beyond that.

One team at the San Francisco office sought to improve pelvic exams by redesigning the speculum. After conducting research with patients and physicians to gain insight about the experience from both perspectives, they also engaged with members from the LGBTQ+ community. frog believes that diverse voices, perspectives, skills sets, and backgrounds—within its organization and across its design process—always create better solutions.

This explains why the company also invited men to imagine themselves in a doctor's office undergoing the procedure and then declare in first-person what the experience was like, calling the exercise "radical empathy." As a result, not only did they design a better speculum for anyone who experiences vaginal healthcare—whether they identify as women or not—but they also improved the exam experience holistically by making changes to the physical space and introducing an app.

The company's commitment to social good is a another reason frog is an empathic organization. The opening sentence of its manifesto reads, "We are fanatical about improving the world." To that end, it launched a social impact practice to design for social innovation. For example, in collaboration with a UN agency, it created the Humanitarian Data Exchange to improve the coordination of relief efforts after a major catastrophe. Since its launch in 2014, it has served 100,000 users in over two hundred locations around the world and has become an essential tool for local governments, the UN, Red Cross, and other NGOs, as well as journalists reporting from the field. Using its design props to save lives is another great example of leveraging empathy on purpose.

KIND

> *Even though people do not traditionally think of being empathetic as a business skill, it can create enormous value.*
>
> —Daniel Lubetzky, CEO, KIND Healthy Snacks

Daniel Lubetzky is a consummate bridge builder who can say "hello, how are you?" in over forty languages. Born in Mexico City to a father who survived three years at Dachau as a teenager, he believes his ancestry highlights what happens when people don't recognize our shared humanity. In his senior thesis at Trinity University in Texas, he argued that Arabs and Israelis should go into business together to create meaningful relationships through vested interests. A few years later, while doing research about economic cooperation in Israel, he founded a "not-ONLY-for-profit" business called PeaceWorks, selling tapenades and spreads to promote Middle East peace.

Fast forward two decades and Lubetzky is now keeping busy as founder and CEO of KIND, a company that sells over one billion snack bars every year. He credits the meteoric rise and ongoing success of the company to great products but also to a culture that incentivizes and rewards empathy and kindness. One example is its longstanding tradition of recognizing team members (KIND is allergic to the word *employee*) who embody and champion kindness at work, dubbed *Kindos*. Lubetzky believes the recognition is "just as high an honor, if not more so, than meeting an important sales goal or other business objective."

In 2016, the KIND Foundation was established with a mission to "foster kinder and more empathetic communities" and announced a twenty-million-dollar investment to incubate Empatico, a free video-conferencing tool for teachers to help primary and middle school students nurture meaningful connections with other children around the world. To date, more than forty thousand educators are registered users, and tens of thousands of children across 155 countries have shared bridge-building activities and lesson plans.

KIND published its first-ever impact report as I was writing this book. It's a document created to celebrate what the organization is doing right, so, admittedly, I read it with a grain of salt. But just as I had discovered after watching interviews with Lubetzky on YouTube and searching what employees (past and present) had to say about the company anonymously online, I kept reaching the same conclusion: The company's effort to promote empathy and kindness is not a marketing gimmick. Of course, it doesn't hurt sales, but the brand promise is legit.

Lubetzky recognizes the fine line his company must walk. On one hand, he says, "If you over-commercialize a social mission, it completely loses its soul." On the other, he sees empathy as an existential question: "It's about the survival of the human race . . . Unless we can join forces and recognize each other's humanity, how can we do business together, let alone make progress on the increasingly complex and difficult problems in society?"

ASHOKA: INNOVATORS FOR THE PUBLIC

In a Changemaker world, empathy becomes as fundamental as reading, writing and math. This creates a new social imperative for societies worldwide to ensure that every child fully develops their own innate capacity for empathy.

—Ashoka website

Unlike traditional entrepreneurship fueled by profit, social entrepreneurs are driven to implement solutions that make our world more peaceful, just, and sustainable. My own doctoral research revealed they're motivated by what I call "empathic action." In 1980, Bill Drayton founded a nonprofit organization dedicated to helping social entrepreneurs scale their efforts. Since then, Ashoka has supported nearly four thousand Fellows across the globe, tackling issues such as human trafficking, biodiversity loss, and prison reform.

Inspired by their impact, other funders including the Schwab Foundation, Skoll Foundation, and Echoing Green have followed suit, and many high-profile competitions such as the Clinton Global Initiative, XPrize, and Hult Prize award millions of dollars every year to scalable social innovations. I recall with enormous pride watching the winning team of McGill MBA students onstage in New York being presented with a seven-figure check to launch Aspire, a social enterprise that combats food insecurity in low-income countries by harvesting insects as an alternative source of protein. The fact that Aspire still exists, has scaled, and even spawned Legendary Foods, a spinoff company on a different continent led by one of the original team members, says plenty about the viability and sustainability of social ventures. To my mind, social entrepreneurship exemplifies the practical application of purposeful empathy in business.

After four decades analyzing the behavior of the world's leading social entrepreneurs, Drayton has drawn a couple of conclusions: All changemakers are skilled collaborators. And all effective collaboration requires empathy. That's why Ashoka believes empathy is as fundamental as reading, writing, and math and puts it centerstage in all its granting and programming. "The course of human history has been moving towards a more and more empathy-based society," according to Drayton. "It's the only way to have real equality."

PARTICIPANT

A film can have the power to spur conversation and spark an audience's empathy, passion, and curiosity . . . to create meaningful impact.

—Jim Berk, former CEO of Participant

When you think of an LA-based film production company with eighty-two Academy Award nominations and twenty-one wins, does a string of red-carpet celebrities come to mind? Probably faster than a roster of movies that inspire social action, right? It turns out Participant films not only star A-listers including Tom Hanks, Julia Roberts, Jamie Foxx, Kate Winslet, and George Clooney, but they also address some of society's most vexing problems, including systemic racism, sexual harassment, and climate change.

With a slate of more than one hundred feature and documentary films, including *Spotlight*, *Lincoln*, *An Inconvenient Truth*, and *Contagion*, Participant's mission is to produce social impact entertainment. What makes the company unique—apart from being founded and initially bankrolled by billionaire Jeff Skoll—is that for as many as five films per year, it creates social impact campaigns in partnership with advocacy groups to inspire viewers into action. "We like to say there's a fourth act to our movies, which is the impact," says CEO David Linde.

Take Oscar-winning *Roma*, for example. Released in 2018, the film offers a poignant glimpse into the life of an Indigenous domestic worker in Mexico. According to the International Labour Organization (ILO), Cleo is one of sixty-seven million domestic workers worldwide who lacks benefits and other basic labor protections. In partnership with the National Domestic Workers Alliance (NDWA) in the United States and a similar NGO in Mexico, Participant created video campaigns to support Alia, a portable benefits platform for domestic workers. The film's star and representatives from both partner NGOs also went to Geneva to attend a two-day event focused on domestic worker rights to advocate for the Mexican government to ratify Convention 189 of the ILO, which sets labor rights and protections, including minimum wage, decent work, rest hours, and protection against violence. Two months later, Mexico's Congress passed legislation to support the rights of domestic workers, and in 2020, it became the thirtieth member state to ratify the convention.

Linde is careful to point out that legislative action was not an overnight result of the film's commercial success. But Monica Ramirez, NDWA's gender justice campaigns director, acknowledges the film's social impact campaign raised public awareness. Moreover, human rights activist Bonnie Abaunza believes the Participant partnership "serves as a prime example of how pop culture and social change practitioners can work together to shift attitudes and create the cultural conditions needed to sustain lasting social change."

Other campaigns have included Represent Justice to change the hearts and minds of audiences in support of criminal justice reform, based on the work of attorney Bryan Stevenson, as depicted in *Just Mercy*, as well as *Ingredients for Change*, a yearlong initiative that brought *Food Inc.* to leaders and decision makers in low-income communities facing food insecurity and provided support to local initiatives that combat child obesity. *Waiting for Superman* was followed by a three-year campaign to reform public education in America, and *North Country* is credited for having led to the renewal of the Violence Against Women Act in the US Congress. All that is to say Participant films take audiences from empathy to action, and often what follows is social change.

When Skoll began shopping around the idea of a prosocial media company, people told him, "The surest way to become a millionaire is to start by being a billionaire and go into the movie industry." Thankfully, he ignored the warnings. In the early years, studios were also wary about Participant's social action campaigns, but thanks to their overwhelming success, they have often become contractually required. This means films grounded in purposeful empathy are making it in Hollywood.

THE FUTURE OF EMPATHIC ORGANIZATIONS

In 2017, Participant became a Certified B Corporation, joining the ranks of a new type of company committed to leveraging the power of business to solve social and environmental problems. Its Declaration of Interdependence reads, "We envision a global economy that uses business as a force for good. As Certified B Corporations and leaders of this emerging economy, we believe: That we must be the change we seek in the world; That all business ought to be conducted as if people and place mattered; That, through their products, practices, and profits, businesses should aspire to do no harm and benefit all; and To do so requires that we act with the understanding that we are each dependent upon another and thus responsible for each other and future generations."

Imagine how the world would look if all companies espoused this credo. In one of its publications, *B the Change Weekly*, the company wrote, "Empathy is a powerful emotion that the Certified B Corporation community can use to redesign and rebuild capitalism." No wonder some see B Corps as leaders of a more equitable and regenerative economy.

In this chapter, I have described how six organizations put empathy to work in different ways. The constant is the degree to which their leaders appreciate its value holistically. Empirically, we know that empathic organizations have more loyal, productive, and engaged employees who suffer from fewer mental health problems. They design better products and services and have more respect for the unwritten social contract they hold with citizens at large. Of course, some companies are empathy-washers and may succeed at faking it in the short term. But it's only a matter of time until their customers and employees put pressure on them to walk the talk.

Practicing purposeful empathy is never a done deal. It's perpetual work in progress. This means organizations will always have room for improvement, including the companies lauded above. But make no mistake: The demand for empathic organizations is on a steep and urgent ascension. Victor Hugo famously said, "All the forces in the world are not so powerful as an idea whose time has come." Given what humanity is up against, I think we can all agree that it's time for a tidal wave of empathic organizations to emerge.

PURPOSEFUL EMPATHY PRACTICES

The following exercises can be completed as standalone activities or combined into a team-building retreat. They are meant to help you and your team achieve three things: become better listeners—an essential skill for empathic communication and leadership; evaluate the potential for empathic practices and policies within your organization; and articulate how you would like to engage in purposeful empathy as an organization. For maximum benefit, dedicate a couple of hours as a team for each exercise. You can download a free workbook from my website.

1. With three to five members of your team, participate in an empathy circle to hone your listening skills and emotional intelligence. According to the Center for Building a Culture

of Empathy, "An Empathy Circle is a structured dialogue process based on mutual active listening. The process increases constructive dialogue and mutual understanding by ensuring that each person feels fully heard to their satisfaction."

Circles typically run ninety to 120 minutes, including time to cover instructions. At first, they may feel robotic or mechanical, but once you get the hang of the process, it gets easier and feels more natural. Each speaker has four to five minutes to speak before assuming a different role. Participants in the circle should rotate roles more or less evenly without being too prescriptive. Finally, it helps to have a guiding question to kick off the practice. Each speaker can answer the same question when it's their turn, or the conversation can unfold organically after the original question has been answered.

Below are detailed instructions as provided by The Center for Building a Culture of Empathy. To learn more about the practice or become trained as a facilitator, visit https://www.empathycircle.com/.

Speaker

- You can choose to speak to anyone in the group.

- The intention is for you to feel heard to your satisfaction by the person to whom you are speaking.

- You have the full attention of the circle.

- Pause often to give the listener a chance to reflect back what they heard you say.

- Remember that you are guiding the listener to hear you to your satisfaction. You are "teaching" them how to listen and empathize with you the way you want to be heard.

- When you are finished speaking, you can say something like "I feel fully heard" to indicate that you are finished and it's the listener's turn to speak.

Active Listener

- You want to accompany and follow the speaker where they want to go, not steer or guide them.

- Check your understanding of what the speaker is saying. You can do this by reflecting back, summarizing, paraphrasing, conveying the meaning you get, or using a combination of these options.

- Keep your attention on the speaker's meaning rather than your own interpretations. Refrain from asking questions, judging, analyzing, detaching, diagnosing, advising, or sympathizing.

- Relax. There is no right and wrong way. You are not being judged. Do the best you can. You are simply working to make the speaker feel heard to their satisfaction.

- If the speaker does not feel heard to their satisfaction, they can repeat what they said, and you can try again until the speaker feels heard to their satisfaction.

Silent Listener(s)

- You are invited to listen and be present for the empathic listening taking place between each speaker and active listener. You will soon have a turn to actively listen and speak.

2. As an organization, take the *B Impact Assessment*. Used by more than 150,000 businesses, the assessment is a digital tool that can

help measure, manage, and improve positive impact performance for environment, communities, customers, suppliers, employees, and shareholders. Receiving a minimum verified score of 80 points on the assessment is also the first step toward B Corp Certification.

3. Revisit the purposeful empathy diagram and five key questions for reflection posed in chapter 3. There are two approaches to this exercise: option 1) As a group, respond to the questions below, adapted for group work; option 2) Respond to the original questions as individuals first. Then share your responses with your group and find synergies and common ground.

- What issue(s) do we most care about?

- How do those issue(s) we care about align with the most pressing challenges facing the world?

- What do we want to learn, and how do we want to grow?

- What system(s) need(s) to change, and what is our role?

- How can we be kind to ourselves while practicing purposeful empathy?

Once complete, draft a purposeful empathy mission statement for your team or organization. Recommendations include keeping it short, concise, and declarative; making it aspirational but not implausible; and inviting feedback from a larger group of colleagues to increase organizational buy-in. Finally, create a plan to bring your ideas and insights to life. Codifying, operationalizing, and aligning with already existing strategic plans will increase the likelihood of success.

PART III

6

EMPATHY AND TECHNOLOGY

Empathy is certainly harder to muster when you're typing onto a screen instead of looking into someone's eyes.

—Kaitlin Ugolik Phillips

Invented in 1440, Guttenberg's printing press is arguably the first major technology that elevated our collective empathy. With the mass production of books came widespread literacy and the ability to inhabit the lives and minds of others. This marked a seismic change for most people in the pre-industrial age who, until then, had never interacted with anyone outside their village.

Fast forward six centuries, and empathy in tech is all the rage. The fourth industrial revolution—which will blur the boundaries between our physical, digital, and biological worlds—is also on track to challenge what it means to be human, upend the global economy, and disrupt the political world order. What does this mean for our superpower?

The potential of new technology is extraordinary. Even Stephen Hawking believed that achieving artificial intelligence (AI) would be the biggest event in human history. "Unfortunately," he warned, "it might also be the last. Unless we learn how to avoid the risks." Not surprisingly, technophiles are much more optimistic. For example, when speaking about virtual reality, Chris Milk said, "Through this machine, we become more compassionate, we become more empathetic, and we become more connected. And ultimately, we become more human."

Really? To me that's like implanting iTunes into a nightingale and believing it will sing sweeter songs. Maybe I'm cynical because I've always had a thorny relationship with technology. But I know I'm not the only skeptic out there. As far back as ancient Greece, Socrates worried that the stylus, an early writing instrument, would destroy his generation. More recently, Shelly Turkle, director of the MIT Initiative on Technology and Self, cautions us, "Technology is taking us places we don't want to go."

To be clear, I don't doubt that some innovations will lead to great things. After all, I'm not writing this book with an ink plume or a typewriter. But that doesn't negate the risks of Industry 4.0, which includes the erosion of empathy—precisely when we need it most. "The very qualities that define us as human beings could disappear in this transformation," writes Franklin Foer of *The Atlantic*. That's why stress-testing our brave new world is so important.

ROBOTS AND AI

A few years ago, I attended an event at my university to envision the role of student services fifty years hence. It began with a series of presentations, including one by a group of researchers that rolled out a giant screen hooked up to a computer. "Ladies and gentlemen," they said. "We'd like you to meet Larry." Larry was a digital hologram therapist able to interpret language and read facial expressions in real time. One of their software engineers pulled up a chair to face the avatar and shared a sad story. When she was done, Larry leaned forward, paused a moment, and gently replied, "So what I'm hearing you say is . . ."

The reaction was immediate and palpable. Half the room responded with *ooohs* and *aaahs*. The other half sucked in their breath, outraged or horrified. I remember thinking, *Did they honestly believe some lines of code and a pixelated face could fake human connection?* The presenters pressed on, explaining how artificial intelligence could help millions of people feeling depressed, anxious, or lonely. They asked the audience: What if an attentive twenty-four-hour online therapy bot could help prevent a mass shooting? Or keep someone from being recruited by the dark corners of the internet?

Intellectually, I understood what they were suggesting, but I couldn't shake a sinking feeling. Machines don't empathize. When humans extend empathy, we produce the hormone oxytocin—a neurotransmitter known to facilitate trust and cooperation between people. No matter how sophisticated they become, no machine in the world will ever be able to do that.

That's not to say the potential of AI and robotics isn't remarkable. After inventing mind-controlled wheelchairs, biomedical engineer Jordan Nguyen is now on a mission to scale inclusive human-augmented technology. That's fantastic. I also admire award-winning computer scientist Angelica Lim's determination to build robots that are just, kind, and compassionate.

But how will society adjust to massive, destabilizing unemployment across the globe when robots replace hundreds of millions of jobs? And what will happen when our grandparents befriend their machine caregivers and our children start loving their family bots? US troops already hold funerals for robots they've lost in combat. And researchers at Kyoto University have found neurophysiological evidence that humans empathize with robots perceived to be in pain. What if sex with robots becomes popular or even the norm? That may sound farfetched today, but sexbots can already perform fifty automated sexual positions, and as they anthropomorphize, taboos will surely shatter. Already, up to two-thirds of men say they'd have sex with an android, and a quarter of young people would happily date a robot. Soon, swiping left will seem positively endearing.

AI is everywhere. In education, healthcare, banking, and transportation. Our kitchens and bedrooms too. On the plus side, AI is expected to help fight climate change, build smart and sustainable cities, and provide food and water security—all of which is great. It's also hard to refute the upside of AI-powered vehicles that will avert accidents by monitoring drivers for fatigue or distraction. Same for AI healthcare apps that provide early diagnosis of life-threatening diseases, AI voice recognition that identifies PTSD or AI pedagogical tools that offer personalized learning to students. All of which are in the works. But why, then, does techpreneur Elon Musk, a man seeking to colonize Mars, believe "AI is far more dangerous than nukes"?

Dystopian critics claim we're engineering our own demise at the hands of "slaughterbots," whereas utopian proponents argue AI will serve humanity. Who is right? No one knows for sure, but a few years ago, the results of a survey with machine-learning experts was published. In it, researchers predicted AI will outperform humans in language translation by 2024, truck driving by 2027, and (this one really hurt) writing a bestselling book by 2049. In an interview with *Society for Science*, Google's longtime director of engineering Ray Kurzweil said, "By the early 2030s, I believe we'll be able to integrate our neocortex to the cloud, which will have advanced AI." If that sounds ludicrous, consider that his predictions have an 86 percent accuracy rate. Perhaps historian Yuval Harari was right when he said at the 2018 World Economic Forum, "We are probably one of the last generations of homo sapiens."

Here's the thing. When someone like Dr. Grin Lord, a certified psychologist, launches a startup called Empathy Rocks to build human connection through empathic AI, her aim is to apply clinically effective active listening techniques to digital text. Imagine how much relationship anguish could be prevented if AI could detect passive-aggressive messages and suggest alternatives before anyone hits send!

But it's an entirely different story when a company like Emoshape patents an emotional processing unit that can interpret sixty-four trillion possible emotional states every one-tenth of a second and claims to be "bringing AI one step closer to sentient machines." Watch their promo video on YouTube to be enthralled (or terrified) by the possibilities.

Perhaps in the future, client care chatbots will detect frustration in a caller's voice and effortlessly help them down-regulate. Perhaps emotionally intelligent AI healthcare droids will communicate tough diagnoses with pitch-perfect empathy. But what if affective computing also means that gamers in the metaverse can watch and hear their opponents suffer rape or torture with emotional precision? What if kids hone their bullying skills by watching how an avatar reacts to ridicule and shame? The race for empathic machines is on. "To what end?" is the key question.

VIRTUAL REALITY, GAMING, AND THE METAVERSE

For two decades, the Virtual Interaction Lab at Stanford has been at the vanguard of research that explores the prosocial potential of virtual and augmented reality. Yet its director, Jeremy Bailenson, has admitted that addiction to fantasy worlds, videogames, and pornography will be epic since VR is the most psychologically powerful medium ever invented. For example, as VR entertainment taps next-generation 3D simulations originally developed for the military, how will sustained spikes of adrenaline and cortisol affect our bodies, health, and relationships?

Admittedly, in healthcare and education, it's exciting to see how VR apps help us flex our empathy muscles. Caregivers can step into exoskeleton suits to experience the physical effects of aging, and devices at the forefront of "tele-empathy" can simulate movement disorders like Parkinson's, allowing doctors to gain a better understanding of what their patients are going through. Students can also teleport to another place and time for a history or geography lesson and practice perspective-taking. I think all of this is exciting.

Art-meets-tech companies like BeAnotherLab have also developed VR experiences that allow users to feel what it's like to be in another person's body to "promote mutual respect and understanding through an embodied exchange of perspectives." Inspired by its potential to help cultivate empathy for victims of climate change, performance artist Marina Abramović created *Rising*, a VR experience that lets users try to save her avatar from drowning in an apocalyptic world. Finally, since our brains store immersive experiences as memories, VR is also being tested in a variety of contexts to increase empathy toward racialized and other marginalized groups, including survivors of domestic violence; unhoused, unemployed, and transgender people; as well as animals and our natural ecosystems.

All this pro-empathy content may sound promising, but critics vehemently disagree—especially as users are invited to step into refugee camps, disaster zones, and date rape scenarios. VR filmmakers argue these experiences were created precisely to build bridges of understanding and inspire empathic action. Others see them as nothing more than trauma porn. As Robert Yang, assistant arts professor at NYU Game Center, puts it, "VR empathy machines, especially slick UN-sponsored empathy productions built to milk donations from millionaires at Davos, definitely do not foster any kind of critical reflection."

Anna Anthropy, creator of *Dys4ia*, an autobiographical game about being transgender, concurs: "Empathy games rarely address how a privileged audience is complicit in the suffering they're dipping their toes into. And ultimately, the whole process is a congratulatory pat on the back rather than something that leads into actionable behavior." Worse, some critics argue that immersive simulations of Blackness, mental illness, or physical disability perpetuate unjust power dynamics and inequality. Framed that way, it's hard to defend VR as the "ultimate empathy machine."

As for videogames, aficionados have long avowed they're innocuous entertainment, whereas critics have blamed them for a plethora of psychosocial ills, including increased emotional callousness. But a new generation of designers claim their games actually *increase* empathy. Consider Ryan and Amy Noel Green, who cocreated *That Dragon, Cancer* after losing their four-year-old son, Joel, to a brain tumor. In a heartfelt TED Talk, Amy explains how gamers discover what their family endured during his illness and must "prepare themselves to invest emotionally in a story that they know will break their hearts." After watching a two-hour gameplay led by Markiplier, one of the world's most popular YouTubers, and perusing some of the fifty-seven thousand comments about his video, I can appreciate why it's hailed as an "empathy game."

Designed for that purpose, videogames hold promise. That's why I'm a fan of Games for Change, a nonprofit organization that empowers developers and social innovators to create real-world change through gaming and other immersive media. I also admire Jane McGonigal, who believes our collective intelligence can be leveraged through gaming to solve some of our most intractable problems, and has made it her number-one goal in life to see a game designer nominated for a Nobel Peace Prize.

But when Microsoft recently paid sixty-nine billion dollars in cash for Activision Blizzard, the world's third biggest video game publisher, I doubt that developing gamers' empathic proclivities and addressing social injustices were their primary goals. With three billion active players worldwide, gaming is now the largest and fastest-growing form of entertainment, valued at more than $200 billion. Perhaps CEO Satya Nadella was earnest when he said the company plans to "usher in a new era of gaming that puts players and creators first and makes gaming safe, inclusive and accessible to all." But when the global VR gaming market hits its stride, I am confident that violence and misogyny will dominate as usual, and leave empathy in the dust.

The same can be said about the metaverse. When Meta launched Horizon Worlds, a free VR space to play games and socialize with virtual avatars,

Nina Jane Patel was excited to be among its early adopters. As cofounder of Kabuni, a child-safe metaverse for learning, she is generally optimistic about technology. But in a blog posted to Medium about her experience, she wrote about being sexually assaulted by three or four male avatars within a minute of joining. Her story was picked up by the mainstream media, and she immediately started receiving death threats and online abuse. Meta responded by adding security features to prevent harassment. But critics were adamant that wasn't enough. As Caroline Criado Perez writes in her book *Invisible Women*, "When planners fail to account for gender, public spaces become male spaces by default, and the metaverse is dangerously close to becoming a male-dominated space."

Does this mean the metaverse will be all bad? No, of course not. Many expect it to shatter physical and economic accessibility barriers and make immersive entertainment, travel, sports, and pedagogy possible. Some even believe empathic reality (ER) will cultivate connection and enhance empathy, especially as race, gender, and physical (dis)ability become less salient in an avatar-based context. "While many have cautioned against the potential harmful psychological effects of the Metaverse, technological advances are rarely—if ever—reductionistic enough to be either fully dystopian or utopian," writes Marlynn Wei, Harvard- and Yale-trained psychiatrist. "The important conversation to have now is how we and the trailblazers in this industry can all work together to build an ethical and moral framework for the Metaverse grounded in empathic design and social connection." That sounds good to me, but who can guarantee that will happen?

SMARTPHONES AND SOCIAL MEDIA

According to Statista, a leading business data platform, over 3.6 billion people worldwide used social media in 2020—a number that's projected to balloon to 4.4 billion by 2025. With that degree of penetration, no one can dispute its value to users, including me, your resident luddite. That said, things can be valuable and destructive at the same time.

Smartphones and social media increase our anxiety and make us feel lonelier—to say nothing about their nefarious drag on democracy. And as digital and mobile devices have proliferated, our screen habits have deteriorated. Eighty-two percent of respondents in a Pew Research Center study said that taking out their phones during a social interaction not only dampened the conversation but also lessened the empathic connection they felt toward the person with whom they were socializing. Still, the average adult checks their phone ninety-six times per day—once every ten minutes—and spends four to five hours daily on a handheld device, using apps that were reverse engineered to keep us hooked.

To children, phones and tablets are digital drugs. Regular use boosts dopamine and decreases impulse control—just like cocaine. And all that screen time? It's literally changing our kids' brains by reconfiguring their neural networks. There's also mounting empirical evidence that correlates social media use in youth with a disturbing rise in mental health problems, including depression, eating disorders, self-injury, and suicide. And, sadly, as many as one out of four teens says it makes them feel worse about their life.

We knew this intuitively, but it took a brave whistleblower to make it official. What's truly egregious, however, is that the host companies knew it too. "We have seen over and over again in Facebook's research, it's easier to provoke people to anger than to empathy or compassion, so we are literally subsidizing hate on these platforms," Frances Haugen told the British Parliament. Not convinced? I urge you to watch the Netflix documentary *The Social Dilemma* to learn about the phenomenon of "human downgrading." With a business model designed to maximize distraction, misinformation, addiction, polarization, and radicalization, what chance does empathy stand?

Then again, as Leonard Cohen reminds us, "There's a crack in everything—that's how the light gets in." Case in point: Özlem Cekic, one of the first Muslim immigrant women elected to the Danish Parliament, was on the receiving end of xenophobic slurs and death threats during her time in office. She flipped the script by meeting her haters in their homes for coffee and, after thousands of conversations, launched a nonprofit organization called Bridge Builders.

In the same spirit, Dylan Marron, creator of the web series *Sitting in Bathrooms with Trans People*, asked his bullies why they wrote what they did. To his surprise, his question provoked many earnest conversations, which led him to conclude in his TEDx Talk, "Sometimes the most subversive thing you can do is actually speak with people you disagree with, not simply at them."

Of course, that's easier said than done. Most people don't have the psychic bandwidth to take on trolls. Nor can they withstand the magnetic pull of algorithmic rabbit holes, myself included. So to protect our wellbeing, avoid further polarization, and guard our capacity to empathize, the key is to know what triggers us and have self-awareness about our social media habits. That's why "digital wellness" has become a thing.

THE BOTTOM LINE

As always, when it comes to new technology, we can expect breakthrough innovations that will benefit humanity. Likewise, there will be collateral damage. Most futurists believe tech is neither inherently good nor bad. Instead, they insist the issue is how it is used. In other words, *we* are responsible for the outcomes. On one hand, I suppose that's true. Then again, I'm reminded of the progun refrain "Guns don't kill people. People kill people."

It also discounts the fact that today's technological advancements are unfolding within the logic of predatory capitalism. That's why I don't buy the tech neutrality argument. The investment dollars speak for themselves. FANG stocks—Facebook, Amazon, Netflix, and Google—are among the biggest and most influential in human history. The metaverse alone has been estimated as a trillion-dollar revenue opportunity. Finally, "in a world where money is the measure of success, the most successful people will be the most extractive," says technologist Harper Reed. Of course, none of the big tech companies wants to be seen as villainous inventors of digital Frankensteins. That's why they weave empathy-friendly narratives to protect their reputations and expand their customer base.

"In its most pessimistic, dehumanized form, the Fourth Industrial Revolution may indeed have the potential to 'robotize' humanity and thus to deprive us of our heart and soul," writes Klaus Schwab, executive chairperson of the World Economic Forum. "But as a complement to the best parts of human nature—creativity, empathy, stewardship—it can also lift humanity into a new collective and moral consciousness based on a shared sense of destiny. It's incumbent on us all to make sure the latter prevails." Indeed, if we want to keep empathy as our superpower—especially in the face of technological disruption—we have some really important work to do. Nothing less than our humanity is at stake.

LIGHT AT THE END OF THE TUNNEL

For a long time, the development of AI was held uniquely within the purview of programmers, but as it began seeping into our daily lives, critics quickly observed some deleterious social outcomes. That's why Valentine Goddard, founder of the Artificial Intelligence Impact Alliance, is committed to engaging academics, artists, activists, and citizens in dialogue and advocacy to ensure that AI develops with democratic oversight, contributes to the UN SDGs, and, ultimately, serves humanity. Similarly, a mosaic of strategies and initiatives, cutting across technologies, is beginning to emerge to help us prevent, or at least mitigate, some of the negative impacts. Let's consider three of them.

Creating a Culture of Empathy in Tech

"In the world of technology, almost everything is code," writes Silicon architect Sebastien Ahmed. That's why coders should always ask themselves, "Will another human understand this? What information will help them?" Unfortunately, empathic code, meaning code that's imbued with humility and concern for future coders, is an industry anomaly. In *Empathy-Driven Software Development*, Andrea Goulet describes how the world of programming has historically been a space in which shame and contempt reign supreme. Legacy code, for example, which is source code inherited from someone else, is rife with disdain, if not outright malice, for future coders. She believes engineers, designers, and technologists deserve to work with psychological safety and a sense of belonging, especially if we expect them to use empathic design principles.

In response to the culture of "bro-gramming," April Wensel founded Compassionate Coding to promote emotional intelligence in the tech sector and cultivate a collaborative culture that would spawn more socially conscious products. In a 2016 blog, she wrote, "Software may be built on machines, but it's built by, with, and for human beings." That's why their training approach integrates compassion, mindfulness, and ethics.

Initiatives like hers matter for organizational culture, employee engagement, and wellbeing. But it has direct bottom-line implications as well. More than half of female software engineers leave their jobs within a decade, citing hostility and isolation in the workplace as the primary motivation for quitting. Turnover like that is disruptive and expensive. Studies also show that only 50 percent of software projects are successful, and team dynamics are often blamed as the major factor impeding success. Industry veteran Luke Heath believes that "software development is too complicated and interconnected to be hampered by a lack of empathy." Increasingly, tech companies are catching on.

Advancing EDI in Tech

Women and people of color are chronically underrepresented in the technology sector. Despite being nearly half of the total US workforce, women make up only a quarter of the tech industry. And according to a 2019 survey conducted by *Wired*, Black, Hispanic, and Indigenous people made up only 5 percent of Silicon Valley firms. McKinsey also reported that the proportion of BIPOC women receiving computing degrees had dropped by 40 percent over the prior decade, from a paltry 7 percent down to a measly 4 percent.

Ensuring greater equity, diversity, and inclusion in tech is a no-brainer for three reasons. First is the business case: heterogenous groups make better decisions than homogeneous ones. Second is the justice case: underrepresented and marginalized voices have more to lose in the fourth industrial revolution as inequality is expected to worsen. Third is the social impact case: when implicit biases are coded into technology, many people face significant consequences, including increased surveillance and many forms of illegal discrimination (i.e., employment, housing, etc.).

In response, the tech giants are beginning to invest serious dollars into EDI efforts, including recruitment and training, funds for Black-owned businesses and suppliers, and donations to educational initiatives to address the so-called "pipeline problem." In addition, many organizations have been created to increase representation in the tech industry. These are positive signs of things moving in the right direction, but a sense of greater urgency is needed, especially post-COVID-19. More than half of the racially and ethnically diverse women in the tech sector rate their work-life balance as "extremely poor," and one out of three plans to leave their jobs in tech within the next two years.

Increasing Our Digital Wellness

Netflix CEO Reed Hastings is on record for having said that his company's biggest competitor is sleep. Meanwhile, in 2021, *doomscrolling* was named by the *Oxford English Dictionary* as one of the words of the year. Before things go from bad to worse, we need an intervention. *Digital wellness* refers to holistic physical, mental, and social health that occurs with mindful engagement with our digital world. Much like good nutrition and enough exercise, digital wellness requires effort and personal responsibility. It's also an ongoing process that can be continually improved.

To that end, Nina Hersher founded the Digital Wellness Institute. She believes that in a world where our attention is an extractable resource, we must pursue a healthier and more intentional relationship with technology. Some adjustments that she suggests include using a digital-free alarm clock instead of our mobile phone, resisting the urge to check our phone for the first thirty minutes of the day, scheduling regular breaks into our calendar and treating them like a meeting, not eating in front of a screen, blocking two days per week for "deep work," and using auto replies to communicate digital boundaries. In short, even though the tech deck is stacked against us, we can assert greater control over our time and psychic energy to protect our wellbeing as well as our capacity to empathize.

ONLY HUMANS CAN ACHIEVE EMPATHIC CONSCIOUSNESS

Every semester, I invite my students to participate in a simple two-minute eye-gazing exercise. They sit in pairs, facing each other, without saying a word. In a debrief afterward, some tell me they don't remember the last time they looked into someone else's eyes. And many admit how special it was to *really* see a classmate and *be* seen. Despite all their digital connectivity, they are craving human connection.

Whenever we do this exercise, I think about Albert Einstein, who believed humans are delusional because we think we're separate from the whole. As a remedy, he suggested "widening our circle of compassion to embrace all living creatures and the whole of nature in its beauty." I love the idea that a Nobel Prize-winning physicist was promoting global empathic consciousness—something that no technology in the world will ever achieve.

I also agree with Amar Peterman, director of the Center for Empathy in Christian and Public Life, who says, "The redemptive and empathic possibilities of the internet ultimately are not found on our screens, but rather in our physical bodies and relationships with one another through tangible actions of seeking justice, acting mercifully, practicing compassion, and loving both our neighbors and our enemies." In our high-tech world, these are words worth remembering.

PURPOSEFUL EMPATHY PRACTICES

The following tools and exercises are meant to inspire introspection about the impact of technology on your life and your capacity to empathize. You can download a free workbook from my website.

1. Take the *Digital Flourishing Survey* developed by the Digital Wellness Institute. It was designed to assess "digital flourishing" across the following six categories: mental health, physical health, productivity, relationships, wellbeing, and digital citizenship. Upon completion of the survey, you will receive a personalized summary and access to a set of tips. After you've had time to digest them, create a plan to increase your digital flourishing in the categories where there's room for improvement. Consider enrolling an accountability buddy too.

2. Engage with the following empathy games and apps:

   - *Random App of Kindness* (RAKi), designed to help increase empathic habits. In 2011, Sara Konrath published a meta-analysis that showed a 40 percent decrease in empathy among students since 1979, especially after 2000. After completing the study, she became depressed and decided to focus on ways to increase empathy in young people. This app is the result of her efforts.

   - *Daily Haloha* tackles loneliness, fosters empathy, and improves wellbeing by asking thought-provoking questions to the whole world every day. Created as an antidote to social media, users answer the daily prompts without fear of judgment and can scan the Haloha Wall "for a story-portrait of what it's like to be us."

- *RealLives* exposes players to how other human beings live across the world in different cultures and socioeconomic categories and how challenges framed by the seventeen UN SDGs have a real impact on human lives.

- *Jaago* is described as "the world's first and only Empathy Gym app." Its vision is to help create a world of greater mutual understanding.

3. Watch *Feel That Network*, the provocative trailer for *Collaborative Foresight: How to Game the Future*, a free online course taught by Jane McGonigal. After watching the video, consider these questions for reflection:

- How did you feel watching the four vignettes? Excited about the possibilities? Concerned about potential pitfalls? A mix of curiosity and apprehension?

- Do you agree with McGonigal that thinking about the future today better prepares us to be "upstanders" tomorrow?

- Given the pace of technological change and what's at stake, what steps can you take today to help cocreate a better future?

7

THE SPIRIT OF EMPATHY

All differences in this world are of degree, and not of kind, because oneness is the secret of everything.

—Swami Vivekananda

In 2004, I visited the Persian city of Mashhad. Known as a sacred place of religious pilgrimage, it attracts more than twelve million visitors per year. Many go to pay homage to the eighth imam of Shia, whose tomb sits in a stunningly ornate room located in the heart of the sprawling complex. Once inside, it's considered auspicious to latch on to the metal grids protecting the tomb and make a wish or say a prayer. I was keen to do this; the only problem was the impenetrable wall of bodies in the way. On my first attempt to reach the structure, I could barely breathe and was terrified of tripping on the *chador* I was wearing and being trampled to death. But after studying the rhythm of the crowd, which moved in waves like a school of fish, I tried again and was successful. With my right hand, I gripped on tightly to the bars, and the room fell immediately silent, despite hundreds of guests heaving. It was an unmistakable quiet that left me feeling as though I was communing directly with omnipotence.

That wasn't the first time I've had a transcendent experience. I have a vivid memory from Thailand, standing in a rice field on a very hot and humid day, hearing the sound of dragonflies and feeling as though I was one with the world. I also felt divine energy the first time my daughter and I locked eyes while I was nursing her. Regardless of context, it's always been a peaceful, loving, and life-affirming feeling.

Our species is known as *homo sapiens*, derived from Latin to mean "wise man." But at times like those, I believe *homo sentiens* is a more appropriate term, given that *sentience* means "the capacity to feel." These sacred moments also remind me of something Jesuit priest Pierre Teilhard de Chardin once said: "We are not human beings having a spiritual experience; we are spiritual beings having a human experience."

In the introduction, I named seven issues that require our urgent attention: predatory capitalism, political polarization, the mental health crisis, consumerism and the cult of celebrity, Cartesian thinking, a dated model of leadership, and the need to decolonize our hearts and minds. These issues all inhibit us from flourishing as human beings and are destructive to humanity as a whole. They also disregard our inner worlds, interconnectedness, and inherent spiritual nature. Brené Brown defines spirituality as "recognizing and celebrating that we are all inextricably connected to each other by a power greater than all of us, and that our connection to that power and to one another is grounded in love and compassion." I believe the spiritual dimension of empathy is what unites us in our shared humanity.

THE CIRCLE

I have been studying the power of empathy for a long time, and the most paradigm-shifting insight I've gained can be traced back to Elif Gokcigdem, a Turkish-born Islamic arts historian and founder of the Organization of Networks of Empathy (ONE). In a stirring conversation, she explained why the circle is a beautiful metaphor for the phenomenon. I'll try to do her explanation justice, but first let's revisit some basic geometry. The culmination is worth it, so stay with me.

Lines and circles are elementary shapes. Technically speaking, a line is a straight one-dimensional figure that extends infinitely in both directions, and a circle is a kind of line or, more accurately, a line segment that's bent until its ends join, with all the points along that curved line being equidistant to the center. Over geography and time, studies of the circle have inspired mathematical innovations, including geometry, astronomy, and calculus. And in the material world, the circle led to the wheel, which helped make much of modern civilization possible.

In the transcendental arena, the circle has long been considered a perfect shape, endowed with sacred symmetry and divine balance. "From the time of the earliest known civilisations—including the Assyrians and ancient Egyptians, those in the Indus Valley and along the Yellow River in China, and the Western civilisations of ancient Greece and Rome during classical Antiquity—the circle has been used directly or indirectly in visual art," writes Jean-François in *The Circle from East to West*. It's also been used to express spiritual and metaphysical ideas, perhaps explaining why humans have always been drawn to circles. Think of Hindu mandalas, the Chinese yin-yang symbol, Stonehenge, the Mayan zodiac, and the Indigenous medicine wheel. Not to mention wedding rings, crop circles, and the Olympic logo.

Islamic artists and craftspeople were prohibited from using physical representations of people in holy sites, so they developed an aesthetic that combines repeated and overlapping shapes to form complex geometric patterns. Circles figure prominently. According to Gokcigdem, the circle symbolizes an important Sufi concept called "unity in diversity," a oneness without hierarchy in which plurality begets the whole. Moreover, since all forms, without exception, can be contained within a circle, the latter also symbolizes union, encompassing everything within all of creation.

With no beginning or end, the circle is also made up of an infinite number of connecting dots. In fact, it's impossible to count how many dots exist along a circle's circumference, and adding one more—or ten thousand—simply expands the circle's size. Significantly, each dot has equal proximity to the center but also has a different perspective vis-à-vis the center. Two dots side by side, or even relatively close, may see the center in similar ways but never *exactly* the same way. And dots on opposite sides have vastly different perspectives. This is where empathy comes into play.

If we imagine that every person on the planet represents a dot along the circumference of a circle, all equidistant to the center, equality is plain to see. If we assign the name *God*, *Allah*, or *Buddha* to the epicenter, or what others might describe as the Big Bang or the generative force that gave us life, we can see that each of us has intrinsic value by virtue of having been born. In addition, given our myriad positionalities along the circle, we also see that no two people in the world share exactly the same perspective. In short, the circle is a sublime metaphor for empathy because it allows us to understand humanity's oneness while transcending otherness, without denying or discounting lived experience.

"Empathy shows that the concept of separateness is an illusion," writes Steve Taylor, a British transpersonal psychologist. "Empathy is simply the experience of our true connectedness, the exchange of feeling through the channel of shared consciousness which unites not just all human beings, but all living and non-living things." If you let his words and the circle metaphor sink in for a moment, can you feel your heart soften a little? Do you have access to a little more tenderness, compassion, and kindness? Can you dig a little deeper to where forgiveness and healing are possible? *That* is the spirit of empathy.

TRADITIONS OF ONENESS

In *The Perfume of Silence*, Francis Lucille, a guru of the Advaita Vedanta tradition, writes, "The realization of oneness means being constantly open to the possibility that we are like two flowers looking at each other from two different branches of the same tree, so that if we were to go deep enough inside to the trunk, we would realize that we are one." That's why the concept of oneness has always been revered by spiritual leaders. Let's consider three traditions.

Interbeing: Everything Relies on Everything Else in Order to Manifest

Zen master Thich Nhat Hanh was born in Vietnam in 1926 and was ordained as a monk at the age of sixteen. He left his monastery during the war to advocate for peace and toured America to "describe the aspirations and the agony of the voiceless masses." Nominated for the Nobel Peace Prize by Martin Luther King Jr., he was also threatened with arrest by the Vietnamese government. He lived in exile in Plum Village, France, until his death in the early days of 2022.

More than three decades ago, he coined the term *interbeing* to express the idea of mutual interdependence. In his words, "We do not exist independently . . . we inter-are with one another and with all of life." To him, the human body is not a solitary entity but rather a community of cells. Likewise, the earth is one giant living organism with all its parts working in symbiosis, otherwise known as the Gaia hypothesis.

In a simile called *clouds in each paper*, he described the concept of interbeing as follows: "If you are a poet, you will see clearly that there is a cloud floating in this sheet of paper. Without a cloud, there will be no rain; without rain, the trees cannot grow; and without trees, we cannot make paper. The cloud is essential for the paper to exist. If the cloud is not here, the sheet of paper cannot be here either. So we can say that the cloud and the paper inter-are." Thich Nhat Hanh devoted his life to advancing the idea that we can free ourselves from a false belief of separation and experience profound connection through the conscious recognition of interbeing.

In the Nguni Bantu language spoken in South Africa, the word *ubuntu* is often translated to mean "I am because you are." When relationships are imbued with reciprocal respect, two people, or two groups of people, may see the world differently and have vastly dissimilar lived experiences, but a recognition of their mutual humanity is assured. We all need love, friendship, and a sense of belonging to be happy. We all seek joy, growth, and pleasure to feel satisfied. And we all want to rise above guilt or shame through forgiveness and redemption. To honor our interbeing, we must value what we have in common and let that nurture our relationships.

Nonduality: One without a Second

Duality means "two." In dualism, you and I are separate from the world, separate from each other, and our souls and material bodies are separate too. The Cartesian worldview is grounded in dualism. In contrast, *nonduality*— which is derived from Sanskrit, meaning "not two"—assumes there is one eternal spirit in existence from which everything in the universe is inseparable and interconnected. Nondualist beliefs can be found in all the world's great faiths, including Hinduism, Buddhism, Taoism, Sufism, Kabbalism, and the Abrahamic religions.

Imagine nonduality through the analogy of a clear blue sky hidden by white puffy clouds of all shapes and sizes. Although the clouds move and morph across the sky, the sky behind them is always there, unchanged. Similarly, while our thoughts, actions, relationships, and experiences come and go like moving clouds, the backdrop of our lives is unchanged and ever present. Practitioners believe that to properly understand nonduality, we must be in a state of expanded consciousness beyond words and thinking. This nondual awareness requires us to silence our minds and be grounded by the present moment. In the absence of thoughts, we can sense that oneness is the true nature of reality and basis for all human connection.

Psychoanalyst Sigmund Freud argued that maturity involves freeing ourselves from the "oceanic feeling" of "being one with the external world as a whole," as first encountered with our mothers. Empathy encourages the opposite. In *One Mind*, Larry Dossy writes, "A felt unity with all other minds conveys meaning, purpose, and possibility and a sense of the sacredness of all things." We must overcome our limited and self-absorbed ego to see that separateness is an illusion. Whenever we do, empathy is immediately accessible.

Interconnectedness: All My Relations

It would be foolish and impertinent to say there is one Indigenous worldview when hundreds of millions of Indigenous people, from a wide array of traditions, live on all four corners of the planet, with different histories, languages, cultures, and contexts. Yet it would be fair to say that a fundamental attribute of Indigenous worldviews is a holistic, integrated, and generative view of life. As Australian Aborigine writer Mudrooroo wrote, "Our spirituality is a oneness and an interconnectedness with all that lives and breathes, even with all that does not live or breathe."

Writing from the Canadian context, interconnectedness is a central tenet of the Inuit, Metis, and First Nations ways of knowing. Inherent to their belief systems is the idea that all people, including ancestors and future descendants, are inextricably linked to their communities, the land upon which they live, and all the plants and animals that live on it with them— hence, the concept of "all my relations." This interconnectedness with all living things, including Mother Earth, the universe, and the Great Spirit, is called the Sacred Circle of Life. Why am I not surprised?

According to the Haudenosaunee (commonly referred to as Iroquois or Six Nations), the Seventh Generation Principle urges the current generation of humans to consider the potential impact of decisions they make on those of seven generations hence. Assuming an average life span of seventy-five years, that means having empathy for people hundreds of years into the future. Given the unsustainable world we are bestowing upon our children and grandchildren, we would be wise to adopt this principle with a greater sense of urgency.

CHALLENGING THE SOCIAL ORDER

The second most compelling insight I have gained about empathy has to do with its activation—which, I have come to refer to as *empathic action*. Since delving into this research, I have always believed empathy is the most powerful emotion in the world, second only to love. And when empathy is brought to bear *en masse*, it's a formidable force indeed. "It would be difficult to fully explain many major shifts in political history—especially the expansion of rights regimes—without including the role of empathy," writes Roman Krznaric in *The Empathy Effect: How Empathy Drives Common Values, Social Justice and Environmental Action*. Obvious examples are the abolition of slavery, women's suffrage, and the civil rights and LGBTQ+ movements.

Regrettably, sustained empathic action is not a regular part of our daily lives because we're locked into a paradigm of distraction, extraction, neocolonialism, systemic racism, and other forms of oppression—all antithetical to empathy. As Dr. King wrote, "Our abundance has brought us neither peace of mind nor serenity of spirit . . . We have guided missiles and misguided man." Indeed, as I type these words, the devastating invasion of Ukraine rages on. That's why empathy is not just spiritual by nature; it is inherently political too.

Put plainly, empathy is a beautiful and powerful force, but to create positive change in the world, it is never enough. Instead, *purposeful* empathy unleashes its full potential because it requires us to confront social injustices—not as spectators but as participants committed to putting an end to indignity and suffering. I credit Brazilian educator Paulo Freire for this belief and will attempt to summarize two of his major contributions to critical pedagogy and how they relate to empathy.

Conscientização (Portuguese)/Conscientization (English): "Coming to Consciousness"

Paulo Freire was born in Brazil in 1921. His father died during the Great Depression, which left his family destitute. Having lived the dehumanizing effects of poverty and hunger, Freire devoted his life to improving the social and economic conditions of oppressed people, including the children and grandchildren of the formerly enslaved. After his own formal education was complete, he began working with uneducated peasants in the late '40s and within twenty years had organized a popular movement to eradicate illiteracy. He spent his life encouraging humans to become *more human* through education.

Freire was taken by the Marxist idea of false consciousness, which refers to members of the working class mistakenly believing that they're not being exploited or that by working harder, they may one day gain economic freedom. To overcome this form of internalized oppression, Freire called for *conscientização*. To him, conscientization is the process by which oppressed people develop awareness about their class and lack of power in society and gain agency to transform their reality. Echoes of conscientization can be found in liberation theology as well as social justice activism since both center the social, political, and economic needs of marginalized groups and see everyone's full emancipation as the end goal.

Social psychologist Kenneth B. Clark, best known for research about the self-image of Black children (who, when given a choice between white and Black dolls, preferred white ones), wrote, "The essential aspect of empathy is the capacity of an individual to feel into the needs, the aspirations, the frustrations, the joys, the sorrows, the anxieties, the hurt, indeed, the hunger of others as if they were his own." To do this, we must recognize our intersectional positionality and strive toward allyship. In *New Forms of Transformative Education*, Anne Curry-Stevens writes that deconstructing one's privilege is a "spiritual awakening that allows learners to expand their circle of compassion while at the same time feeling profoundly interconnected with others."

Praxis: Theory and Practice in Synthesis

Freire is also credited with having popularized the term *praxis*, another Marxist concept, which he described as "the action and reflection of men and women upon their world in order to transform it." In his classic text *Pedagogy of the Oppressed*, Freire argues that it's not enough for people to simply study the world; they are also responsible for taking action to transform it so that all humans have the opportunity to flourish. To him, praxis is a prerequisite to freedom, and liberatory struggles must not reside in social critique only. Instead, they must be galvanized by hope and possibility.

We are all beholden—albeit to different degrees—to the hegemonic forces of consumerism, neoliberalism, and the military industrial complex. We have internalized an egoistic and materialist worldview, replete with normalized violence and warfare—all of which is making us sick and miserable and putting our planet in peril. Freire would say that we must develop awareness of the oppressive regimes that govern us before we can change them.

Likewise, I see purposeful empathy as a necessary precondition for social change. "Empathy can trigger the urge to help others, sure enough; but it cannot be the ultimate guide to alleviating human suffering. It can be a place to start, but not to finish," writes professor of philosophy J. D. Trout in *Why Empathy Matters*. Social progress is only possible as the result of empathy exercised intentionally. *Purposeful* empathy is what counts.

As we've seen throughout the history of social movements—from the salt marches in India to Greta's Friday for Future—when people come together to change systems, protect the planet, and enlarge the rights and liberties of others, the potential for an empathic social order is made real. Recall from my purposeful empathy diagram that the fourth element is "social progress," and the question posed is: what system(s) need(s) to change, and what is my role? We are being called upon to collectively free ourselves from inertia and fatalism through praxis like never before, and we must rise to the occasion.

SPIRITUAL ACTIVISM

Just as clapping occurs when both hands work in concert, purposeful empathy manifests when oneness and action coalesce. All over the world, activists, artists, educators, scientists, social entrepreneurs, and policymakers are deploying what could otherwise be called *spiritual activism* to achieve peace, justice, equity, and sustainability. Here are three inspiring examples.

Revolutionary Love Project

Shortly after Donald Trump was elected, Sikh activist and lawyer Valarie Kaur gave a rousing six-minute address at a watch night church service in Washington that went viral with over forty million views worldwide. Fifteen years earlier, her family friend was murdered in the days following 9/11. On the heels of her loss, she began documenting hate crimes against Sikh and Muslim Americans. Today, she leads the Revolutionary Love Project to "reclaim love as a force for justice." The nonprofit organization produces educational tools, training courses, artwork, films, music, and mass mobilizations that center the voices of BIPOC communities. Their pledge includes: "We vow to see one another as brothers, sisters, and siblings. Our humanity binds us together, and we vow to fight for a world where all of us can flourish."

Kaur believes this is possible through the practice of "seeing no stranger." That is, looking upon the face of another and choosing to say: you are a part of me that I do not yet know. In her memoir, *See No Stranger*, she writes that this always starts with wonder: "It can be a place to start, but not to finish."

Network of Spiritual Progressives

The Network of Spiritual Progressives (NSP) was founded by Rabbi Michael Lerner, Sister Joan Chittister, and Cornel West—three of the most provocative public intellectuals in America today. Rabbi Lerner is a lifelong activist and educator. In *Revolutionary Love*, he writes, "Unless we simultaneously transform our economic and political arrangements to overcome class-stratified society, patriarchy, and racism, our compassion, empathy, and generosity will not stop the destruction of the Earth." Sister Chittister is a spiritual leader and prolific writer. In *The Time Is Now*, she writes, "Our world waits for you and me, for spiritual people everywhere—to refuse to be pawns in the destruction of a global world for the sake of national self-centeredness." Finally, West is an outspoken socialist. In the twenty-fifth anniversary edition of *Race Matters*, he writes,

"We live in one of the darkest moments in American history—a bleak time of spiritual blackout and imperial meltdown . . . Our last and only hope is a prophetic fightback—a moral and spiritual awakening that puts a premium on courageous truth telling and exemplary action by individuals and communities."

The mission of the NSP is "to build a social change movement—guided by and infused with spiritual and ethical values—to transform our society to one that prioritizes and promotes the well-being of the people and the planet, as well as love, justice, peace, and compassion over money, power and profit." They do this through their Caring World philosophy and by promoting policies such as basic income, adequate food and shelter, quality and affordable healthcare and education, meaningful work for a living wage, integrative health care (i.e., spiritual, physical, intellectual, emotional), and debt-free college or trade school.

Presencing Institute

Founded in 2006 by Otto Scharmer, a senior lecturer at MIT Sloan School of Management, the Presencing Institute is an action research platform at the intersection of science, consciousness, and profound social and organizational change. The institute's change framework, called Theory U, has been applied by thousands of organizations and communities across the globe to address the world's most pressing challenges. In 2015, Scharmer cofounded the MITx u.lab, a massive open online course (MOOC), to activate a global ecosystem of changemakers seeking personal and social renewal. It engaged more than 140,000 participants from 185 countries and continues to attract new cohorts to this day.

The website reads, "The COVID-19 pandemic and the climate change crisis make us acutely aware of our profound interdependence. Each breakdown or collapse in this decade is a potential turning point to redirect our evolutionary pathway going forward." Scharmer believes that "awareness-based systems change" may be the number-one leadership challenge of our time: "The only change that will make a difference is the transformation of the human heart."

THE POWER OF EMPATHY

Each of these examples has a different theory of change, but all three put purposeful empathy into practice. As we know from many inspiring examples throughout history, when the spiritual and political dimensions of empathy are coactivated at scale, social progress is inevitable.

In a conversation with Tibetan Buddhist scholar Jinpa Thupten, who served as a translator for His Holiness the Dalai Lama, he told me, "At a fundamental level, we are absolutely the same. And that sameness is rooted in a basic disposition of wanting freedom from suffering and the pursuit of happiness"—for ourselves and for others.

According to Thich Nhat Hanh, however, one of the fourteen precepts of interbeing is "Do not avoid contact with suffering or close your eyes before suffering. Do not lose awareness of the existence of suffering in the life of the world. Find ways to be with those who are suffering, including personal contact, visits, images, and sounds. By such means, awaken yourself and others to the reality of suffering in the world." How can we reconcile this tenet with the universal yearning to be free of suffering?

The answer is twofold. We must expand our empathic consciousness to include all sentient beings. And we must take action to address injustice and alleviate suffering wherever it's expressed or encountered. As Dr. King put it, "Whatever affects one directly, affects all indirectly. I can never be what I ought to be until you are what you ought to be. This is the interrelated structure of reality." That's why the outer ring of my diagram (on the following page) speaks to the inherently spiritual and political nature of purposeful empathy.

Every day in the news, there are stories of people in pain, making it easy for us to feel overwhelmed and despondent. But with so much at stake, we must find courage to step up. Polish poet Stanislaw Lec once said, "Every snowflake in an avalanche pleads not guilty." Some take that to mean "I didn't cause the problem, so it's not my responsibility to fix." Others interpret is as "I'm just one person; what can I possibly do to change things?" In juxtaposition, St. Francis of Assisi, a friar who gave up a life of privilege to be of service said, "All the darkness in the world cannot extinguish the light of a single candle." Meaning, we can all make a difference.

Twinkle Rudberg believes her late husband, Dan, had a premonition an hour before he was killed. While getting ready for their anniversary dinner, he peeled open the shower curtain and asked, "Honey, what would you do without me?" Then, uncharacteristically, he begged her to take off the black dress she was wearing, saying it made her look like a widow.

It was a crisp autumn evening more than forty years ago when the couple was in search of a parking spot in downtown Montreal. They turned up a small street and witnessed a young man assault an elderly woman. Dan immediately put the car into park, checked to see if the woman was alright, and then chased after her assailant. Twinkle drove around the block to catch up with her beloved husband and found him lying in a pool of blood. He'd been stabbed to death by the teen.

A few months later, during a preliminary hearing, Twinkle learned a lot about the kid who killed Dan. Raised by a single mom working three jobs to make ends meet, he had spent most of his days alone, stoned, and watching violent television before deciding to run away from home. The more she learned about *his* story, the more she understood he was a victim too. She wondered, *How can I turn the empathy I feel for this boy into something positive?*

Twinkle launched Leave Out ViolencE (LOVE) as a modest experiment with fifteen kids in the basement of a community college. A quarter century later, her international nonprofit organization has award-winning programs facilitated by professional psychologists and social workers. Thousands of kids previously struggling with addiction, working as child prostitutes, or engaged in crime or self-harm have found a new path forward at LOVE. Today, Twinkle has transcended the greatest loss of her life: "I am more blessed than you can possibly imagine."

It's not every day that murder leads to love, but therein lies the power of empathy—especially when wielded on purpose. Twinkle could have spent her life as a victim. Instead, she was led by the better angels of her nature. Imagine how the world would be transformed if we all followed her lead. Jane Fonda was right: Empathy is revolutionary.

PURPOSEFUL EMPATHY PRACTICES
The following exercises will help you integrate the principles of oneness and praxis and hopefully nudge you toward spiritual activism. You can download a free workbook from my website.

1. Partake in the Japanese practice of *shinrin-yoku*. Otherwise known as *forest bathing* or *ecotherapy*, this practice is part of a group of techniques used to augment awe and wellbeing through immersion in nature. It also helps remind us that we are part of an interdependent whole. Afterward, journal in response to these prompt questions:

   - When you think of humanity as being interconnected, what opens up for you?

   - How does the circle as a metaphor for empathy make you feel?

   - When you breathe deeply in the outdoors and notice all that's alive around you, what do you feel inspired to do?

2. Visit a local museum and immerse yourself in creative and artistic expressions that celebrate our shared humanity. Then, using a medium of your choice, create an artistic expression that symbolizes oneness to you. Possible mediums include a drawing or painting, a poem, photographs, music, crafts, and so on. During both activities, contemplate ways in which you can become a spiritual activist and develop an action plan.

3. Building on the previous exercises, draft a praxis statement—a personal manifesto for spiritual activism—that builds on your purposeful empathy mission statement from chapter 5. For example, "I commit to learning more about food insecurity in low-income neighborhoods and will volunteer every month at a local food bank or homeless shelter" or "I resolve to do my part to mitigate climate change by developing a plan for my company to participate in the circular economy."

8

COMMUNITIES OF EMPATHIC PRACTICE

There is no power for change greater than a community discovering what it cares about.

—Margaret J. Wheatley

Eva and Matt met in Haiti while sifting compost on a farm. She was a teacher, and he worked in community development. Over long conversations about classic rock, world travel, and a calling to help those facing hardship, they fell in love. Three children and one decade later, they attended a retreat for couples, seeking to buoy a stagnating marriage. In the closing session, the facilitator asked everyone to name a dream they had. Without skipping a beat, Matt shared that he wanted to tour the entire United States as a family. Fortunately, Eva was open to the idea.

As kids, they had both traveled abroad on medical missions with their families, from Benin to Bangladesh. "Those experiences invited us to think more globally, and we wanted our kids to have broadened perspectives too," Matt explained. In 2018, after years of planning and saving, the Webb family of five set off from Pasadena, California, on an epic fourteen-month road trip, covering thirty-seven thousand miles across all fifty states. Along the way, they visited forty-five national parks and immersed themselves in the local art, literature, and history—which, on its own, was a significant undertaking. But their road trip had a more profound purpose than that.

Eva, as an educator, and Matt, as a filmmaker, wanted to expose their kids to service learning. They also wanted to cocreate an enduring artifact from their trip, so along the way they recorded seventy-five interviews with youth changemakers with the intention of producing a feature-length documentary. According to their "One Year Road Trip" website, "Our hope is to illuminate the stories of the kids we meet, inspire other children to go change the world, and be transformed as a family by immersing ourselves in the stories of the growing 'Generation of Generosity.'" To say they were transformed by their voyage would be an understatement.

In an interview eighteen months after their return home, the family reminisced about the times they ran out of money to buy gasoline and groceries, which meant having to rely on their faith and the goodwill of others. Much to their surprise, donations came out of nowhere, including cash gifts, places to park their trailer, warm showers, meals, and even the opportunity to do a few loads of laundry. Their eldest child, Jack, told me his spirituality was profoundly deepened by the connection he felt with complete strangers thanks to their random acts of kindness. On the road, Matt and Eva wrote in a blog, "Our own 'tribe of five' is getting closer and closer every day . . . and learning to trust one another in new ways." When I asked the kids if they had any lessons to share about empathy, Solveig, their middle child, replied, "People need to learn more about others, and accept and love one another, because we're really not all that different."

WHY MODELING EMPATHY IS KEY

The residual "warm glow" the Webbs felt about their trip—and each other—is consistent with the literature about families who engage in service work together. Other positive outcomes include deeper familial bonds, newfound appreciation for one another's strengths, and increased overall life satisfaction, mental wellness, sense of gratitude, and empathy—the last of which has beneficial spillover effects at school and into adulthood. For example, children who display more empathy at a young age are less likely to bully their peers and more likely to intervene when they see someone else being bullied. Longitudinal studies also show they're less likely to drop out of school, engage in delinquent behavior, or have substance abuse problems. Finally, evidence points to a significant positive correlation between empathy and creativity, self-esteem, better grades, and civic engagement.

"The problem is that empathy is widely underestimated by moms and dads, as well as the general public, so it's low on most child-rearing agendas," writes Michelle Borba in *Unselfie: Why Empathetic Kids Succeed in Our All-About-Me World*. How ironic since most parents say that raising caring kids is one of their top priorities! Research conducted by Harvard's Making Caring Common Project revealed that four out of five kids across a wide spectrum of races, cultures, and classes agree that their parents convey that being kind to others is important. Yet an overwhelming 80 percent also report that their parents are more concerned with achievement or happiness than caring for others.

That's why the initiative's codirector, Richard Weissbourd, suggests that parents be intentional about modeling empathic behavior at home. "The challenge is for adults to 'walk the talk,' inspiring, motivating, and expecting caring and fairness in young people day-to-day, even at times when these values collide with children's moment-to-moment happiness or achievement," concludes their report, "The Children We Mean to Raise."

This idea is echoed by psychologist Marilyn Price-Mitchell, founder of Roots of Action, an online resource for parents and educators to learn about positive youth development. In *Tomorrow's Change Makers*, she writes that young people often describe how their greatest teachers not only fostered empathy but also inspired them into empathic action, adding that, in many cases, their parents *were* those teachers. This aligns with my own research findings: The common thread across dozens of interviews I conducted with social entrepreneurs about their lives was that their parents had modeled service behavior. Thus, to raise caring kids, experts recommend that parents make empathy a priority, communicate its importance as often as possible, and reward it accordingly. And taking a page from the Webb family playbook, they should also engage in service activities *with* their children. In other words, become a community of empathic practice.

COMMUNITIES OF EMPATHIC PRACTICE

The term *community of practice* (CoP) refers to a self-organizing group of people who share a common concern or passion and come together through joint activities and collaborative learning in the pursuit of a shared human endeavor. During their trip, the Webbs embodied not only a CoP but also a community of *empathic* practice by stepping into the spiritual activism I described in the previous chapter. bell hooks famously said, "I am often struck by the dangerous narcissism fostered by spiritual rhetoric that pays so much attention to individual self-improvement and so little to the practice of love within the context of community." To my mind, any CoP that seeks to ameliorate the lives of others by centering their work in the recognition of our shared humanity is a community of empathic practice—one that intentionally shifts the paradigm from *me* to *we*.

Brooke Dodson-Lavalle, president of the Courage of Care Coalition, writes about the "relationshift" needed to build relational cultures of practice: "To develop social structures that reflect the inherent value of all life, significant internal and inter-personal shifts must accompany systemic changes. We have to practice new ways of being—new cultures—that help us embody alternative systems." This means leaning into what Dr. Martin Luther King Jr. called the "beloved community," an assembly of like-minded people who seek economic and social justice for all, grounded in a universal love of humankind. What's heartening is that these communities of empathic practice are on the ascension. Let me share three compelling examples.

Center for Building a Culture of Empathy

Founded fifteen years ago by Edwin Rutsch, an unassuming but highly committed social and political activist, the Center for Building a Culture of Empathy was created to launch a movement. Today, it engages a global network of twenty thousand empathy enthusiasts and serves as a portal to the world's largest collection of empathy-related resources, including hundreds of expert interviews. More recently, it has deployed "empathy tents" on campuses and at rallies to promote dialogue across ideological divides and is now leading a campaign to train thousands of empathy circle facilitators, of which I am proud to be one.

As a young man, Edwin spent a decade traveling the world as a self-described seeker, inspired by the human connections he made wherever he went. Despite being raised Evangelical, he was swept up by the social movements of the 1960s. Not surprisingly, this caused friction at home, especially since his parents saw wearing jeans as a sign of rebellion. Immediately after high school, he began traveling in search of the meaning of life. "As a Christian, I thought I was saved and going to heaven, and others were going to hell," he admits. "I thought I had the world all figured out. But through my travels, while meeting so many different people from so many different cultures, my religion started to dissipate. I began to realize that people's values were more important. I started seeing the humanity in everyone, including the people in the slums of Indonesia who invited me to stay with them in their homes. I realized if I had been born in Jakarta, I would be Muslim, whereas if I had been born in Delhi, I'd likely be Hindu." Communing with people from all walks of life helped Edwin shed a false sense of superiority, separation, and otherness and ultimately led him to the empathy work he does today.

After years of research, he and some friends working in mediation, conflict resolution, and nonviolent communication codesigned a process of empathic listening called *empathy circles*. As you might recall from one of the practices in chapter 5, it's a structured dialogue with one aim: To listen and reflect back what a speaker is saying until they feel fully heard and understood. When the speaker is satisfied, it becomes the listener's turn to speak to another member of the circle, who then reflects back what they hear. This may sound like an easy formula, but even the most empathically minded people find it challenging, yours truly included. That's because we're such poor listeners! More often than not, when we think we're listening, we're actually preparing to respond—and this is especially true when emotions run high. Think of your most recent argument. Can you honestly say that your primary objective was to *understand* what your partner, child, or colleague was saying? Exactly.

Empathy circles require listeners to turn off their internal dialogue, withhold judgment, and be fully present, which is easier said than done. But when properly executed, the process increases mutual understanding and connection among participants. According to the center's website, "Ideally, out of this newfound connection, the possibility of working creatively together towards positive solutions to our common problems can emerge. Many of our facilitated dialogues and meditations end in hugs between people on opposite sides of the political and social divide."

Edwin has seen this transpire not only within his own politically divided family but also in some of the most hyperpolarized public spaces in America. Indeed, since the 2016 presidential campaign, he and his team have brought empathy tents to the frontlines of contentious political rallies across California and have used empathy circles to engage in constructive dialogue and problem solving with people who hold vastly opposing views. Heartened by their success, they're now on a quest to propagate their impact. This means that anyone in the world with access to Wi-Fi can now join online empathy circles for free and, through their train-the-trainer model, can learn to facilitate them as well. All told, the Center for Building a Culture of Empathy is clearly on a mission to scale communities of empathic practice.

Charter of Compassion

At the age of seventeen, Karen Armstrong joined a convent, where she endured physical and psychological abuse. She left seven years later to pursue studies at Oxford and became an English teacher, an author, and a television broadcaster. In 1984, the British Channel 4 commissioned her to write and narrate a documentary about the life of St. Paul, which involved retracing his steps in Jerusalem. Despite her religious formation, she says it was the first time she truly encountered the two other Abrahamic religions of Judaism and Islam. And in her words, this was a breakthrough experience. After penning several critically acclaimed books about the three monotheistic traditions, she was awarded a TED prize to launch a global *Charter of Compassion*. Her goal was simple: to unite the world around the principle of the golden rule.

In 2008, an open writing process to craft the charter began. People of all faiths, nationalities, and backgrounds from more than one hundred countries submitted ideas. The submissions were then read and commented upon by more than 150,000 visitors to a website created for that purpose. The final text—an elegant six paragraphs—was crafted in Vevey, Switzerland, by the Council of Conscience, a multifaith and multinational group of religious leaders and scholars from Judaism, Christianity, Islam, Hinduism, Buddhism, and Confucianism. The official charter was unveiled in the fall of 2009. Since then, more than two million people have endorsed it, including Pope Benedict XVI, His Holiness the Dalai Lama, and Desmond Tutu.

Karen believes religion is "ethical alchemy" and is more about what you do, than what you believe. That's why one of the charter's major initiatives is the Compassionate Communities program, which has enrolled hundreds of communities taking compassion-driven action. Initiatives have been launched in nearly fifty countries by neighborhoods, schools and colleges, businesses, local governments, and religious groups to address issues ranging from homelessness to teen suicide, healthcare accessibility to environmental sustainability, gang violence to food security, and much more.

Within the United States, Louisville, Kentucky—the seventh city to sign the charter—is a great example. One of its signature annual events involves the whole city devoting a day to service. In 2015, the city broke its own world record, with more than 166,000 volunteers and acts of compassion. Overseas, Botswana offers another example. Its Compassionate Community action focuses on meeting the needs of street kids who have been orphaned by the AIDS epidemic.

Compassionate Communities typically get off the ground organically when a group of like-minded people concerned about a particular issue begin to ask, "What can *we* do about this?" Regardless of what they take on, the collaborative nature of their efforts, grounded in the ethos of spiritual activism, is what makes them communities of empathic practice. And as Coretta Scott King says, "The greatness of a community is most accurately measured by the compassionate actions of its members."

Tribeless Conversations

Gwen Yi is a classic overachiever. She excelled at school and, by graduation, had accumulated more accolades, awards, and distinctions than all her peers combined. At the age of twenty-one, her goal was to revolutionize learning as a techpreneur, so she was thrilled to be accepted into Silicon Valley's Minerva University. Unfortunately, rather than flourish as a student, she floundered. Depression and anxiety kept her from making friends, and before long, she returned home to her native Malaysia: "I had no idea how to talk about my experience in the United States. It was so painful. I was ashamed that I had dropped out and could not face meeting people."

Mired by self-recrimination, she languished at home for months. Then, one day, she hosted a dinner party with people who were strangers to one another. Her goal was to create a safe space for everyone to talk openly about anything they were going through or dealing with. Wanting to emphasize vulnerability, her only rule was "no small talk." She called the gathering a "Tribeless Conversation."

The event was such a success that she went on to curate dozens of similar dinner parties. In so doing, it became clear to her that people were yearning to connect on a meaningful level. After hosting a couple of hundred Tribeless Conversations, she had a eureka moment. The space she had been creating for deep connection through dialogue was essentially an empathy lab. Armed with that insight, she decided to formalize the process, and in 2017, after more than two thousand hours of research and development with participants from 120 nations, she and her team codesigned the Empathy Box. It was launched as a tool to help turn group conversations into immersive experiences that promote active listening, develop emotional intelligence, foster generative conversations, and activate empathy.

The process is simple but powerful. It begins with a participant selecting a word from a set of open-faced cards and telling a personal story associated with that word. Examples include faith, family, and fear. Listeners can only interact with the storyteller by holding up one of the five response cards: "Show some love," to convey appreciation; "Help me understand," to pose a question; "Share an observation," to point something out; "Offer an alternate perspective," to challenge an idea; and a "wild card." Since each storyteller decides what to do if a card is raised by a listener, speakers have control over how their narrative unfolds. Finally, to ensure psychological safety for everyone, the entire experience is guided by three principles: to listen openly, share honestly, and respond kindly.

I have used the Empathy Box in professional contexts, at social gatherings among friends, and within intimate family get-togethers. The outcome is always the same. Participants quickly remove their social masks, listen and share with open hearts, and walk away feeling the afterglow of having been seen and heard. With so much judgment, animosity, and toxicity running rampant in our culture, it's easy to take a defensive stance. To armor up, lash back, or shut down. Gwen and her team have created a process that allows participants to step into their authenticity and vulnerability. And when that's experienced as a community of empathic practice, healing and bridge-building is the natural result.

Empathy Is Good for Us

Communities of empathic practice highlight the relational shift from *me* to *we* that's needed to achieve purposeful empathy at scale. Luckily for us, this comes with a host of personal benefits. For example, a surprising study published by *Harvard Business Review* found that people who devote time to community causes feel they have *more* time in general. Other research has shown that simply being a member of a group improves physical and mental fitness. In fact, *social connectedness*, defined as a sense of belonging to a group, family, or community, has been found to be at least as good for your health as exercise or the cessation of smoking. Finally, people with more social group memberships outlive those with fewer.

In 1986, the National Institute on Aging launched a major investigation called Americans' Changing Lives to explore how neighborhoods, jobs, and social connections impact our health and wellbeing. Two groups were followed: those who do volunteer work and those who don't. According to survey data collected six times over thirty years, those who volunteered were happier and in better physical health, regardless of age. More recently, researchers at Boston College evaluated the effects of volunteering and discovered that it reduces chronic pain and disability, even after several months. Participants admitted that "making a connection" and having "a sense of purpose" were likely responsible for their improved condition. Other studies have shown that volunteers, even those with modest levels of engagement, have fewer risk factors for cardiovascular disease, hypertension, and depression than do nonvolunteers. Finally, adults aged sixty and older may stand to benefit most from volunteering because it's linked to a lower risk of cognitive impairment.

"The benefits of giving back are definitely biological," says bioethicist Stephen Post, coauthor of *Why Good Things Happen to Good People*. "When we do good deeds, we're rewarded by a dopamine pulse. Giving a donation or volunteering in a food bank tweaks the same source of pleasure that lights up when we eat or have sex." There's also an increase in endorphins, which positively impacts our sense of wellbeing. In sum, the physical and psychological upsides attributed to empathic action are convincing.

If we all have the capacity to empathize, can become more empathic with practice, agree the world needs more empathy, and all stand to benefit from elevating our empathic consciousness, an important question surfaces: what's the best approach to pursue purposeful empathy at scale? Communities of empathic practice, such as the ones we met in this chapter, are important sites for movement building. And should inspire us all to get more involved.

PURPOSEFUL EMPATHY PRACTICES

The following exercises are intended to help you and your family, as well as the groups to which you belong, gel as communities of empathic practice. You can download a free workbook from my website.

1. Assemble a group of friends to screen the documentary *Dialogue Lab: America*. The film's description reads, "What happens when twelve Americans from across the political spectrum attempt to have a conversation? Ideos Institute conducted a social experiment to test whether constructive dialogue is possible in today's polarized culture, and if so, how dialogue might be the first step in healing our nation."

    After watching the film together, share your reflections using the empathy circle process, following the instructions at the end of chapter 5.

2. As a family or community group, participate in a service activity and then discuss the shared benefits of the experience and any lessons learned, using these prompt questions:

    •   Who did you help today? And who helped you today? This pair of questions is important to avoid slipping into the pity paradigm of working "for" others. Instead, by honoring our shared humanity, the key is to serve "with."

- How is the volunteer or service work you did today connected to larger systems that are broken and in need of repair?

- To what extent did you live up to Dr. King's vision of a "beloved community"? What could you have done differently?

- What do you commit to doing, both personally and collectively, to create or sustain a community of empathic practice?

3. *Sign the Charter of Compassion* and join or establish a *Compassionate Community* initiative that makes sense for your context (e.g., with your neighbors or a recreational, athletic, artistic, advocacy, or faith group).

The Charter for Compassion

The principle of compassion lies at the heart of all religious, ethical and spiritual traditions, calling us always to treat all others as we wish to be treated ourselves.

Compassion impels us to work tirelessly to alleviate the suffering of our fellow creatures, to dethrone ourselves from the centre of our world and put another there, and to honour the inviolable sanctity of every single human being, treating everybody, without exception, with absolute justice, equity and respect.

It is also necessary in both public and private life to refrain consistently and empathically from inflicting pain. To act or speak violently out of spite, chauvinism, or self-interest, to impoverish, exploit or deny basic rights to anybody, and to incite hatred by denigrating others—even our enemies—is a denial of our common humanity.

We acknowledge that we have failed to live compassionately and that some have even increased the sum of human misery in the name of religion. We therefore call upon all men and women:

- *To restore compassion to the centre of morality and religion;*

- *To return to the ancient principle that any interpretation of scripture that breeds violence, hatred or disdain is illegitimate;*

- *To ensure that youth are given accurate and respectful information about other traditions, religions and cultures;*

- *To encourage a positive appreciation of cultural and religious diversity;*

- *To cultivate an informed empathy with the suffering of all human beings—even those regarded as enemies.*

We urgently need to make compassion a clear, luminous and dynamic force in our polarized world. Rooted in a principled determination to transcend selfishness, compassion can break down political, dogmatic, ideological and religious boundaries.

Born of our deep interdependence, compassion is essential to human relationships and to a fulfilled humanity. It is the path to enlightenment, and indispensable to the creation of a just economy and a peaceful global community.

Bonus if you have children: Take the *Compass Survey for Families* (with kids ages ten to seventeen or with children aged five to nine), created by developmental psychologist Marilyn Price-Mitchell. Then, as a family, discuss the results and decide together what you'd like to do differently.

PART IV

9

EMPATHY SUPERHEROES

One of the deep secrets of life is that all that is really worth doing is what we do for others.

—Lewis Carroll

After two miscarriages, my husband and I were blessed with a baby girl. Throughout our pregnancy, we attended a series of hypno-birthing classes and were supported by a wonderful midwife. My dream was to bring Annika into the world in water. A week before my due date, contractions began. They were relatively mild and spaced apart, so I was told to stay home. By the next morning, they had grown sharper and closer together, so we drove to the birthing center and settled into a large room, listening to the soothing music of Deva Premal. Another full day and night passed without progression, so our midwife broke my water. Still, nothing happened. Finally, after following all the protocols, she recommended that we move to a hospital.

The doctor on duty waited patiently for several more hours as my contractions intensified. Eventually, he said, "Anita, you must be exhausted. Maybe it's time to consider a Caesarean." I had devoted many months to learning about the benefits of natural childbirth, so a C-section was the last thing I wanted to do—even after sixty-five hours of labor pain. "Something else to consider is that your baby's head should be engaged, but right now her chin is in position, as though she's looking up to the sky," the doctor said. Then, with a kindred smile, he asked, "Wouldn't you like to meet your stargazer?"

I could feel his empathy wash over me, and off to the operating room we went.

Our little miracle was born healthy, and we bonded instantly. She slept on my chest throughout the night, and I dozed off between feedings, still high on a cocktail of oxytocin and morphine. My husband went home to get some much-needed sleep, and I savored the unforgettable feeling that all was well with the world. That is, until 3:00 a.m., when I felt an urgent need to pee. Post-surgery, I didn't have the strength to walk across the room alone, so I rang the nurse's station for help. Ten minutes passed, but I assumed everyone was busy, so I held on tight.

I rang a second, third, and fourth time at ten-minute intervals and started to feel anxious that no one was responding. What if there had been a real emergency? Finally, after waiting as long as I could, I peed myself in bed. It was not my finest moment, but what else could I do? As anyone with a sense of irony might guess, a nurse doing her rounds came into my room a few short minutes later. I explained what happened and apologized profusely, but she still scolded me something fierce. I was flooded by shame and humiliation, and her lack of empathy remains an upsetting memory to this day.

As the adage goes, "You may forget their words, but you'll never forget how they made you feel." In that spirit, this chapter is an ode to our empathy superheroes, all those kindhearted warriors called to their vocation by a sense of service. They may not be perfect, but like a peacock fanning its feathers, they put humanity's superpower on full display. You know who I mean. Nurses, doctors, and their colleagues in healthcare. Psychologists and social workers. Humanitarians and social entrepreneurs. And last but not least, teachers.

The nature of these jobs requires the professionals who occupy them to bring their empathy A-game to work every single day. But they're mere mortals just like us, with taxes to pay, laundry to fold, and teeth to floss. Then along came COVID-19, and they all put their lives on the line, working tirelessly in systems under siege. And more than ever before, their risk of burnout and PTSD went through the roof. Given the daily tensions they faced to keep healthy and safe, honor their personal boundaries, and fulfill their duties with grace—regardless of how poorly some people behaved during the crisis—it's a wonder they don't all wear capes by now.

HEALTHCARE PROVIDERS

The United States spends more on healthcare than other developed nations but produces worse outcomes. No wonder 70 percent of Americans believe the system has major problems or is in a state of crisis, and seven out of ten primary care physicians think it needs a fundamental overhaul. There's also broad agreement that empathy is important to the practice of medicine, but only half of patients and doctors believe the healthcare system is caring. In one study that recorded medical encounters, researchers found that doctors regularly miss or dismiss signs of patient distress and provide empathic responses only 22 percent of the time. What's going on?

Empathy in healthcare has always been tricky. Doctors, nurses, and other practitioners encounter emotionally taxing situations—illness, suffering, and dying—on a daily basis. Meanwhile, patients are usually at their most vulnerable. This means healthcare workers must walk a fine line between clinical distance and empathic concern, and the struggle to achieve balance is relentless.

In the 1960s, sociologists began studying how medicine was being practiced and observed that physicians tended to blunt their feelings. At the time, objectivity was seen as the gold standard for effective diagnosis and treatment, and emotional engagement was considered an impediment. As a result, "detached concern" became the modus operandi. Things got progressively worse as the bureaucratic demands of the profession grew. Imagine: for every hour spent with patients, doctors spend two hours doing paperwork. I doubt that's what they had in mind when taking the Hippocratic Oath!

Thanks to empirical research, we know that strong empathic connections between physicians and patients increase job satisfaction and treatment compliance and decrease malpractice complaints. Doctors with higher levels of empathy also experience less stress, cynicism, and burnout. Finally, clinical empathy is associated with improved patient satisfaction and outcomes, including a stronger immune system and better health. In fact, when patients perceive their caregiver as empathic, the duration and severity of the common cold drop.

Nonetheless, the workplace culture in healthcare is notorious for stress, overwork, and self-neglect, all of which contribute to higher rates of burnout and increased numbness to patient suffering. In one pre-COVID-19 study, 86 percent of nurses across emergency, oncology, and intensive care reported moderate to high levels of compassion fatigue, and 83 percent of doctors reported moderate to severe emotional exhaustion. Sadly, throughout the pandemic, frontline workers worldwide experienced devastating increases of insomnia, anxiety, depression, and PTSD. And this holds true for those working in mental health and social work too. Prior to the pandemic, they were already at a greater risk for compassion fatigue and secondary traumatic stress. Once the pandemic hit, their caseloads skyrocketed, and they were called upon to help individuals and families cope with work-life upheaval, social isolation, illness, and death while simultaneously managing their own personal stress and anxiety. It was a completely untenable situation.

Looking back, we relied on empathic care from caregivers, who were just as overwhelmed as the rest of us. We owe them a debt of gratitude, and they also deserve to work in a system in which empathy thrives. With that in mind, here are five initiatives that recognize the power of empathy at distinct points of intervention along a healthcare worker's career.

Narrative Medicine

Listen to your patient; he is telling you the diagnosis.

—William Osler, MD

In 1889, Dr. William Osler became the first physician-in-chief at the newly established Johns Hopkins Hospital. There, he made his mark by introducing the concept of a residency program for medical school students, insisting "the good physician treats the disease; the great physician treats the patient who has the disease." Residencies are now a ubiquitous part of med school training. Unfortunately, multiple studies show that empathy dwindles in year three and continues to wane throughout residency, just as students are starting to engage in patient-care activities. Even north of the border in Canada, a country with a universal public system, 27 percent of healthcare providers reported suicidal ideation during their training, and nearly half screened positive for symptoms of depression by the time they were residents.

By the 1990s, medical educators realized the curriculum focused too much on biomedical sciences and did not sufficiently address the needs and experiences of patients and their families. Plus, the realities of clinical encounters had shifted gears quite dramatically. First, the business side of healthcare was driving physicians to prioritize efficiency over empathy. According to Harvard Medical School, the average doctor's appointment is only twenty minutes. Another study found that physicians listen to their patients an average of eleven seconds before interrupting them. How can anyone properly discuss a health issue within that context? Second, new technologies to diagnose and treat illness began taking center stage. And as Rita Charon concludes in *Narrative Medicine: A Model for Empathy, Reflection, Profession, and Trust,* "Scientifically competent medicine alone cannot help a patient grapple with the loss of health or find meaning in suffering." Clearly, more patient-centered approaches were needed.

Cue narrative medicine. Developed and taught at Columbia University, the practice is described as an "interdisciplinary field that brings powerful narrative skills of radical listening and creativity from the humanities and the arts to address the needs of all who seek and deliver healthcare." The premise is simple. Much like doing a close reading of a novel, practitioners are adept at deciphering body language, interpreting metaphors, and reading between the lines. Empathic engagement with patients is the goal, not detached concern. And this arises naturally when doctors listen to stories without biases, judgments, or assumptions. "If the physician cannot perform these narrative tasks," Charon elaborates, "the patient might not tell the whole story, might not ask the most frightening questions, and might not feel heard."

In 2016, one study concluded that narrative medicine is "a powerful instrument for decreasing pain and increasing well-being related to illness." Furthermore, doctors who receive narrative training—whether they come from genetics counseling, fetal cardiology, or surgical training—derive pleasure from the practice. Finally, as physicians begin to incorporate a patient's lived reality into their care plans, they also begin to address issues of structural inequality and social justice in healthcare. As such, narrative medicine is a holistic practice that meets the emotional needs of patients while simultaneously looking to mend a broken and inequitable system.

E.M.P.A.T.H.Y

Empathy training is the key transformative education.

—Helen Riess, MD

A famous study conducted by body language expert Albert Mehrabian revealed that during face-to-face conversations, 55 percent of communication is nonverbal facial expressions, 38 percent is tone of voice, and only 7 percent is the spoken word. This became known as the 7-38-55 rule. In *The Empathy Effect*, Dr. Helen Riess, director of the Empathy and Relational Science Program at Massachusetts General Hospital, writes, "In my own profession, I saw an urgent need to teach the nonverbal aspects of communication to foster better understanding between physicians and patients." In response, she developed a web-based training program called E.M.P.A.T.H.Y, based on insights from the neurobiology and physiology of emotions. Let's unpack the acronym to better understand each component.

"E" is for "eye contact." Anecdotally, from the eye-gazing exercise I do in my classes and workshops, I know how meaningful it is to look someone deeply in the eyes and also be seen. Eyes are, after all, the windows to the soul. Unfortunately, eye contact is becoming increasingly uncommon in a world full of screens and digital devices. But in professions like healthcare, it is key to promoting trust and improving interpersonal communication.

"M" is for "muscles of facial expression." According to a Danish study, people who scored higher on an empathy questionnaire had better empathic accuracy when reading facial expressions. This builds on the pioneering work of Paul Ekman, who codified facial expressions into seven universal "families" of emotions. There are, of course, important cultural differences, so it's not a perfect science, but healthcare providers can improve their capacity to discern facial reactions and expressions through training and learn to respond to their patients with greater empathy.

"P" is for "posture." "I always try to convey my respect and openness through my body language. When I sit with patients, I turn my body toward them, lean forward and sit at eye level. I use mirroring and nonverbal cues. All of this conveys I'm attentive and interested on a personal level," writes Riess. As it turns out, the same areas of the brain light up during the perception of facial expressions and body positioning, so both are important to an empathic exchange.

"A" is for "affect." *Affect* is the scientific term for emotion. In *Atlas of the Heart: Mapping Meaningful Connection and the Language of Human Experience*, Brené Brown writes, "When we don't understand how our emotions shape our thoughts and decisions, we become disembodied from our own experiences and disconnected from each other." To communicate empathically, healthcare professionals must be adept at discerning emotions.

"T" is for "tone of voice." The popular refrain "It's not *what* you said; it's *how* you said it" captures perfectly why managing our tone of voice is important. According to personal development guru Tony Robbins, "Words that may seem neutral can become provoking if spoken with a sarcastic, demeaning or contemptuous tone of voice, causing the listener to feel hurt and disrespected. A soft tone of voice is often interpreted as lack of confidence—but too loud, and you'll be seen as aggressive." Paying attention to pitch, pace, volume, and timbre can help healthcare workers become better communicators.

"H" is for "hearing the whole person." Reminiscent of narrative medicine, the goal is to listen empathically without judgment while also reading between the lines. In two separate studies investigating the E.M.P.A.T.H.Y approach, Riess and her research team discovered that when doctors learn how to "hear the whole person" in clinical encounters, their patients ranked them much higher on empathy scales.

Finally, "Y" is for "your response." Since emotions are contagious, it's easy to get triggered by someone else's affective state, especially if it's intense. That's how conversations go sideways and conflicts quickly escalate. Healthcare providers with self-awareness are in a better position to respond empathically to anxious or angry patients and to help them down-regulate.

The E.M.P.A.T.H.Y approach has been validated as highly effective; both physicians and medical residents who followed the program outperformed those who didn't on patient-rated empathy scores. This is great news since empathic relationships are known to improve health outcomes. Riess is also excited that other professions are beginning to benefit from her model, including educators, police officers, and management professionals.

Vital Talk

Vital Talk began as a training organization for oncology caregivers. According to their research, 99 percent of doctors agreed that advance care planning conversations were important, but fewer than half knew what to say, and 14 percent skipped the conversation altogether. "Just as no doctor is born knowing how to handle a scalpel, the same is true for how to communicate effectively with seriously ill patients and their families," reads their website. Today, the organization offers culturally sensitive and evidence-based communication training to clinicians who care for patients living with a range of serious illnesses.

Ed-U-CARE

During college, Sharyn Fein was her mother's sole caregiver. This spawned a lifelong passion for senior care. Founded to meet the needs of both elderly patients and their caregivers, Ed-U-CARE hosts an annual Compassion Fatigue Symposium and provides a wide variety of training programs, including one devoted to cultural competency that sheds light on the unique issues and discrimination that older LGBTQ+ Americans face. The organization also runs a Bridge-Building Network to serve marginalized communities and manages a Hearts and Hands program that pairs seniors with trained volunteers to engage in conversation over manicures.

3rd Conversation

Christine Bechtel, cofounder of 3rd Conversation, which seeks to infuse empathy and humanity back into healthcare, believes the lived experiences of patients, clinicians, and administrators vary considerably, but the system takes a serious toll on everyone. By curating opportunities for these three groups to engage in dialogue outside the context of medical visits, they can forge a human connection through bidirectional empathy. And because the sessions are described by all three stakeholder groups as therapeutic, they also make healing possible.

Each of these five initiatives is purposeful about injecting more empathy into medicine. But as virtual and AI-driven healthcare interactions increasingly supplant in-person communication for millions of patients, there's a risk that the system will become even more impersonal and transactional than it already is. In 2019, the global telehealth market was sixty-one billion dollars. By 2027, it's expected to balloon to $560 billion. If we genuinely believe in health*care*, we would be wise to insist that empathy features prominently.

EDUCATORS, HUMANITARIANS, ACTIVISTS, AND SOCIAL ENTREPRENEURS

Incredibly, up to 50 percent of American teachers burn out within five years of starting their careers.

During the pandemic, over half a million public school educators left their jobs, and according to a National Education Association poll of its membership, 55 percent of them were planning to leave. This is a national crisis atop a national tragedy.

The toll on teachers is well documented. For years, they've faced intense pressure thanks to standardized testing and shrinking budgets. And the ubiquity of phones and technology has changed classrooms forever. Sadly, thirty-five million American children have experienced one or more types of childhood trauma. Can we really expect educators to also be psychologists? More recently, increasing parental and political surveillance of curriculum is causing new stress and anxiety. Finally, teachers are expected to manage kids who were out of school for months (and, in some cases, years) at a stretch due to the pandemic. One-third of teachers polled by the American Psychological Association reported having endured verbal harassment or threats from students during the 2020–2021 school year, and 14 percent said they were the victim of physical violence. No wonder burnout and attrition is sky-high.

Regarding the second group, the purpose of humanitarian aid is to help people in emergency situations such as natural and humanmade disasters, including floods, tsunamis, earthquakes, and war. Rachel Kiddell-Monroe has devoted her career to working alongside people who have suffered mass trauma and loss, including in Rwanda, Somalia, the Democratic Republic of Congo, Indonesia, and refugee camps across Europe. Despite having witnessed unspeakable tragedy, after more than two decades with Doctors without Borders, she remains optimistic about the human condition but reminds us, "We have everything to give; and they have nothing to lose."

There's no question that providing humanitarian relief requires empathy and resilience. Seeing the magnitude of suffering and social injustice in the world must be disheartening at the best of times and, on a bad day, must make aid workers apoplectic or inconsolable, or both. That's why they suffer from burnout and mental illness at more than double, and sometimes even triple, the rate of the general population, according to the CHS Alliance, a global network of humanitarian and development organizations. Unfortunately, women, younger professionals, and people of color are disproportionately affected.

The same can be said about activists. In one study that examined the mental health of human rights advocates, researchers found that one in five met the criteria for PTSD, another 20 percent for subthreshold PTSD, and 15 percent for depression. This means more than half were in the grip of a serious mental health issue. Similar disconcerting findings were published in a staff wellbeing review at Amnesty International. Finally, in another study, more than half the activists interviewed felt disillusioned or hopeless about the work they were doing. In fact, up to 87 percent of peace activists had quit activism within six years of getting involved. And once again, burnout was found to be most prevalent among activists of color, who must cope with the daily stresses of activism in addition to living in a society plagued by systemic racism.

Finally, there are social entrepreneurs—the dedicated impact innovators, changemakers, and systems disruptors inspired into empathic action. According to research conducted by the Social Impact Award (SIA), an organization empowering youth to make a difference, two out of five of social entrepreneurs said they experienced burnout with lasting periods of stress, and one in five faced persistent problems including anxiety and disordered sleeping. A full 5 percent had to stop working altogether, feeling pressure that "someone could die tomorrow if I take a break."

Nonprofit organizations like Focusing Initiatives International provide mental health and wellness programming to support care providers working in communities of distress. This includes body-centered training rooted in Indigenous traditions to heal complex personal and community traumas. Similarly, The Wellbeing Project was created to instill a culture of inner wellbeing for changemakers, cofounded by six social change organizations. Through personal development programming, convening, connecting, and storytelling, the collaborative seeks to support those working on the front lines of social change. According to a research report about their work, "Wellbeing inspires welldoing." When social entrepreneurs are kind to themselves, they reject the hero model of success, become more emotionally resilient, and adopt practices of self-care.

COMPASSION SATISFACTION

According to Mark Brennan, the UNESCO chair of Community, Leadership, and Youth Development at Penn State University, "In times of emergency, providing empathy, kindness and compassion to our fellow citizens is the single most important factor in surviving the initial stages of disaster, limiting suffering, protecting the vulnerable, and quickly recovering in the aftermath of the crisis." At the same time, compassion fatigue is an occupational hazard for all our empathy superheroes.

Characterized by deep physical, emotional, and spiritual exhaustion, this silent epidemic is the result of secondhand trauma caused by working with traumatized individuals. Symptoms include extreme anxiety, a sense of hopelessness, difficulty concentrating, and irritability, all of which affect performance and wellbeing. Thanks to COVID-19, compassion fatigue has ripped across our schools and hospitals, in the field and over Zoom. Worse, recovery—both individually and collectively—is moving at glacial speed.

Compassion satisfaction, on the other hand, is defined as the joy and meaning that a caregiver derives from doing good work and contributing to the wellbeing of others. It's the secret ingredient to balancing professional service and personal renewal. When caregivers and frontline service providers see that they're having a positive impact on someone's life, family, or community, they are motivated by their work. It's also a major factor in their capacity to handle the stress of their day-to-day jobs and contributes to overall fulfillment in their careers.

It's been empirically shown that empathy training can increase compassion satisfaction, reduce burnout, and even prevent secondary traumatic stress. Plus, compassion satisfaction is known to be a protective factor for mental health and is tied to positive self-worth. Taken together, it's a no-brainer that empathy should play a central role in professional development across every caretaker's career. And we, the public, should advocate on their behalf to make that happen with a greater sense of urgency. Given the heavy emotional burden they shoulder, it's the least we could do.

PURPOSEFUL EMPATHY PRACTICES

The following tools and exercises are meant to inspire a sense of gratitude for our empathy superheroes, help you determine if you're at risk for compassion fatigue, and provide you with a couple of resources to help reduce stress in your life. You can download a free workbook from my website.

1. Thank some caregivers in your life. Buy a pack of thank-you cards and write notes of appreciation to those you feel have gone above and beyond their professional roles over the past couple of years. During the first wave of COVID-19, groups of volunteers came together to prepare and distribute sandwiches and baked goods for exhausted frontline healthcare providers. That was great, but it shouldn't take a pandemic to appreciate the emotional heavy lifting all our empathy superheroes do on behalf of society.

2. Determine your level of stress and if you're at risk for burnout, secondary trauma, or compassion fatigue by using one of the assessment tools made available by *Professional Quality of Life* (proQOL), which is "intended for any helper—healthcare professionals, social service workers, teachers, attorneys, emergency response, etc. Understanding the positive and negative aspects of helping those who experience trauma and suffering can improve your ability to help them and your ability to keep your own balance."

3. Learn more about inner wellbeing by tapping into these two resources:

- *Super Soul Sunday* videos or podcasts to "awaken, discover and connect to the deeper meaning of the world around you. Hear Oprah's personal selection of her interviews with thought-leaders, best-selling authors, spiritual luminaries, as well as health and wellness experts. All designed to light you up, guide you through life's big questions and help bring you one step closer to your best self."

- *Yoga with Melissa* was created to promote "real yoga for real people" to buck the trend of athletic yoga for bikini bodies. Her YouTube channel boasts hundreds of free classes to help practitioners restore balance, harmony, and wellbeing in their lives.

10

PURPOSEFUL EMPATHY IS A MARATHON

The person who starts the race is not the same person who finishes the race.

—A popular marathon spectator sign

I entered the seminar room feeling frazzled. I was late, and everyone was already seated on mats and bolsters doing a deep breathing exercise. It was my first visit to Kripalu, a wellness center in the Berkshires, and I was there to attend a retreat called "Women Who Do Too Much." After settling in, our workshop facilitator, named Jennifer, asked everyone to open their eyes and introduce themselves, saying where they were from and why they were there. Some were social workers or therapists describing textbook symptoms of burnout. Others were C-suite executives raising a child with a disability or caring for a parent with Alzheimer's. As each woman shared her story of exhaustion, guilt, and self-reproach, we all nodded in solidarity. We also felt empathy permeate the room, uniting us in somatic entanglement.

After hearing from everyone, Jennifer shared the following story that touched a collective nerve: Once upon a time there was an old woman in a village who fetched two pails of water every day from a well on the outskirts of town. The bucket on her right leaked all the way back and was empty by the time she got home. Some neighbors took pity on her and bought a shiny new one, a gesture she genuinely appreciated. Nonetheless, to their surprise, she refused the gift and pointed to the side of the road. "On the walk home, my leaky pail waters all those flowers as far as your eyes can see," she said. "I haven't replaced my bucket because I want their beauty to brighten your day."

Jennifer slowly panned the circle with a tender-hearted smile on her face and said, "Like that kind, old woman, each of you faithfully tends to the needs of others. But now it's time to take care of yourself and let your own healing journey begin." With that, the floodgates opened, and we all cried a river of tears.

Given the competing demands on our time and energy, it's easy to run on empty—especially if you do any kind of emotional labor. And let's face it: if you have parents, children, neighbors, friends, a boss, colleagues, or direct reports, you're doing some emotional heavy lifting! That's why practicing self-empathy is so important.

Having empathy for oneself means looking to the past, present, and future with soft eyes. Honoring our personal history, including our traumas, and being intentional about healing from them. Respecting our current needs, boundaries, and limits—which can take a variety of forms like saying no, ending a relationship, or asking for help. Finally, imagining the best possible future for ourselves, without pressure or striving.

Purposeful empathy, on the other hand, centers the best interests of others. It's about wielding the power of empathy to achieve greater peace, justice, and sustainability in the world. It's about making decisions that take into account what we bestow upon our progeny. It's about leadership that develops innate gifts and talents in service to the greater good. It's about defying the status quo with moral courage and elevated consciousness on behalf of those without power or privilege. It's about leaning into humility, mutuality, reflexivity, and tenacity in the spirit of collective action. Finally, it's about extending an empathic embrace far and wide, knowing we all share a common humanity. That's why sustained purposeful empathy is a marathon.

With that in mind, this chapter explores six approaches that address the question "How can I be kind to myself *while* practicing purposeful empathy?"

SELF-COMPASSION

Give yourself permission to treat yourself kindly.

—Kristen Neff

The term *self-compassion* was mainstreamed by Kristen Neff, an associate professor of educational psychology. Initially, she leaned on the concept as a personal coping mechanism. Today, after having devoted many years to validating the construct empirically, she's on a mission to raise public awareness about its many benefits—which include better health, improved relationships, and a more satisfying life overall.

Not to be confused with self-pity, Neff describes self-compassion as "a way of relating to the ever-changing landscape of who we are with kindness and acceptance—especially when we fail or feel inadequate." It means treating ourselves with the same degree of benevolence that we would a good friend while recognizing that life is hard on everyone.

The threat-defense system of our reptilian brain is triggered whenever it perceives danger. This includes being judged or criticized by someone else, as well as any form of self-recrimination. In 2007, Neff's son was diagnosed with autism. He suffered regularly from public meltdowns and tantrums, and she recalls getting dirty looks from strangers. In those moments, she felt paralyzing shame and a crushing sense of desperation.

She learned to self-soothe and down-regulate by tapping into what she describes as the three elements of self-compassion: kindness (being warm to ourselves when in pain and looking upon our shortcomings with forgiveness), common humanity (recognizing that suffering and failure are part of the human condition), and mindfulness (sensing negative emotions without judgment, suppression, or exaggeration).

We live in a high-performance and image-based culture, where shame and fear of judgment run rampant. Our toxic social media landscape is also replete with hurtful and unfiltered comments. Cyberbullying is now so prevalent that it's considered a public health problem. Our amygdala, which is located deep in our brain, imprints all our experiences and stores them by emotional relevance. That's what makes triggers so powerful. When something happens in the present moment that reminds us of a past pain or threat, our body is put on high alert, and an emotional chain reaction quickly follows. In those moments, self-compassion is important to help ease heightened emotions and kneejerk reactions. Studies have also found that members of racialized groups and the LGBTQ+ community are better able to cope with discrimination and harassment if they practice self-compassion because it bolsters resilience.

LOVING KINDNESS

Compassion doesn't mean we don't fight. It means we don't hate.

—Sharon Salzberg

Raised in New York City during the 1950s, Sharon Salzberg experienced a difficult childhood. At the age of four, her father abandoned the family, and five years later, her mother passed away. By the time she was sixteen, she had lived in five different households and suffered from chronic anxiety. In college, she took an Asian philosophy class and fell in love with Buddhism. This led her to Bodh Gaya, India, where she discovered the healing power of meditation during a ten-day *vipassana* (insight) retreat. Enraptured by its potential for posttraumatic growth, she immersed herself in a form of meditation called *mettā bhāvanā*, meaning "loving kindness." After years of study, she returned home to America and cofounded the Insight Meditation Society, which is now one of the leading centers for contemplative practice in the Western hemisphere.

According to Salzberg, "The practice of loving-kindness is about cultivating love as a strength, a muscle, a tool that challenges our tendency to see people (including ourselves) as disconnected, statically and rigidly isolated from one another." By dissolving the us-versus-them paradigm, it's also a gateway to greater empathic consciousness.

In *The Force of Kindness*, Sharon suggests repeating the following phrases silently to yourself for a few minutes as a *mettā* meditation practice:

> May you live in safety, without fear of injury;
> May you have mental happiness, including a sense of peace and joy;
> May you have physical happiness, including good health and
> freedom from pain; and

May you live with ease, such that daily life, work and family do
   not pose any struggles.

Ideally, you would repeat these phrases for different groups, beginning with
your inner circle and then extending your empathic embrace outward. For
example:

Someone you love or who has been generous to you;
A friend who is going through a tough time;
A neutral person for whom you have no strong feelings of like or
   dislike; and finally
Someone who has hurt you or with whom you have a conflict.

While it may seem odd, and often difficult, to wish strangers or foes loving
kindness, research shows that in addition to fostering empathy, reciting *mettā*
phrases also provides many physical and psychological benefits, including
less stress, depression, anxiety, and chronic pain and fewer migraines.

FOREST BATHING

Nature itself is the best physician.

—Hippocrates

Exposure to natural environments enhances vitality by as a much as 40
percent, and spending time indoors does the opposite. Nonetheless, the
average American spends 93 percent of their time inside—87 percent in
buildings and 6 percent in cars. Meanwhile, the United Nations predicts that
two-thirds of humanity will live in cities by 2050. This does not bode well for
human flourishing since cities are associated with higher rates of loneliness
and stress, as well as several mental illnesses.

In 1982, the Japanese Ministry of Agriculture, Forestry, and Fisheries
began to promote *shinrin-yoku* as a form of ecotherapy. Known in English
as *forest bathing*, the mindful immersion into nature was meant as an
antidote to the tech-boom burnout that many Japanese workers were
facing at the time.

The practice is simple: Go to the woods, breathe deeply, and pay attention to your five senses. The focus is on the journey, not the destination. Anecdotally, forest bathers insist the practice inspires greater wellbeing, creativity, and mental clarity—possibly thanks to the aromatic oils released by trees and plants known as phytoncides, which boost our immune system.

Dr. Qing Li, the world's leading authority on forest medicine at Tokyo's Nippon Medical School hospital, has found that the practice combats depression and anxiety, lowers blood pressure, improves sleep, and fights cancer, strokes, and gastric ulcers. With that kind of healing potential, no wonder forest bathing is gaining traction, especially in the pandemic's aftermath.

SELF-CARE

Self-care is not selfish or self-indulgent. We cannot nurture others from a dry well.

—Jennifer Louden

As a young woman, Jennifer Louden dreamed of becoming a screenwriter and movie director but was rejected by the School of Cinematic Arts at USC. For the two decades that followed, she battled imposter syndrome, feeling beholden to what she thought her writing "should" be. But after having what she describes as "a moment of grace," she began to write from the heart. Today, as a bestselling author, she's considered a pioneer of the self-care movement.

According to the World Health Organization, "self-care is what people do for themselves to establish and maintain mental health, and to prevent and deal with illness." This can take many forms, including reading for pleasure, getting exercise or playing a sport, taking a bath, getting enough sleep, journaling, or simply resting without justification. The essence of self-care is making conscious decisions that optimize our physical and psychological wellbeing.

Unfortunately, many caregivers and activists report feeling guilt and shame when tending to their own needs. To them, self-care is in conflict with the intended selflessness of their calling. Louden's body of work dispels the notion that self-care is akin to self-indulgence, and through her books and retreats, she has inspired a generation of women to tend to their emotional, physical, and spiritual lives as part of a regenerative care regime that lets them continue serving the communities they love, as well as the world at large. I know this firsthand, having participated in the Kripalu retreat she facilitated, in which I narrowly escaped a major burnout.

That said, since the late 1980s, self-care has been hijacked by commercial interests. A quick search of the self-care hashtag on Instagram and TikTok reveals wall-to-wall beauty routines and superficial wellness practices. Not only is today's global wellness business category valued at five trillion dollars; much of it carries a vapid, neoliberal, "boss babe" ethos that proclaims wellness can be achieved through conspicuous consumption. That's why in *The Empathy Effect*, Roman Krznaric proposes an empathy-based model "to shift identities from 'buying' to 'belonging,' where more people find their personal wellbeing and sense of self from having strong relationships (intrinsic values) than from financial success, shopping and social status (extrinsic values)."

COMMUNITIES OF CARE

Caring for myself is not self-indulgence; it is self-preservation, and that is an act of political warfare.

—Audrey Lorde

The self-care movement has a second origin story that often gets overlooked. Throughout the 1970s, Black people began prioritizing their health and wellbeing as a strategy to fight systemic racism. This included the Black Panther Party's community-led Survival Programs in food distribution, pediatric clinics, legal aid, and education. Since self-care doesn't remedy the trauma of hatred, discrimination, and injustice, Communities of Care are often considered a better alternative.

GirlTrek is a contemporary example of community care in action. According to national data, two-thirds of African-American women engage in little to no leisure time or physical activity—due primarily to the demands of balancing work, childcare, and other responsibilities. As a result, four out of five are overweight, and 59 percent are obese. The consequences of which are dire: Black women experience higher rates of hypertension and diabetes, and their life expectancy is five to ten years shorter.

Since most healthcare campaigns fail to acknowledge intergenerational trauma and systemic racism, GirlTrek was created as "a global movement of Black women leveraging the historic legacy of walking and the power of self-care as a pathway to heal and transform our lives." Members have retraced Harriet Tubman's hundred-mile journey to freedom and the historic fifty-four-mile civil rights walk from Selma to Montgomery. Today, representing 7 percent of the African American women's population, their 1.3 million members agree that walking thirty minutes a day is a "radical act of self-love and the root of a cultural revolution."

Another manifestation of community care is found in *mutual aid*, a term that traces back to nineteenth-century anarchist Peter Kropotkin, who explored the Siberian wilderness to investigate how different animals united against common struggles. Unlike charity, which involves a one-way flow of resources from the haves to have nots, mutual aid involves bilateral support grounded in an ethos of solidarity. Instead of the mantra "every man for himself," mutual aid assumes everyone has something to contribute *and* everyone has a need.

COVID-19 inspired a renaissance of mutual aid societies. At least four thousand groups were launched in the United Kingdom alone during the first eighteen months of the pandemic, and they were considered an indispensable part of the public response to the crisis. They took many forms of support, including grocery shopping and delivery, collection of prescriptions, dog walking, library services, emotional support by telephone and email, informational support on existing public services, community gardening, and much more.

One great example is Out in the Open, a nonprofit organization that supports the LGBTQ+ community in rural America. As wealthier individuals moved from cities into rural areas during the first phase of the pandemic, rental prices began to soar. And as smaller public transportation options disappeared, queer and trans folk faced unprecedented levels of social isolation. The organization set up a mutual aid fund to support its members with groceries, housing and medical support, and other vital necessities.

Another non-COVID-19 example is Mutual Aid Disaster Relief, a national, decentralized, and grassroots network across the United States composed of environmentalists, Black liberation organizers, and activists of all stripes who "provide disaster relief based on the principles of solidarity, mutual aid, and autonomous direct action."

SOMATIC EXPERIENCING

Trauma is not what happens to us. But what we hold inside in the absence of an empathetic witness.

—Peter Levine

In 1996, the Centers for Disease Control and Prevention undertook a longitudinal study with more than seventeen thousand people known as the Adverse Childhood Experiences (ACEs) to understand the effects of complex trauma. They discovered a significant relationship between "adverse experiences" in childhood, such as neglect or abuse of any kind, and negative health outcomes later in life, including depression, self-harm, suicidality, substance abuse, obesity, and chronic illnesses like diabetes, cancer, and heart disease. Since then, additional studies have confirmed that trauma hinders the capacity for trust, connection, and mutuality—in other words, our ability to be in relation with others. In response, over the past couple of decades, somatic therapy techniques and healing modalities have been advanced.

In parallel, healing professionals have also been studying ways to treat intergenerational and historical trauma. In the 1960s, psychologists in Canada began to notice that a disproportionate number of children of Holocaust survivors—overrepresented by 300 percent compared to the general population—were seeking mental help in clinics across the country. Since then, similar collective trauma has been discovered among descendants of African Americans forced into slavery, Native American genocide survivors, refugees, and victims of domestic violence or war, and many other groups that have experienced collective distress.

Just like individual trauma, cultural trauma manifests in many dysfunctional ways. Symptoms include substance abuse; addiction to food, sex, and entertainment; and media overuse. Thomas Hübl is a spiritual teacher and cofounder of the Pocket Project, an international organization that raises awareness about collective trauma and its impacts. He writes, "Collective trauma energetically fragments and alienates, trapping us in a concussed field of static separation."

Developed by Peter Levine, somatic experiencing (SE) is a body-oriented form of therapy to treat trauma and other stress-related disorders by directing practitioners to internal sensations as opposed to thoughts and emotions. Informed by physiology, psychology, biology, neuroscience, Indigenous healing practices, and medical biophysics, the SE approach helps determine where a person is stuck in the fight, flight, or freeze response. Then, through a variety of body practices including dance and other forms of movement, witnessing, sensing, visualization, breath work, and attunement, SE helps release traumatic shock and restore interpersonal connection. The essence of trauma-informed care asks not "What's wrong with you?" Instead, it asks, "What happened to you?" That reframing offers a pathway to integration and healing and, at an aggregate level, ideally lends itself to elevated empathic consciousness.

REJECTING THE DOCTRINE OF INDEPENDENCE

I defended my dissertation more than a decade ago, and since then, we have lived through many traumatic events, including a massive earthquake in Japan and a camp massacre in Norway (2011); Hurricane Sandy and Malala Yousafzai nearly shot to death in Pakistan (2012); the Boston Marathon bombing and a factory collapse in Bangladesh (2013); the Russian annexing of Crimea, an Ebola breakout in West Africa, and mass protests in Ferguson (2014); the Syrian refugee crisis and Paris terrorist attacks (2015); Brexit, Donald Trump's election, the Pulse nightclub mass shooting, and the water crisis in Flint, Michigan (2016); Colin Kaepernick taking a knee, the Harvey Weinstein sex abuse scandal, the Rohingya crisis, and North Korea launching twenty-three missiles (2017); #MeToo going global, the Brett Kavanaugh hearing, the humanitarian crises in Venezuela and Yemen, and the Pittsburgh synagogue shooting (2018); mass protests in France and Hong Kong and the New Zealand mosque terror attack (2019); Australian bushfires, the explosion in Beirut, the COVID-19 pandemic, and George Floyd's murder (2020); the US Capitol riot, and the Taliban takeover of Afghanistan (2021); and, finally, until the time of this writing, Russia's invasion of Ukraine, and the school shooting in Uvalde, Texas (2022). In light of all of this and much, much more, it's no wonder that we're feeling physically, psychologically, emotionally, and spiritually whiplashed.

In 2016, a group of spiritual activists came together to launch the Courage of Care Coalition. Their goal was to strengthen relational ties within communities, organizations, and movements that have been severed by trauma and systems of oppression. Anchored by a belief that we can neither meditate nor legislate our way forward, they are committed to fostering relational culture as the antidote to what ails us.

Practically speaking, they partner with schools, trauma clinics, human rights organizations, healthcare centers, activists, organizers, and social service professionals to engage in practices that center healing, connection, and care. Using a five-part model, their approach "weaves together somatic, trauma-informed, healing-centered, relational practices designed to foster the stamina necessary for engaging in authentic community building across positionality, faith and age cohort." This is precisely what we need more of in the world today.

Another example is Weave: The Social Fabric Project, an initiative co-led by *New York Times* columnist David Brooks and the Aspen Institute that "aims to build social trust to address the root cultural cause behind many of America's social problems." Brooks may not be the most obvious poster child for communities of care. Yet, after a midlife crisis described in *The Second Mountain*, he began meeting people who "radiate an inner light." He refers to them as *weavers* because they're knitting back together the social fabric that's being torn apart by hyper-individualism. According to him, instead of asking themselves "What do I want from life?" they ask, "What is life asking of me? How can I match my intrinsic talent with one of the world's deep needs?"

According to Weave's *The Relationalist Manifesto*, "The central problems of our day flow from this erosion: social isolation, distrust, polarization, the breakdown of family, the loss of community, tribalism, rising suicide rates, rising mental health problems, a spiritual crisis caused by a loss of common purpose, the loss—in nation after nation—of any sense of common solidarity that binds people across difference, the loss of those common stories and causes that foster community, mutuality, comradeship, and purpose." In response, their mission is to invite new weavers into the fold and help shift our culture from one that values personal achievement to one that honors deep relationships and community success. Again, initiatives like this are desperately needed in our social sphere.

PURPOSEFUL EMPATHY PRACTICES

The following tools and exercises underscore that purposeful empathy can only be practiced sustainably when you're kind to yourself and feel connected to others, ideally within a community of care. You can download a free workbook from my website.

1. Much like a book club meeting, host a gathering among friends or neighbors to discuss these two documents that highlight the importance of community:

    a. *Relationshift: The CourageRISE Model for Building Relational Cultures of Practice*, by Brooke Lavelle, Abra Vigna, Zack Walsh, and Ed Porter

    b. *The Relationalist Manifesto*, by Weave: The Social Fabric Project

2. Read the *Mutual Aid 101 Toolkit* cocreated by Congresswoman Alexandria Ocasio-Cortez and community organizer Mariame Kaba during COVID-19.

3. Make time for self-compassion, *mettā* meditation, and contemplation.

    a. Listen to a weekly episode of the *Metta Hour* podcast, hosted by Sharon Salzberg, which "brings Buddhist wisdom to everyday life." Alternatively, the *Loving-Kindness Meditation*, by the Greater Good Science Center at Berkeley.

    b. When you find yourself flooded by shame or upset about a mistake you've made, listen to these *Self-Compassion Guided Meditations*, created by Kristen Neff.

c. Start your day with this guided meditation adapted from
    the Courage of Care Coalition. Ideally, instead of reading it
    every morning, play a recording of yourself reading the text
    slowly. Be sure to include short pauses after every line. The
    running time should be about seven minutes.

Part I

Find a quiet place and a comfortable position.
It starts now—we don't need a bell.
Take a moment to find your center of gravity.
Take some time to let awareness come to you naturally, in your own way.
Ask yourself: what is connecting me with the land and ground beneath me?
You might notice your legs, feet, and toes. Feel what's grounding you.
Welcome that moment of grounding.
Notice how that grounding is always available to you.
Attend to the qualities of the land.
For example, What does this land like to grow?
Who else has lived on, loved, and stewarded this land?
What feels loving to this land?
What possibilities exist for a loving relationship with the land?
What commitments can you make to affirm that kind of relationship?
Rest gently into the mutual support that exists between you and the ground.

Part II

Call the lineages to mind.
All the leaders, healers, wisdom-keepers, and ancestors who came before
    you.
Feel a hand on your shoulder.
Call that person whose hand is on your shoulder vividly to mind.
Sense their body. See the expression on their face. Hear their tone of voice.
Connect with their qualities.
Love, joy, empathy, and kindness.
See if you can be drawn into those qualities.
Awaken those qualities in you.

Be empowered by the lineage to continue the work of care.

When you're ready, allow those images to fade and rest in a place of care.

Part III

Sense yourself in relation to the people you know.

Sense your neighbors, your colleagues.

Sense how we are all deeply connected to one another.

Sense our longing to be more deeply connected to one another.

Sense how we are a collective "we."

Sense how generosity, compassion, and gratitude spring from this relationality.

Sense the sorrow that comes from the loss of any relationship.

Sense a longing for deeper connection.

Sense the quality of mutuality.

Sense your heart opening, deepening.

Allow space for this feeling to grow.

Allow your arms and hands to open. Invite deeper connection.

Open your heart to its natural capacity to care.

Open your heart to its innate desire to be held, seen, and heard.

Part IV

From a space of allowing and being . . .

Aware of our deepest intentions . . .

Allowing whatever has arisen . . .

In this practice . . . On this land . . . In our body . . .

Aware of our lineages and whoever we brought with us today . . .

Use it as a call home. A call forth. A guidepost that orients your life.

As you begin to bring this practice to a close . . .

I invite you to notice the moment of transition as you shift back to routine.

How would it feel to allow this practice to reverberate in your body throughout the day?

Imagine what it would be like to allow the community of care vibration to flow through your being forever more.

CONCLUSION

The only thing that will save us is a universal increase in empathy.

—Kenneth B. Clarke

According to legend, Malaysia's Pulau Tioman is the resting place of a beautiful dragon princess, who, on her first visit, fell in love with its white-sand beaches and aquamarine seawaters and never left. Instead, she took the form of an island and pledged to offer shelter and comfort to passing travelers forever after.

As a graduate student in Singapore, I spent many wonderful weekends there, paying as little as four dollars per night for a beachfront cabin with an overhead fan and fresh papaya for breakfast. What made those visits truly priceless, though, were the encounters I had with fellow backpackers.

One day, I got into a heated debate with a young British man about how to create a better world. He gave me an oral treatise about all the political and economic systems that would need massive overhaul. I argued that we only needed one thing: a universal commitment to human dignity. In retrospect, I see that we were both right.

In *The Empathic Civilization*, Jeremy Rifkin wrote, "The ability to recognize oneself in the other and the other in oneself is a deeply democratizing experience. Empathy is the soul of democracy. It is an acknowledgment that each life is unique, unalienable, and deserving of equal consideration in the public square. The evolution of empathy and the evolution of democracy have gone hand in hand throughout history. The more empathic the culture, the more democratic its values and governing institutions. The less empathic the culture, the more totalitarian its values and governing institutions."

If that sounds prescient, consider the cocktail of hegemonic forces we are all beholden to that are perpetually weakening our innate capacity to empathize and destroying our personal and planetary wellbeing. As I've argued throughout this book, for us to flourish as human beings, and our organizations and ecosystem to thrive, we must elevate our empathic consciousness and center purposeful empathy in our daily lives.

THE NEXT GENERATION IS WAY AHEAD OF US

In the spring of 2021, as a Fellow with the International Woman's Forum, I participated in an executive education program at Harvard Business School. Using the case methodology, we analyzed the parent organization that produces *Sesame Street*. Our goal was to determine why the nonprofit had faced years of steady financial decline. By the end of our class discussion, we reached three major conclusions: the organization had been complacent, had ignored major changes in the external environment, and had failed to recognize that it was part of a living system.

The second half of the case explored what a new CEO did to turn things around. It was compelling, but I was locked in deep reflection about my undergraduate students and alumni. The longer I pondered our diagnosis of *Sesame Network's* losing streak, the more parallels I saw with "business as usual." What seemed obvious in retrospect about the organization's steady downfall was reminiscent of many conversations I'd been having with younger Millennials about how we organize society today. In their eyes, we are being equally complacent and myopic. Not to mention selfish and short-sighted.

Consider the fact that *everything* is more expensive for them than it was for their parents and grandparents, including housing, healthcare, and education. And their tax dollars continue to subsidize big business and the fossil fuel industry which will come back to bite them in the form of austerity and cuts to their pension and social security. Not to mention climate change.

On a planet with finite resources, the idea of extractive growth doesn't make sense to them. So there's no question about transitioning to zero-emission energy and protecting our planet's biodiversity. And to younger people, it's only fair that we evolve to a more equitable system founded on collective wellbeing, not individual greed. Who can blame them when it's been calculated that the seventeen UN SDGs could be achieved by 2050 at an estimated cost of $230 billion a year—a fraction of the $1.3 trillion the world's governments spend annually on their military? To the next generation, it's crystal clear that a massive paradigm shift is needed. What's confusing to them is our ambivalence.

A few years ago, Greta Thunberg punctured our collective consciousness with her "How dare you?" speech at the UN General Assembly. In some circles, she was celebrated for calling out world leaders. Others were appalled: How dare a kid—a girl no less—publicly upbraid statespeople like that? I believe that beneath a veneer of anger, one usually finds fear, pain, or grief. Viewed in that light, Greta's message ought to be understood as a cry for help.

Greta wasn't the champion of a hostile social movement; she was the unlikely spokesperson for her generation, pleading for empathy and begging for action. The same holds true for education activist Malala Youssef, the teens behind *March for our Lives*, and anyone who's stood in solidarity with *Black Lives Matter*, *Standing Rock*, or *#MeToo*. These campaigns were not motivated by rebellion. They were inspired by the hopeful possibility of widespread purposeful empathy.

WHERE DO WE GO FROM HERE?

I admit that the magnitude of changes required to save our species from catastrophe can feel overwhelming. But we can be mindful of what Lao Tzu said: "A journey of a thousand miles begins with a single step." Let's consider all the small-scale empathy shifts we can make on a daily basis.

At one point during my PhD studies as I was learning about the neuroscience of empathy, I found myself in a long queue at a FedEx store. After an extended wait, I was greeted rudely by a sales agent. I could have easily snapped back at her but instead I tried something different. I took a deep breath, caught her gaze, and asked sincerely, "Are you OK?" After a pregnant pause, I watched her stern face soften and her eyes well up with tears. "My kid is at home sick and I've been doing double-shifts for two weeks' straight. It's 3pm and I haven't had a lunch break. I'm flat-out exhausted," she sobbed. After a few minutes of venting, she regained her composure, thanked me for listening, and served me with efficiency and grace. Our exchange was brief but profound. And all these years later, I remember with fondness the spontaneous human connection we forged through a simple act of purposeful empathy.

Moments like those come up for all of us, all the time. One day, we might be having a tough go at life and could use a little dose of empathy to lighten our load. On another day, we have the bandwidth to be empathic. Empathy not only disarms us, it unites us in our shared humanity. And remember, extending an empathic embrace not only feels good, it is good for us!

The second path to a more empathic world calls for learning from nature. In *Designing Regenerative Cultures*, Daniel Christian Wahl writes, "In mature ecosystems the health of the whole system is optimized by creating symbiotic relationships between diversity of species in the system." Imagine that—when every entity in a system is given the opportunity to flourish and collaborate, the entire system functions at its best.

Thanks to breakthroughs in biological and ecological research, the flaws of economic theories of separation and scarcity are now being exposed. Instead, "[T]he *systems view of life*, as a fundamentally collaborative interconnected process, is inviting us to redesign the human presence on Earth based on our new understanding of the way life unlocks abundance through collaboration," Wahl adds. No wonder leaders around the world are beginning to deploy regenerative agriculture and regenerative finance and economics. Recognizing that we all serve to benefit when each of us is at our best provides insight into how we should treat one another: the Golden Rule should reign supreme, underpinned by empathy.

Finally, in a provocative and inspiring article called *Quantum Empathy: An Alternative Narrative for Global Transcendence*, Kathryn Pavlovich, a professor of strategic management based in New Zealand, makes the case for quantum empathy to help us address issues including climate change, wealth inequality, and social injustice. She writes, "Quantum physicists posit that thoughts are waves of information traveling through space at the sub-atomic level and that when we are fully present and self-aware we are capable of receiving those thoughts." She refers to this harmonic frequency as *quantum empathy* and asks rhetorically, "Is this the experience of the sacred that most religious texts refer to, this mystical feeling of awe and connectedness?" She then argues that tapping into quantum empathy through mindfulness practices could help shift our human consciousness. Moreover, as a macrolevel organizing system, quantum empathy could promote participation in a "shared world of possibility where everyone has the opportunity to grow and prosper." I believe that's worth a try, don't you?

We are in the nascent days of studying human consciousness from a scientific perspective. Nonetheless, neuroscientists and physicists are already coming to the same conclusions reached by spiritual leaders, mystics, and sages over the millennia: we are all interdependent and part of an eternal "oneness." Expanding our empathic consciousness goes hand in hand with expressing our spiritual natures. Whatever you can do in the arena of transcendence—be it yoga, meditation, forest bathing, prayer, the arts—takes us one step closer to the realization of our collective empathic potential.

2021 marked the tenth anniversary of the World Happiness Report, which summarized how nine million people in more than 150 countries around the world evaluated their own lives. After two years of COVID-19, what became clear is the extent to which both benevolence and trust contributed to wellbeing during the pandemic. John Helliwell, a professor at the University of British Columbia and coauthor of the report, said:

> We found during 2021, remarkable worldwide growth in all three acts of kindness monitored in the Gallup World Poll. Helping strangers, volunteering, and donations were strongly up in every part of the world, reaching levels almost 25% above their pre-pandemic prevalence. This surge of benevolence, which was especially great for the helping of strangers, provides powerful evidence that people respond to others in need, creating in the process more happiness for the beneficiaries, good examples for others to follow, and better lives for themselves.

Evidence of purposeful empathy may be the silver lining of the pandemic—with important lessons we must integrate, especially in the face of climate change. The good news is that for as long as we *homo sapiens* have been alive, empathy has been our saving grace. Now it's time for us to revitalize that legacy.

> *Do not be dismayed by the brokenness of the world. All things break.*
>
> *And all things can be mended. Not with time, as they say, but with intention.*
>
> *So go. Love intentionally, extravagantly, unconditionally.*
>
> *The broken world waits in the darkness for the light that is you.*
>
> —L. R. Knost

> *Another world is not only possible, she is on her way.*
>
> *On a quiet day, I can hear her breathing.*
>
> —Arundhati Roy

PURPOSEFUL EMPATHY PRACTICES

The last three exercises of this book invite you to assess your level of purposeful empathy today and one year into the future, consider the world you'd like to bestow upon future generations, and reflect on your personal legacy. You can download a free workbook from my website.

1. Take my *Purposeful Empathy Survey* to establish a baseline and see where there's room for improvement. Then set a calendar reminder to take it again one year from now to evaluate your purposeful empathy progress.

2. Create a social fiction vision board. In 2013, onstage at the Skoll World Forum, Nobel Peace Prize winner Muhammad Yunus, famous for having introduced microfinance to the world, challenged hundreds of social entrepreneurs to engage in "social fiction." He explained that science fiction has often preceded reality, so there's an opportunity to envision a world of solutions to the most vexing social and environmental problems so that social fiction can manifest too.

Instructions:

- Set a timer for five minutes and create a list of at least fifty issues that cause hardship, injustice, or suffering in some way. For each issue listed, imagine how the world would look if that issue were no longer of concern.

- Next find an image online to represent that social fiction. For example, if one of your issues is food insecurity, imagine what it would look like if everyone had access to healthy food. One social fiction could be a happy group of people seated around a picnic table with a bounty of food to eat.

- Assemble all your social fiction pics into a mosaic of images and save it as your social fiction vision board. Feel free to share it with the *purposeful empathy* community.

- Respond to these questions for reflection:

  - How did it feel to search out your social fiction images?

  - What can you do to help turn your social fiction into reality?

  - How can you encourage others to join you in that effort?

3. Write your own eulogy. On April 11, 2015, the *New York Times* published a piece by David Brooks called "The Moral Bucket List." Here are some excerpts:

   About once a month I run across a person who radiates an inner light . . . A few years ago I realized that I wanted to be a bit more like those people . . . It occurred to me that there were two sets of virtues, the resumé virtues and the eulogy virtues. The resumé virtues are the skills you bring to the marketplace.

The eulogy virtues are the ones that are talked about at your funeral—whether you were kind, brave, honest or faithful . . . We all know the eulogy virtues are more important than the resumé ones. But our culture and our educational systems spend more time teaching the skills and the strategies you need for career success than the qualities you need to radiate that sort of inner light.

In the spirit of what Brooks wrote, draft a five hundred-word eulogy for yourself. (Or longer if you're so inclined.) Please don't see this exercise as morbid. Instead, consider it an opportunity to articulate your most cherished eulogy virtues. Once you're done, consider making changes in your day-to-day life to better align with those eulogy virtues. Create a list of at least ten changes and make a commitment to start living in alignment with your moral bucket list.

EMPATHY RESOURCES

BOOKS

To learn more about empathy, I am pleased to share a curated list of books with you, organized into the following categories: General; Business and Leadership; Call to Action; Neuroscience; Psychology and Morality; Philosophy and Politics; Technology; Self-Help; Empaths (aka Highly Sensitive People); Skeptics and Contrarians; *Purposeful Empathy*-Adjacent; Compassion-focused; Raising and Educating Children and Youth; and Children's Books about Empathy. All the descriptions were culled from Amazon or Goodreads (sometimes, with minor modifications), and the books are listed in order of publication date, starting with the most recent.

A star (*) next to an author's name means I interviewed them for my *Purposeful Empathy* podcast. You can watch those episodes (and many more) on my YouTube channel or listen to them on your favorite audio platform, including Spotify and Apple. Since new books about empathy are regularly being published, and new episodes of my podcast are uploaded weekly, please visit my website (anitanowak.com) to access my most up-to-date empathy resources.

General

> *The Power of Kindness: Why Empathy Is Essential in Everyday Life*
> *Brian Goldman, MD (HarperCollins, 2019)

As an experienced emergency room physician, Dr. Brian Goldman spent time pondering whether he was the same caring doctor he was at the beginning of his career, after years of helping patients amidst medical emergencies. In *The Power of Kindness*, Goldman leaves the comfortable, familiar surroundings of the hospital in search of his own lost compassion through MRIs, researchers, and stories of the world's most empathic people.

Empathy: A History
Susan Lanzoni (Yale University Press, 2018)

In *Empathy*, Susan Lanzoni tells the fascinating and largely unknown story of the first appearance of "empathy" in 1908 and tracks its shifting meanings over the following century. This meticulously researched book uncovers empathy's historical layers, offering a rich portrait of the tension between the reach of one's own imagination and the realities of others' experiences.

I Feel You: The Surprising Power of Extreme Empathy
Cris Beam (HarperOne, 2018)

In *I Feel You*, Cris Beam carves through the noise with a revelatory exploration of how we perform empathy, how it is learned, what it can do—indeed, what empathy is in the first place. A cogent, gorgeous examination of empathy, illuminating the myths, the science, and the power behind this transformative emotion.

The Empathy Instinct: How to Create a More Civil Society
Peter Bazalgette (John Murray, 2017)

Empathy is a fundamental human attribute, without which mutually co-operative societies cannot function. In *The Empathy Instinct*, full of entertaining stories that are underlined by the latest scientific research, Peter Bazalgette mounts a passionate defense of arts and popular culture as a means of bridging the empathy gap.

Assessing Empathy

*Elizabeth A. Segal, Karen E. Gerdes, Cynthia A. Lietz, M. Alex Wagaman & Jennifer M. Geiger (Columbia University Press, 2017)

In *Assessing Empathy*, Elizabeth A. Segal and colleagues marshal years of research to present a comprehensive definition of empathy, one that links neuroscientific evidence to human service practice.

Empathy: Why It Matters, and How to Get It

Roman Krznaric (TarcherPerigee, 2015)

In *Empathy*, Roman Krznaric argues that our brains are wired for social connection. Empathy, not apathy or self-centeredness, is at the heart of who we are. By looking outward and attempting to identify with the experiences of others, he argues we can become not only a more equal society, but also a happier and more creative one.

Empathy: What It Is and Why It Matters

David Howe (Springer, 2012)

In *Empathy*, David Howe invites readers on an illuminating journey of discovery into how empathy was first conceptualised and how its influence has steadily risen and spread. He captures the growing significance of empathy to many fields, from evolutionary psychology and brain science to moral philosophy and mental health.

The Age of Empathy: A Nature's Lessons for a Kinder Society

Frans De Waal (Crown, 2010)

Using research from the fields of anthropology, psychology, animal behaviour, and neuroscience, in *The Age of Empathy*, Frans De Waal brilliantly argues that humans are a group of animals—highly cooperative, sensitive to injustice, and mostly peace-loving—just like other primates, elephants, and dolphins. Through a better understanding of empathy's survival value in evolution, he suggests that we can work together toward a more just society based on a more generous and accurate view of human nature.

Why Empathy Matters: The Science and Psychology of Better Judgment

J. D. Trout (Penguin Books, 2010)

Drawing on his sweeping and innovative research in the fields of psychology, behavioral economics, and neuroscience, philosopher and cognitive scientist, in *Why Empathy Matters*, J. D. Trout explains how our empathic wiring actually undermines the best interests of individuals and society. Trout offers a tantalizing proposal—how to vault that gap and improve the lives of not just ourselves but the lives of everyone all around the world.

Born For Love: Why Empathy Is Essential—and Endangered

Maia Szalavitz & Bruce D. Perry (William Morrow Paperbacks, 2011)

In *Born For Love*, psychiatrist Bruce D. Perry and award-winning science journalist Maia Szalavitz interweave research and stories from Perry's practice with cutting-edge scientific studies and historical examples to explain how empathy develops, why it is essential for our development into healthy adults, and how to raise kids with empathy while navigating threats from technological change and other forces in the modern world.

Realizing Empathy: An Inquiry into the Meaning of Making

*Seung Chan Lim (Self-Published, 2013)

In *Realizing Empathy*, Seung Chan Lim analyzes and reflects on his embodied research into the disciplines of craft as well as the visual and performing arts, to tell the story of how realizing empathy is the heart of the creative process we call "making."

Business and Leadership

Tell Me More About That: Solving the Empathy Crisis One Conversation at a Time

*Rob Volpe (PageTwo, 2022)

In *Tell Me More About That*, Rob Volpe draws on his years of market research, conducting thousands of in-home interviews with everyday people, to illustrate the 5 Steps to Empathy—the actions you can use in everyday interactions to build a strong and reflexive empathy muscle.

The Empathetic Workplace: 5 Steps to a Compassionate, Calm, and Confident Response to Trauma on the Job

*Katharine Manning (HarperCollins, 2021)

In *The Empathetic Workplace*, Katharine Manning provides an overview of the prevalence and effect of trauma at work, then covers her LASER process for responding effectively to trauma on the job: Listen. Acknowledge. Share. Empower. Return. She also guides supervisors of any level through an understanding of how stories of trauma impact the brain of both the survivor and the listener, as well as the tools to handle the interaction appropriately, to help the listener, the organization, and most importantly, the survivor.

Leading with Empathy: Understanding the Needs of Today's Workforce

*Gautham Pallapa (Wiley, 2021)

In *Leading with Empathy*, Gautham Pallapa delivers an inspiring call to action on becoming an empathic leader. Organized into three parts, the book begins with a candid acknowledgement of the adversity facing people worldwide as they suffer through recent events, including the COVID-19 pandemic, unemployment, Black Lives Matter protests, and the economic downturn.

Mindful Empathy: The Mindset of Success for Leaders of the Future
*Dani Rius and Wayne Duncan (Independently Published, 2020)

Personal leadership coach Dani Rius and Wayne Duncan team up to help readers develop the skills that allow for greater understanding of human behavior and how to harness the power of mindfulness and empathy to create positive, trusting relationships.

Softening the Edge: How Humanity's Oldest Leadership Trait Is Changing Our World
*Mimi Nicklin (The Dreamwork Collective, 2020)

Empathetic influence is this decade's most critical human and scientifically validated skill set. In *Softening the Edge*, Mimi Nicklin shows readers how to successfully harness emotional intelligence to influence and genuinely connect with people on a deeper level.

The Empathy Edge: Harnessing the Value of Compassion as an Engine for Success
*Maria Ross (Page Two Books, 2019)

In *The Empathy Edge*, a practical playbook for businesses of all types, Maria Ross proves that empathy is not just good for society—it's great for business, and may transform you at a personal level, too. She also shows why your business needs to cultivate more empathy now, and shares the habits and traits of empathetic leaders who foster more productivity and loyalty.

Applied Empathy: The New Language of Leadership
*Michael Ventura (Atria Books, 2019)

Empathy is not just about being nice. It's not about pity or sympathy either. It's about understanding—your consumers, your colleagues, and yourself—and it's a direct path to powerful leadership. For leaders of all levels, *Applied Empathy*, by Michael Ventura, lays the foundation to establish a diverse, inventive, and driven team that can meet the challenges of today's ever-evolving marketplace.

Empathy (HBR Emotional Intelligence Series)
Daniel Goleman, Annie McKee & Adam Waytz
(Harvard Business Review, 2017)

Psychologist Daniel Goleman, author Annie McKee, and psychologist Adam Waytz are each featured in this volume of Harvard Business Review's Emotional Intelligence Series. *Empathy* helps you understand what empathy is, why it's important, how to surmount the hurdles that make you less empathetic—and when too much empathy is just too much.

Practical Empathy: For Collaboration and Creativity in Your Work
Indi Young (Rosenfeld Media, 2015)

Empathy is a mindset that focuses on people, helping you to understand their thinking patterns and perspectives. In *Practical Empathy*, technologist Indi Young shows readers how to gather and compare these patterns to make better decisions, improve strategy, and collaborate successfully.

The Empathic Leader: An Effective Management Model for Enhancing Morale and Increasing Workplace Productivity
Dwayne L. Buckingham (RHCS Publishing, 2014)

In *The Empathic Leader*, Dwayne L. Buckingham presents a model that can be applied by any leader for life-changing management styles to address increased workplace violence, burnout, job dissatisfaction, and employee turnover. He also reveals how leaders can enhance morale and increase workplace productivity by embracing and applying The 5 Skills of Highly Empathic Leaders.

Well-Designed: How to Use Empathy to Create Products People Love

Jon Kolko (Harvard Business Review Press, 2014)

Successful companies understand that emotional connection is critical to product development. And they use a clear, repeatable design process that focuses squarely on consumer engagement rather than piling on features for features' sake. In *Well-Designed*, product design expert Jon Kolko maps out this process, demonstrating how it will help you and your team conceive and build successful, emotionally resonant products again and again.

The Empathy Factor: Your Competitive Advantage for Personal, Team, and Business Success

Marie R. Miyashiro (PuddleDancer Press, 2011)

Building on the latest research in brain science, emotional intelligence, and organizational theory, Marie R. Miyashiro, in *The Empathy Factor*, answers questions about the true definition of empathy. This groundbreaking exploration into business productivity and office management offers both real-world insights and practical ways to build transformative empathy skills organization-wide.

Wired to Care: How Companies Prosper When They Create Widespread Empathy

By Dev Patnaik (FT Press, 2009)

In *Wired to Care*, Dev Patnaik tells the story of how organizations of all kinds prosper when they tap into a power each of us already has: empathy, the ability to reach outside of ourselves and connect with other people.

Call to Action Books

Empathy: Turning Compassion into Action

David Johnston (Signal, 2023)

Empathy offers proof of the inherent goodness of people, and shows how exercising the instinct for kindness creates societies that are both smart and caring. David Johnston (the 28th Canadian Governor General) looks at a host of issues that demand our attention, from education and immigration, to healthcare, the law, policing, business ethics, and criminal justice. Convinced that empathy is the fastest route to peace and progress in all their forms, he ends each short chapter with a set of practical steps the reader can take to make the world better, one deliberate action at a time.

Radical Empathy: Finding a Path to Bridging Racial Divides
*Terri E. Givens (Policy Press, 2021)

To bridge our divides, renowned political scientist Terri Givens calls for "radical empathy"—moving beyond an understanding of others' lives and pain to understand the origins of our biases, including internalized oppression. Deftly weaving together her own experiences with the political, in *Radical Empathy*, she offers practical steps to call out racism and bring about radical social change.

Empathy for Change: How to Create a More Understanding World
*Amy J. Wilson (New Degree Press, 2021)

In *Empathy for Change*, former White House entrepreneur-in-residence Amy J. Wilson dives into the intricate science of empathy, debunking common myths and sharing practical uses for a better society.

The War for Kindness: Building Empathy in a Fractured World
Jamil Zaki (Crown, 2019)

In *The War for Kindness*, Jamil Zaki shares cutting-edge research, including experiments from his own lab, showing that empathy is not a fixed trait—something we're born with or not—but rather a skill that can be strengthened through effort.

Humanity on a Tightrope: Thoughts on Empathy, Family, and Big Changes for a Viable Future

Paul R. Ehlrich & Robert E. Ornstein (Rowman & Littlefield Publishers, 2010)

In *Humanity on a Tightrope*, Paul R. Ehlrich and Robert E. Ornstein present a unique approach to what it means to belong to one human family. The book underlines a basic element for solving the human predicament—quickly spreading the domain of empathy. It explains how civilization is unlikely to persist unless many more people learn to put themselves in the shoes of others to keep society balancing on the tightrope to sustainability—a tightrope suspended over the collapse of civilization.

The Empathic Civilization: The Race to Global Consciousness in a World in Crises

Jeremy Rifkin (TarcherPerigee, 2009)

Jeremy Rifkin shows that a disconnect between our vision for the world and our ability to realize that vision lies in the current state of human consciousness. *The Empathic Civilization* addresses how the emergence of empathetic consciousness has implications for the future that will likely be as profound and far-reaching as when Enlightenment philosophers upended faith-based consciousness with the canon of reason.

Neuroscience

The Empathy Effect: 7 Neuroscience-Based Keys for Transforming the Way We Live, Love, Work, and Connect Across Differences

*Helen Riess (Sounds True, 2018)

In *The Empathy Effect*, Helen Riess presents a definitive resource on empathy: the science behind how it works, new research on how empathy develops from birth to adulthood, and tools for building your capacity to create authentic emotional connection with others in any situation.

The Altruistic Brain: How We Are Naturally Good
Donald W. Pfaff (Oxford University Press, 2014)

In *The Altruistic Brain*, Donald Pfaff provides the latest, most far-reaching argument in support of this revolution, explaining in exquisite detail how our neuroanatomical structure favors kindness toward others. He also synthesizes all the most important research into how and why—at a purely physical level—humans empathize with one another and respond altruistically.

Empathy: From Bench to Bedside
Jean Decety (The MIT Press, 2014)

Empathy covers a wide range of topics in empathy theory, research, and applications, helping to integrate perspectives as varied as anthropology and neuroscience. Taken together, the contributions significantly broaden the interdisciplinary scope of empathy studies, reporting on current knowledge of the evolutionary, social, developmental, cognitive, and neurobiological aspects of empathy and linking this capacity to human communication, including in clinical practice and medical education.

The Science of Evil: On Empathy and the Origins of Cruelty
Simon Baron-Cohen (Basic Books, 2012)

In *The Science of Evil*, Simon Baron-Cohen draws on decades of research to develop a new, brain-based theory of human cruelty and kindness. He examines social and environmental factors that can erode empathy, including neglect and abuse.

The Social Neuroscience of Empathy
Jean Decety & William Ickes (MIT Press, 2011)

In *The Social Neuroscience of Empathy*, American French neuroscientist Jean Decety and social psychologist William Ickes use various contributions to the social neuroscience approach to empathy to show how this new discipline bridges disciplines and levels of analysis.

The Empathic Brain: How the Discovery of Mirror Neurons Changes Our Understanding of Human Nature

*Christian Keysers (CreateSpace Independent Publishing Platform, 2011)

The discovery of mirror neurons has caused an unparalleled wave of excitement amongst scientists. *The Empathic Brain* makes you share this excitement. Through intellectually rigorous but powerfully accessible prose, Christian Keysers makes us realize just how deeply mirror neurons change our understanding of human nature.

Mirroring People: The Science of Empathy and How We Connect with Others

*Marco Iacoboni (Picador, 2009)

Marco Iacoboni, a leading neuroscientist, explains the groundbreaking research into mirror neurons, the "smart cells" in our brain that allow us to understand others. *Mirroring People* is the first book for the general reader on this revolutionary new science.

Psychology and Morality

Social Empathy: The Art of Understanding Others

*Elizabeth A. Segal (Columbia University Press, 2018)

When we are socially empathic, we not only imagine what it is like to be another person, but we consider their social, economic, and political circumstances and what shaped them. In *Social Empathy*, Elizabeth A. Segal explains the evolutionary and learned components of interpersonal and social empathy, including neurobiological factors and the role of social structures.

*Cultivating Empathy: The Worth and Dignity of Every Person—
Without Exception*

Nathan C. Walker (Skinner House Books, 2016)

In *Cultivating Empathy*, Nathan C. Walker presents a collection of essays about his wrestlings with personal and cultural conflicts and his commitment to stop "otherizing"—which occurs when we either demonize people or romanticize them. His remedy for these kinds of projections is to employ the moral imagination as an everyday spiritual practice. As he experiments with this approach, he shows a model that can help us all nurture greater empathy for those we have previously held in contempt.

*Entangled Empathy: An Alternative Ethic for Our Relationships
with Animals*

Lori Gruen (Lantern Publishing & Media, 2015)

In *Entangled Empathy*, scholar and activist Lori Gruen argues that rather than focusing on animal "rights," we ought to work to make our relationships with animals right by empathetically responding to their needs, interests, desires, vulnerabilities, hopes, and unique perspectives. She describes entangled empathy as a type of caring perception focused on attending to another's experience of well-being.

The Empathy Exams: Essays

Leslie Jamison (Graywolf Press, 2014)

Beginning with her experience as a medical actor who was paid to act out symptoms for medical students to diagnose, Leslie Jamison's visceral and revealing essays ask essential questions about our basic understanding of others: how should we care about each other? She draws from her own experiences of illness and bodily injury to engage in an exploration that extends far beyond her life, spanning wide-ranging territory—from poverty tourism to phantom diseases, street violence to reality television, illness to incarceration—in its search for a kind of sight shaped by humility and grace.

The Moral Dimensions of Empathy: Limits and Applications in Ethical Theory and Practice

Julinna C. Oxley (Palgrave Macmillan, 2011)

In *The Moral Dimensions of Empathy*, Julinna C. Oxley argues that empathy is often instrumental to meeting the demands of morality as defined by various ethical theories. This multifaceted work links psychological research on empathy with ethical theory and contemporary trends in moral education.

The Ethics of Care and Empathy

Michael Slote (Routledge, 2007)

In *The Ethics of Care and Empathy*, moral philosopher Michael Slote argues that care ethics presents an important challenge to other ethical traditions and that a philosophically developed care ethics should offer its own comprehensive view of morality. He successfully moves empathy from the margins to the center of ethics.

CAKE: A Guide to Reciprocal Empathy for Couples

*Ashok Bhattacharya (Authorhouse, 2006)

In *CAKE*, psychiatrist Ashok Bhattacharya argues that the most enduring relationships have reached reciprocal empathy. Written in four sections, he uses Challenge, Action, Knowledge, and Empathy, to show readers how they can achieve "oneness" in a long-term relationship.

Empathy and Moral Development: Implications for Caring and Justice

Martin L. Hoffman (Cambridge University Press, 2001)

In *Empathy and Moral Development*, Martin L. Hoffman explores empathy's contribution to altruism and compassion for others in physical, psychological, or economic distress; feelings of guilt over harming someone;

feelings of anger at others who do harm; feelings of injustice when others do not receive their due.

Philosophy and Politics

Empathy

Heidi Maibom (Routledge, 2020)

In *Empathy*, Heidi Maibom explores: the nature of empathy and key themes in the literature; empathy as a way of understanding others, particularly "simulation theory" and "perspective-taking;" empathy, emotional contagion, and sympathy; empathy's role in moral understanding or motivation; empathy and art appreciation, with examples from film, music and fiction; and empathy and mental disorder, such as psychopathy and autism.

Empathy: Philosophical and Psychological Perspectives

Amy Coplan & Peter Goldie, Eds. (Oxford University Press, 2014)

Empathy draws together nineteen original chapters by leading researchers across several disciplines, together with an extensive Introduction by the editors, Amy Coplan and Peter Goldie. The individual chapters reveal how important it is, in a wide range of fields of enquiry, to bring to bear an understanding of the role of empathy in its various guises.

Politics of Empathy: Ethics, Solidarity, Recognition

Anthony M. Clohesy (Routledge, 2014)

Politics of Empathy argues that empathy is a necessary condition for ethical subjectivity and the emergence of a more compassionate world. Anthony M. Clohesy discusses that empathy is ethically significant because, uniquely, it allows us to reflect critically on the nature of our own lives and sense of identity.

Empathy Imperiled: Capitalism, Culture, and the Brain

Gary Olson (Springer, 2012)

The most critical factor explaining the disjuncture between empathy's revolutionary potential and today's empathically impaired society is the interaction between the brain and our dominant political culture. In *Empathy Imperiled*, Gary Olson argues that the crucial missing piece in this conversation is the failure to identify and explain the dynamic relationship between an empathy gap and the hegemonic influence of neoliberal capitalism, through the analysis of the college classroom, the neoliberal state, media, film and photo images, marketing of products, militarization, mass culture and government policy.

Empathy and Democracy: Feeling, Thinking, and Deliberation

Michael E. Morrell (Penn State University Press, 2010)

In *Empathy and Democracy*, Michael Morrell argues that empathy plays a crucial role in enabling democratic deliberation to function the way it should. Drawing on empirical studies of empathy, including his own, he offers a "process model of empathy" that incorporates both affect and cognition. He shows how this model can help democratic theorists who emphasize the importance of deliberation answer their critics.

Empathy in the Global World: An Intercultural Perspective

Carolyn Calloway-Thomas (Sage Publications, 2000)

In *Empathy in the Global World*, Carolyn Calloway-Thomas examines the nature, practices, and potential of empathy for understanding and addressing human problems on a global scale. Violence and acts of hatred worldwide—from the bombing of the World Trade Center on September 11, 2001 to wars in Iraq, Afghanistan, Pakistan, Sri Lanka, Darfur, and Palestine—call attention to the critical importance of empathy in human affairs.

Technology

Empathy-Driven Software Development

*Andrea Goulet (Pearson, 2023)

In *Empathy-Driven Software Development*, Andrea Goulet presents a practical framework and specific practices for software developers to use in their daily development. The patterns, frameworks, and practices in this book are complementary on any software project, regardless of tech stack, and will help teams supercharge their collaboration.

Empathy in Action: How to Deliver Great Customer Experiences at Scale

Tony Bates & Natalie Petouhoff (Ideapress Publishing, 2022)

Long-time technology leader Tony Bates teams up with researcher and customer experience evangelist, Natalie Petouhoff, to define a new path forward to put empathy into action. In *Empathy In Action*, they predict empathy is the next frontier in technology. The book is aimed at sparking an industry-wide conversation about how exponential technologies like AI and cloud can enable a more empathetic world.

The Empathy Diaries: A Memoir

Sherry Turkle (Penguin Press, 2021)

For decades, Sherry Turkle has shown how we remake ourselves in the mirror of our machines. Here, she illuminates our present search for authentic connection in a time of uncharted challenges. Turkle has spent a career composing an intimate ethnography of our digital world; now, marked by insight, humility, and compassion, we have her own. In this vivid and poignant narrative, Turkle ties together her coming-of-age and her pathbreaking research on technology, empathy, and ethics.

The Future of Feeling: Building Empathy in a Tech-Obsessed World
*Kaitlin Ugolik Phillips (Little A, 2020)

In *The Future of Feeling*, Kaitlin Ugolik Phillips discusses how although empathy has facilitated our lives, technology is undoubtedly eroding one of our most human traits: empathy. In an effort to preserve empathy, this cautionary book shows it is not too late to preserve something so vital to a peaceful, healthy, and productive society.

Heartificial Empathy: Putting Heart into Business and Artificial Intelligence
*Minter Dial (DigitalProof Press, 2018)

In *Heartificial Empathy*, Minter Dial attempts to lay out the business case and a path for putting more heart and empathy into business and machines for a healthier and more profitable future. It also looks at some of the pioneering work being done on making bots and machines more sentient and empathic.

The Empathic Enterprise: Winning by Staying Human in a Digital Age
Mark A. Brown (Merchant Trask Press, 2016)

In *The Empathic Enterprise*, Mark A. Brown describes the trade-offs we make between empathy and trust when we rely too much on it, and offers suggestions for better balance between "tech" and "touch" in both our business and personal lives.

Self-Help

Currency of Empathy: The Secret to Thriving in Business & Life
*Dr. Jacqueline Acho (The Acho Group, 2020)

In *Currency of Empathy*, Jaqueline Acho re-examines our modern myths about how we work, what "quality time" at home really means, and why the age-old battle of the sexes persists. This book looks to these healing capacities in order to conquer the widespread empathy deficit taking over our lives.

Little Book of Empathy
Cyndi Dale (Llewellyn Publications, 2019)

In *Little Book of Empathy*, Cyndi Dale shares effective solutions for working through your under- or over-empathic tendencies, and shows how you can process the underlying issues that lead to manipulation. You will also learn about the different kinds of empathy: physical, emotional, mental, and spiritual.

Finding the Lost Art of Empathy: Connecting Human to Human in a Disconnected World
Tracy Wilde-Pace (Howard Books, 2017)

In *Finding the Lost Art of Empathy*, Tracy Wilde addresses the reasons why we struggle with showing empathy toward others and explains why we ultimately avoid it—and even avoid contact with others altogether. She also inspires us to self-reflect and remove whatever obstacles from our lives that may be blocking our way to true fulfillment in our relationships.

7 Steps to Spiritual Empathy: A Practical Guide
Jenny Florence (A-Z of Emotional Health, 2016)

In *7 Steps to Spiritual Empathy*, Jenny Florence invites readers on a 7-day journey of transformation. Designed to be read in just 15 to 20 minutes a day for seven days, this deeply philosophical and highly transformational book guides readers through a seven-day journey of emotional discovery.

How to Practice Empathy: Connect Deeply with Others and Create Meaningful Relationships

David Leads (Relationship Up, 2014)

Empathy is the number one skill to know and practice in order to create meaningful relationships. In *How to Practice Empathy*, David Leads describes how empathy is different from other similar emotions and feelings.

The Art of Empathy: A Complete Guide to Life's Most Essential Skill

Karla McLaren (Sounds True, 2013)

In *The Art of Empathy*, Karla McLaren teaches us how to perceive and feel the experiences of others with clarity and authenticity—to connect with them more deeply and effectively. Empathy is the skill that builds bridges—a skill that not only creates connection, but that helps us to be more effective in all areas of our lives.

For Empaths (aka Highly Sensitive People)

The Empath's Survival Guide: Life Strategies for Sensitive People

*Judith Orloff (Sounds True, 2018)

Judith Orloff believes that having empathy means our hearts going out to others, but for empaths, it is so much more. *The Empath's Survival Guide* is an invaluable resource for empaths and anyone who wants to nurture their empathy and develop coping skills in our high-stimulus world—while fully embracing their gifts of intuition, compassion, creativity, and spiritual connection.

Empath: A Complete Guide for Developing Your Gift and Finding Your Sense of Self

Judy Dyer (Pristine Publishing, 2017)

In *Empath*, Judy Dyer offers to guide a new empath through their journey. This book will usher your spirit to embrace the many blessings of being an empath. It will also open new doors of opportunity for you to live your life abundantly.

The Strength of Sensitivity: Understanding Empathy for a Life of Emotional Peace & Balance

Kyra Mesich (Llewellyn Publications, 2016)

In *The Strength of Sensitivity*, Kyra Mesich explores the causes of empathic and psychic connections, providing techniques for developing and coping with sensitivity in a positive way.

The Spiritual Power of Empathy: Develop Your Intuitive Gifts for Compassionate Connection

Cyndi Dale (Llewellyn Publications, 2014)

The Spiritual Power of Empathy presents an expanded awareness of what empathy is, how it works, and the myriad ways it manifests. Cyndi Dale invites you to develop deeper connections with your loved ones, use specialized techniques for screening and filtering information, and gain insights on how to overcome the difficulties empaths often face.

Empowered by Empathy: 25 Ways to Fly in Spirit

Rose Rosetree (Women's Intuition Worldwide, 2001)

In *Empowered by Empathy*, Rose Rosetree empowers you to be of greater service to others. With less suffering and more skill.

Empathy Skeptics/Contrarian Perspectives

The Dark Sides of Empathy

Fritz Breithaupt (Cornell University Press, 2019)

In *The Dark Sides of Empathy*, Fritz Breithaupt contends that people often commit atrocities not out of a failure of empathy but rather as a direct consequence of over-identification and a desire to increase empathy. Breithaupt looks at a wide-ranging series of case studies—from Stockholm syndrome to Angela Merkel's refugee policy and from novels of the romantic era to helicopter parents and murderous cheerleader moms—to uncover how narcissism, sadism, and dangerous celebrity obsessions alike find their roots in the quality that, arguably, most makes us human.

Against Empathy: The Case for Rational Compassion
Paul Bloom (Ecco, 2018)

In *Against Empathy*, Paul Bloom argues that the natural impulse to share the feelings of others can lead to immoral choices in both public policy and in our intimate relationships with friends and family. This book shows us that, when it comes to both major policy decisions and the choices we make in our everyday lives, limiting our impulse toward empathy is often the most compassionate choice we can make.

Purposeful Empathy-Adjacent

Atlas of the Heart: Mapping Meaningful Connection and the Language of Human Experience
Brené Brown (Random House, 2022)

In *Atlas of the Heart*, Brené Brown takes us on a journey through 87 of the emotions and experiences that define what it means to be human. As she maps the necessary skills and an actionable framework for meaningful connection, she gives us the language and tools to access a universe of new choices and second chances—a universe where we can share and steward the stories of our bravest and most heartbreaking moments with one another in a way that builds connection.

See No Stranger: A Memoir and Manifesto of Revolutionary Love
Valerie Kaur (One World, 2021)

Drawing from the wisdom of sages, scientists, and activists, in *See No Stranger*, Valerie Kaur reclaims love as an active, public, and revolutionary force that creates new possibilities for ourselves, our communities, and our world. She helps us imagine new ways of being with each other—and with ourselves—so that together we can begin to build the world we want to see.

Real Change: Mindfulness to Heal Ourselves and the World
Sharon Salzberg (Flatiron Books, 2021)

In *Real Change*, Sharon Salzberg, shares sage advice and indispensable techniques to help free ourselves from these negative feelings and actions. She teaches us that meditation is not a replacement for action, but rather a way to practice generosity with ourselves and summon the courage to break through boundaries, reconnect to a movement that's bigger than ourselves, and have the energy to stay active.

Humankind: A Hopeful History
Rutger Bregman (Little, Brown and Company, 2020)

In *Humankind*, Rutger Bregman provides a new perspective on the past 200,000 years of human history, setting out to prove that we are hardwired for kindness, geared toward cooperation rather than competition, and more inclined to trust rather than distrust one another.

HumanKind: Changing the World One Small Act at a Time
Brad Aronson (LifeTree, 2020)

Inspired by the many demonstrations of "humankindness" that supported their family through his wife's recovery from cancer, Brad Aronson writes about the people who rescued his family from that dark time, often with the smallest of gestures. *HumanKind* also features resources to provide guidance and organizations to help readers channel their own acts of kindness.

Age of Union: Igniting the Changemaker

Dax Dasilva (Anteism Books, 2020)

Dax Dasilva presents a guide to take simple measures to promote our collective well-being and union. *Age of Union* is a compelling guide for igniting today's changemakers—those ready to take action for our planet and its inhabitants.

Human(Kind): How Reclaiming Human Worth and Embracing Radical Kindness Will Bring Us Back Together

Ashlee Eiland (Random House, 2020)

Human(Kind) invites us to chart our own formative journeys and recognize our inherent value, cultivating empathy so we may once again see the image of God shining brightly within one another. In this compelling collection of essays, Ashlee Eiland shares her story of being a Black woman living on two sides of the fence: as the token Black girl in majority-White spaces and as the "whitewashed" Black girl in majority-Black spaces.

Radical Kindness: The Life-Changing Power of Giving and Receiving

Angela Santomero (Harper Wave, 2019)

Radical Kindness goes beyond The Golden Rule and entreaties to "be nice," contending that kindness is the key to recognizing others, and ourselves, as worthy of love and understanding. Much like gratitude, Angela Santomero contends we need a kindness practice. A practice in which we learn to see with our hearts and act from a place of compassion.

Revolutionary Love: A Political Manifesto to Heal and Transform the World

Michael Lerner (University of California Press, 2019)

Revolutionary Love proposes a method to replace what Michael Lerner terms the "capitalist globalization of selfishness" with a globalization of generosity, prophetic empathy, and environmental sanity.

All About Love: New Visions

bell hooks (William Morrow Paperbacks, 2018)

In *All About Love*, bell hooks reveals what causes a polarized society, and how to heal the divisions that cause suffering. Here is the truth about love, and inspiration to help us instill caring, compassion, and strength in our homes, schools, and workplaces.

Completely Connected: Uniting Our Empathy and Insight for Extraordinary Results

Rita Marie Johnson (Rasur Media, 2019)

In *Completely Connected*, Rita Marie Johnson shares the Connection Practice, a unique method for connecting with ourselves and others that is supported by scientific research and testimony from people around the world. Johnson's vision is a world where every person practices the art of connection and passes this gift on to the next generation.

A Manifesto for Social Progress: Ideas for a Better Society

Marc Fleurbay (Cambridge University Press, 2018)

In *A Manifesto for Social Progress*, Marc Fleury outlines how to rethink and reform our key institutions—markets, corporations, welfare policies, democratic processes and transnational governance—to create better societies based on core principles of human dignity, sustainability, and justice.

Spiritual Activism: Leadership as Service

Alastair McIntosh & Matt Carmichael (Green Books, 2015)

Drawing on a rich history of spirituality and activism, from The Bhagavad Gita, to the Hebrew prophets, to Carl Jung, *Spiritual Activism*, by Alastair McIntosh and Matt Carmichael, is both guide and inspiration for people involved in activism for social or environmental justice. It contains case studies of inspirational spiritual activists, which demonstrate the transformative power of spiritual principles in action.

Intellectual Empathy: Critical Thinking for Social Justice

Maureen Linker (University of Michigan Press, 2014)

In *Intellectual Empathy*, philosophy professor Maureen Linker provides a step-by-step method for facilitating discussions of socially divisive issues. In contrast to traditional approaches in logic that devalue emotion, she acknowledges the affective aspects of reasoning and how emotion is embedded in our understanding of self and other.

The Force of Kindness: Change Your Life with Love and Compassion

Sharon Salzberg (Sounds True, 2010)

Distill the great spiritual teachings from around the world down to their most basic principles, and one thread emerges to unite them all: kindness. In *The Force of Kindness*, Sharon Salzberg offers practical instruction on how we can cultivate this essential trait within ourselves.

Born to Be Good: The Science of a Meaningful Life

Dacher Keltner (W.W. Norton Company, 2009)

Illustrated with more than fifty photographs of human emotions, *Born to Be Good* takes us on a journey through scientific discovery, personal narrative, and Eastern philosophy. Positive emotions, Dacher Keltner finds, lie at the core of human nature and shape our everyday behavior—and they just may be the key to understanding how we can live our lives better.

Power and Love: A Theory and Practice of Social Change
Adam Kahene (Berrett-Koehler Publishers, 2009)

In *Power and Love*, Adam Kahane delves deeply in the dual nature of power and love, exploring their complex and intricate interplay. With disarming honesty he relates how, through trial and error, he learned to balance between them, shifting from one to the other as though learning to walk—at first falling, then stumbling forward, and finally moving purposefully toward true, lasting reconciliation and progress.

Being Generous: The Art of Right Living
Lucinda Vardey & John Dalla Costa (Vintage Canada, 2009)

Married couple Lucinda Vardey and John Dalla Costa are inspired by generosity. In *Being Generous*, they argue that if we are truly trying to help this troubled world, we must investigate other possibilities for being generous, by helping those we interact with every day: our children, colleagues, parents, friends and the homeless men and women we encounter when out and about in our cities.

The Engaged Spiritual Life: A Buddhist Approach to Transforming Ourselves and the World
Donald Rothberg (Beacon Press, 2006)

In *The Engaged Spiritual Life*, Donald Rotherberg brings together social change and the depth of human consciousness to reveal how they require one another. He weaves together basic spiritual teachings, real-life examples, social context, and exercises, and provides a clear, thorough, and compelling guide for those interested in connecting inner and outer transformation.

Social Intelligence: The New Science of Human Relationships

Daniel Goleman (Macmillan Audio, 2006)

In *Social Intelligence*, Daniel Goleman explores an emerging science with startling implications for our interpersonal world. Its most amazing discovery: we are "wired to connect," designed for sociability, constantly engaged in a "neural ballet" that connects us, brain to brain, with those around us. Goleman's heartening news is that humans have a built-in bias toward empathy, cooperation, and altruism, provided we develop the social intelligence to nurture these capabilities in ourselves and others.

Compassion-Focused

Fierce Self-Compassion: How Women Can Harness Kindness to Speak Up, Claim Their Power and Thrive

Kristin Neff (Harper Wave, 2021)

Drawing on a wealth of research, her personal life story and empirically supported practices, Kristin Neff demonstrates how women can use fierce and tender self-compassion to succeed in the workplace, engage in caregiving without burning out, be authentic in relationships, and end the silence around sexual harassment and abuse. In *Fierce Self-Compassion*, she shows women how to reclaim balance within themselves, so they can help restore balance in the world.

Succeed the Right Way: What Every Compassionate Business Person Must Know

*Paul L. Gunn Jr (Leaders Press, 2021)

Qualities such as empathy, compassion, and kindness have long been seen as weaknesses in business, but in *Succeed the Right Way*, Paul L. Gunn Jr. demonstrates how these qualities can be the most powerful forces in achieving success.

Radical Compassion: Learning to Love Yourself and Your World with the Practice of RAIN

Tara Brach (Penguin Life, 2020)

In *Radical Compassion*, Tara Brach offers an easy-to-learn four-step meditation that quickly loosens the grip of difficult emotions and limiting beliefs. Each step in the meditation practice is brought to life by memorable stories shared by Tara and her students as they deal with feelings of overwhelm, loss, and self-aversion, with painful relationships, and past trauma—and as they discover step-by-step the sources of love, forgiveness, compassion, and deep wisdom alive within all of us.

Compassionomics: The Revolutionary Scientific Evidence That Caring Makes a Difference

Stephen Trzeciak and Anthony Mazzarelli (Studer Group, 2019)

In *Compassionomics*, physician scientists Stephen Trzeciak and Anthony Mazzarelli uncover the eye-opening data that compassion could be a wonder drug for the 21st century. Using research showing that health care is in the midst of a compassion crisis, their rigorous review of the science demonstrates that human connection in health care does matter, and it does in astonishing and measurable ways.

The Compassionate Connection: The Healing Power of Empathy and Mindful Listening

David Rakel (W. W. Norton & Company, 2018)

In *The Compassionate Connection*, Dr. David Rakel explains how we can strengthen our bonds with others—all the while doing emotional and physical good for ourselves. These tools guide us to improve our connections—whether between doctor and patient, husband and wife, parent and child, or boss and employee—and live with clarity, wisdom, and good health.

The Compassionate Achiever: How Helping Others Fuels Success
Christopher L. Kukk (HarperOne, 2017)

In *The Compassionate Achiever*, Christopher L. Kukk identifies the skills every compassionate achiever should master—listening, understanding, connecting, and acting—and outlines how to develop each, with clear explanations, easy-to-implement strategies, actionable exercises, and real-world examples.

Altruism: The Power of Compassion to Change Yourself and the World
Matthieu Ricard (Back Bay Books, 2016)

In *Altruism*, Matthieu Ricard makes a passionate case for altruism—and why we need it now more than ever. It is, he believes, the vital thread that can answer the main challenges of our time: the economy in the short term, life satisfaction in the mid-term, and environment in the long term.

A Fearless Heart: How the Courage to Be Compassionate Can Transform Our Lives
Thupten Jinpa (Avery, 2016)

In *A Fearless Heart*, Thupten Jinpa shows us that we actually fear compassion. We worry that if we are too compassionate with others we will be taken advantage of, and if we are too compassionate with ourselves we will turn into slackers. Using science, insights from both classical Buddhist and western psychology, and stories both from others and from his own extraordinary life, he shows us how to train our compassion muscle to relieve stress, fight depression, improve our health, achieve our goals, and change our world.

The Compassionate Life: Walking the Path of Kindness
*Marc Ian Barasch (Healing Path Books, 2014)

In *The Compassionate Life*, Marc Barasch sets out on a journey to the heart of compassion, discovering its power to change who we are and the society we might become. He provides up-to-the-minute research to timeless spiritual truths, and weaves a stirring, unforgettable story of the search for kindness in a world that clearly needs it.

Self-Compassion: The Proven Power of Being Kind to Yourself
Kristin Neff (William Morrow Paperbacks, 2011)

In *Self-Compassion*, Kristin Neff offers expert advice on how to limit self-criticism and offset its negative effects, enabling you to achieve your highest potential and a more contented, fulfilled life.

Twelve Steps to a Compassionate Life
Karen Armstrong (Anchor, 2011)

Karen Armstrong believes that while compassion is intrinsic in all human beings, each of us needs to work diligently to cultivate and expand our capacity for compassion. In *Twelve Steps to a Compassionate Life*, she sets out a program that can lead us toward a more compassionate life.

Visions of Compassion: Western Scientists and Tibetan Buddhists Examine Human Nature
Richard Davidson & Anne Harrington (Oxford University Press, 2001)

Richard Davidson and Anne Harrington examine how Western behavioral science—which has generally focused on negative aspects of human nature—holds up to cross-cultural scrutiny, in particular the Tibetan Buddhist celebration of the human potential for altruism, empathy, and compassion. Resulting from a meeting between the Dalai Lama, leading Western scholars, and a group of Tibetan monks, *Visions of Compassion* includes excerpts from these extraordinary dialogues as well as engaging essays exploring points of difference and overlap between the two perspectives.

Raising and Educating Children and Youth

The Empathy Advantage: Coaching Children to Be Kind, Respectful, and Successful

*Lynne Azarchi (Armin Lear Press, 2022)

Lynne Azarchi's easy to use guide will help parents, educators, and caregivers teach children, tweens, and teens the ability to "walk in someone else's shoes"—skills that last a lifetime and helps kids become caring adults with the people skills needed for relationships and career success. The goal of *The Empathy Advantage* is help youth make better pro-social choices with self-compassion and empathic concern.

UnSelfie: Why Empathetic Kids Succeed in Our All-About-Me-World

Michele Borba (TouchStone, 2017)

UnSelfie is a blueprint for parents and educators who want kids to shift their focus from *I, me,* and *mine* . . . to *we, us,* and *ours.* Michele Borba pinpoints the forces causing the empathy crisis and shares a revolutionary, researched-based, nine-step plan for reversing it.

Roots of Empathy: Changing the World Child by Child

Mary Gordon (Thomas Allen Publishers, 2012)

In *Roots of Empathy,* Mary Gordon explains the value of and how best to nurture empathy and social and emotional literacy in all children—and thereby reduce aggression, antisocial behavior, and bullying.

Teaching Empathy: A Blueprint for Caring, Compassion, and Community

David Levine (Solution Tree, 2009)

In *Teaching Empathy*, David Levine gives educators the tools to teach the pro-social skill of empathy to help create a culture of caring in their schools.

Empathic Intelligence: Teaching, Learning, Relating

Roslyn Arnold (University of New South Wales Press, 2005)

Roslyn Arnold explains what makes an educator exceptional. The theory of empathic intelligence affirms the practice of those who are attuned to others and gifted in developing others' potential. *Empathic Intelligence* argues for the importance of creating a dynamic between thinking and feeling in a climate of intelligent caring.

Children's Books About Empathy

Empathy Is Your Superpower: A Book About Understanding the Feelings of Others

Cori Bussolari (Rockridge Press, 2021)

Cori Bussolari's introduction to empathy, *Empathy Is Your Superpower*, for kids 5–7 shows that learning to understand and care about the feelings of others is one of the most important steps in a child's development—and it's never too early to start helping them learn these skills.

A Little SPOT of Empathy: A Story About Understanding and Kindness

Diane Alber (Self-published, 2021)

A Little SPOT of Empathy by Diane Alber invites kids to see things from another person's perspective. Readers will see that when we do that it is so much easier to show kindness toward them.

My Camel Wants to Be a Unicorn: A Children's Book About Empathy and a Mopey Camel

Julia Inserro (Self-published, 2019)

In *My Camel Wants to Be a Unicorn*, Julia Inserro introduces the concept of empathy, and how important it is to not make assumptions about others, rather to ask and observe.

You, Me and Empathy: Teaching Children About Empathy, Feelings, Kindness, Compassion, Tolerance and Recognising Bullying Behaviours

Jayneen Sanders (Educate2Empower Publishing, 2017)

In *You, Me and Empathy*, Jayneen Sanders uses a little person called Quinn to model the meaning of empathy. Throughout the story, Quinn shows an abundance of understanding, compassion and kindness toward others. Showing empathy toward others is a learnt trait, and one to nurture and cherish with the children in our care.

Teach Your Dragon Empathy: Help Your Dragon Understand Empathy

Steve Herman (DG Books Publishing, 2019)

Steve Herman, author of the *My Dragon Books* series, seeks to produce books that effortlessly teach social-emotional learning. *Teach Your Dragon Empathy* shows children the importance of empathy, compassion, and kindness through using a pet dragon who can do just about anything, even learn empathy.

LINKS FOR PURPOSEFUL EMPATHY PRACTICES

Chapter 1
Implicit Association Test
implicit.harvard.edu/implicit/takeatest.html

Chapter 2

The Empathy Quiz
greatergood.berkeley.edu/quizzes/take_quiz/empathy

The Empathy Quotient
www.autismresearchcentre.com/tests/empathy-quotient-eq-for-adults/

The Interpersonal Reactivity Index
fetzer.org/sites/default/files/images/stories/pdf/selfmeasures/EMPATHY
-InterpersonalReactivityIndex.pdf

Wheel of Life
https://quenza.com/wheel-of-life/

Chapter 3

Personal Values Assessment
www.valuescentre.com/tools-assessments/pva/

Meaning in Life Questionnaire (MLQ)
www.michaelfsteger.com/wp-content/uploads/2013/12/MLQ-description
-scoring-and-feedback-packet.pdf

Self-Actualization Scale
scottbarrykaufman.com/characteristics-of-self-actualization-scale/

Chapter 4

Human Library
humanlibrary.org/

HUMAN Documentary
www.youtube.com/watch?v=fC5qucSk18w

Teach with Movies
teachwithmovies.org/discussion-questions-for-use-with-any-film-that-is-a
-work-of-fiction/

This is Civity
www.civity.org/podcast/

Chapter 5
Empathy Circles
www.empathycircle.com/

Empathy Tents
www.empathytent.com/

B Impact Assessment
www.bcorporation.net/en-us/programs-and-tools/b-impact-assessment/

Chapter 6
Digital Flourishing Survey
sgiz.mobi/s3/digitalflourishing

Random App of Kindness
rakigame.com/

Daily Haloha
dailyhaloha.com/

RealLives
reallivesworld.com/

Jaago
jaago.life/

Feel that Network
www.coursera.org/lecture/collaborative-foresight/scenario-the-feelthat
-network-xauqU

Chapter 8
Documentary *Dialogue Lab: America*
ideosinstitute.org/dla

Charter of Compassion
charterforcompassion.org/affirm-and-share-the-charter-for-compassion

Compassionate Community
charterforcompassion.org/communities/communities-partners

Compass Survey for Families
www.rootsofaction.com/surveys/

Chapter 9
Level of Stress Assessment
proqol.org/#6d43dca3-1f06-414d-a26e-6ea9ef18c7d4

Super Soul Sunday
www.oprah.com/app/supersoul-sunday-full-episodes.html
podcasts.apple.com/us/podcast/oprahs-super-soul/id1264843400?mt=2

Yoga with Melissa
melissawest.com/

Chapter 10
Relationshift
courageofcare.org/wp-content/uploads/2021/11/RelationSHIFT-The
-CourageRISE-Model-for-Building-Relational-Cultures-of-Practice_The
-Arrow-Journal-2021.pdf

The Relationist Manifesto
www.aspeninstitute.org/blog-posts/the-relationalist-manifesto/

Mutual Aid Toolkit
cdn.cosmicjs.com/09a653b0-7545-11ea-be6b-9f10a20c6f68-Mutual-Aid
-101-Toolkit.pdf

Metta Hour Podcast
www.sharonsalzberg.com/metta-hour-podcast/

Loving-Kindness Meditation
ggia.berkeley.edu/practice/loving_kindness_meditation

Self-Compassion Guided Meditations
self-compassion.org/category/exercises/#exercises

Purposeful Empathy Survey
anitanowak.com/

FEATURED PEOPLE AND ORGANIZATIONS

Preface
Tubahumerize
http://rwandanwomencan.org/

Chapter 1
Project Implicit
https://www.projectimplicit.net/#:~:text=Project%20Implicit%20is%20a
%20non,group%2Dbased%20biases.

Chapter 2
Multidisciplinary Association for Psychedelic Studies (MAPS)
https://maps.org/

Veterans for Peace
https://www.veteransforpeace.org/

Chapter 3
John Wood
https://www.johnjwood.com/

Room to Read
https://www.roomtoread.org/

U-Go
https://ugouniversity.org/

Artistri Sud
https://www.artistrisud.org/

Ray Zahab
https://www.rayzahab.com/

H2O Africa
https://water.org/

impossible2Possible
https://www.impossible2possible.com/

Elsa-Marie D'Silva
http://www.elsamariedsilva.com/

Safecity
https://www.safecity.in/

Red Dot Foundation
https://reddotfoundation.org/

Chapter 4

Petre Shotadze Tbilisi Medical Academy
https://www.tma.edu.ge/eng/

Roots of Empathy
https://rootsofempathy.org/

Dialogue Social Enterprise (DSE)
https://www.dialogue-se.com/

In Your Shoes
https://www.inyourshoesproject.org/

Radical Empathy
https://www.terrigivens.com/

LASER Method
https://www.katharinemanning.com/

Empathic Intervision
https://empathicintervision.com/

Moral Courage
https://www.moralcourage.com/

Chapter 5

Unilever
https://www.unilever.ca/

Goalcast
https://www.goalcast.com/

Frog
https://www.frog.co/

KIND
https://www.kindsnacks.com/

Empatico
https://empatico.org/

Ashoka
https://www.ashoka.org/en-ca

Schwab Foundation
https://www.schwabfound.org/

Skoll Foundation
https://skoll.org/

Echoing Green
https://echoinggreen.org/

Aspire
https://www.aspirecig.com/

Participant
https://participant.com/

Alia
https://www.myalia.org/

Represent Justice
https://www.representjustice.org/

B-Lab (Benefit Corporation)
https://www.bcorporation.net/en-us/

Chapter 6

Jordan Nguyen
https://www.drjordannguyen.com/

Empathy Rocks
https://www.empathy.rocks/about

Virtual Interaction Lab
https://stanfordvr.com/

BeAnotherLab
http://beanotherlab.org/

Marina Abramovic
https://mai.art/

Dys4ia
https://freegames.org/ca/dys4ia/

That Dragon, Cancer
http://www.thatdragoncancer.com/

Games for Change
https://www.gamesforchange.org/

Jane McGonigal
https://janemcgonigal.com/

Brobyggerne: Center for Dioalogkaffee
https://brobyggerne.dk/en/home/

Sitting in Bathrooms with Trans People
https://www.dylanmarron.com/video

Artificial Intelligence Impact Alliance
http://allianceimpact.org/?lang=en

Andrea Goulet
https://andreagoulet.com/

Compassionate Coding
https://compassionatecoding.com/

The Digital Wellness Institute
https://www.digitalwellnessinstitute.com/

Center for Empathy in Christian Public Life
https://ideosinstitute.org/cecpl

Chapter 7
Organization of Networks of Empathy
https://oneempathynetwork.com/

Thich Nhat Hanh
https://thichnhathanhfoundation.org/

Paulo Freire
https://www.freire.org/paulo-freire

Revolutionary Love Project
https://valariekaur.com/revolutionary-love-project/

Network of Spiritual Progressives
https://spiritualprogressives.org/

Presencing Institute
https://www.presencing.org/

Leave Out ViolencE (LOVE)
https://loveorganization.ca/

Chapter 8
One Year Road Trip
https://oneyearroadtrip.com/

Making Caring Common Project
https://mcc.gse.harvard.edu/

Roots of Action
https://www.rootsofaction.com/

Courage of Care Coalition
https://courageofcare.org/

Center for Building a Culture of Empathy
http://cultureofempathy.com/

Charter of Compassion
https://charterforcompassion.org/

Tribeless
https://www.tribeless.co/

The Empathy Box
https://empathybox.co/

Chapter 9
Narrative Medicine at Columbia
https://sps.columbia.edu/academics/masters/narrative-medicine

E.M.P.A.T.H.Y
https://empathetics.com/

Vital Talk
https://www.vitaltalk.org/

Educare
https://www.educare.co.uk/

3rd Conversation
https://www.3rdconversation.org/

Médecins Sans Frontières (Doctors Without Borders)
https://www.doctorswithoutborders.ca/

CHS Alliance
https://www.chsalliance.org/

Focusing Initiatives International
https://focusinginternational.org/

The Wellbeing Project
https://wellbeing-project.org/

Chapter 10
Self-Compassion
https://self-compassion.org/

Sharon Salzberg
https://www.sharonsalzberg.com/

Insight Meditation Society
https://www.dharma.org/

Jennifer Louden
https://jenniferlouden.com/

GirlTrek
https://www.girltrek.org/

Out in the Open
https://www.weareoutintheopen.org/

Mutual Aid Disaster Relief
https://mutualaiddisasterrelief.org/

The Pocket Project
https://pocketproject.org/

Somatic Experiencing International
https://traumahealing.org/

Courage of Care Coalition
https://courageofcare.org/

Weave: The Social Fabric Project
https://www.aspeninstitute.org/programs/weave-the-social-fabric-initiative/

Conclusion
International Women's Forum
https://iwforum.org/

NOTES

INTRODUCTION

top-ten most empathic companies: "The Most Empathetic Companies, 2016," *Harvard Business Review*, March 26, 2018, https://hbr.org/2016/12/the-most-and-least-empathetic-companies-2016

less likely to have a heart attack: Jeffrey A. Burr, Sae Hwang Han, and Jane L. Tavares, "Volunteering and Cardiovascular Disease Risk: Does Helping Others Get 'Under the Skin?'," *Gerontologist* 56, no. 5 (October 2016): 937–947.

Children are more likely to succeed: Michele Borba, *Unselfie: Why Empathetic Kids Succeed in Our All-About-Me World* (New York: Touchstone, 2016).

employees would work longer hours: Ruth Umoh, "60% of Employees Surveyed Would Take a Pay Cut to Work for This Type of Company," CNBC, June 19, 2018, https://www.cnbc.com/2018/06/12/60-percent-of-workers-would-take-a-pay-cut-to-work-for-an-empathetic-company.html

decreases turnover and drives productivity: 2020 State of Workplace Empathy, "Workplace Empathy: What Leaders Don't Know Can Hurt Them," *Businesssolver*, 2020, https://cdn2.hubspot.net/hubfs/378546/2020-empathy-special-report-what-leaders-dont-know/businesssolver-empathy-ceo-special-report.pdf

rate their workplaces: "State of Workplace Empathy," *Businesssolver*, 2021, https://www.businesssolver.com/resources/state-of-workplace-empathy

empathy drives better business outcomes: "State of Workplace Empathy."

According to the World Food Program: World Food Programme, "2019 Hunger Map," August 14, 2019, https://www.wfp.org/publications/2019-hunger-map

extra eleven billion dollars: David Laborde Debucquet, Livia Bizikova, Tess Lallemant, and Carin Smaller, *Ending Hunger: What Would It Cost?* (Winnipeg, Manitoba, Canada: International Institute for Sustainable Development [IISD], 2016), http://www.iisd .org/sites/default/files/publications/ending-hunger-what-would-it-cost.pdf

The World Health Organization reports: World Health Organization, "Sanitation," March 21, 2022, https://www.who.int/news-room/fact-sheets/detail/sanitation

lack access to safe drinking water: World Health Organization, "1 in 3 People Globally Do Not Have Access to Safe Drinking Water—UNICEF, WHO," 2019, https://www.who.int /news/item/18-06-2019-1-in-3-people-globally-do-not-have-access-to-safe-drinking -water-unicef-who#:~:text=Some%202.2%20billion%20people%20around,lack%20 basic**%20handwashing%20facilities

1.6 million people die from diarrheal disease: Bernadeta Dadonaite, "More than Half a Million Children Die from Diarrhea Each Year. How Do We Prevent This?," Our World in Data, August 16, 2019, https://ourworldindata.org/childhood-diarrheal-diseases

planet's population grows: "Population: The Numbers," Population Matters, https:// populationmatters.org/population-numbers

demand for freshwater: "Water Used This Year," Worldometers, https://www.worldometers .info/water/

modern-day slaves: International Labour Organization, "Global Estimates of Modern Slavery," 2017, https://www.ilo.org/global/publications/books/WCMS_575479/lang --en/index.htm?fbclid=IwAR2jxSpR0Lw-pP5ludbT0JCSWkpNgkLn1Zt_Wm2si UNgupsEQm0jacZM6Wk

child soldiers: Human Rights Watch, "Child Soldiers," 2013, https://www.hrw.org/topic /childrens-rights/child-soldiers#

According to the International Labour Organization: International Labour Organization, "Forced Labour, Modern Slavery and Human Trafficking," 2017, https://www.ilo.org /global/topics/forced-labour/lang--en/index.html

Oxfam International reports: Oxfam International, "Ten Richest Men Double their Fortunes in Pandemic while Incomes of 99 percent of Humanity Fall," January 17, 2022, https:// www.oxfam.org/en/press-releases/ten-richest-men-double-their-fortunes-pandemic -while-incomes-99-percent-humanity

executive director Gabriela Bucher: Oxfam International, "Ten Richest Men."

economic impacts of the virus: Esmé Berkhout, Nick Galasso, Max Lawson, Pablo Andrés Rivero Morales, Anjela Taneja, and Diego Alejo Vázquez Pimentel, *The Inequality*

NOTES

Virus (Oxford: Oxfam, 2021), https://oxfamilibrary.openrepository.com/bitstream/handle/10546/621149/bp-the-inequality-virus-250121-en.pdf

rate of depression in industrialized countries: Brandon H. Hidaka, "Depression as a Disease of Modernity: Explanations for Increasing Prevalence," *Journal of Affective Disorders* 140, no. 3 (2012): 205–214.

average age for the onset of depression: "Age at Onset of Mental Disorders Worldwide: Large-Scale Meta-Analysis of 192 Epidemiological Studies," *Molecular Psychiatry* 27 (2021): 281–295, https://www.nature.com/articles/s41380-021-01161-7#citeas

Global temperatures: California Institute of Technology, "The Effects of Climate Change," Global Climate Change, NASA, last updated May 3, 2022, https://climate.nasa.gov/effects/

climate refugees: World Bank Group, "Groundswell Part 2: Acting on Internal Climate Migration," 2021, https://openknowledge.worldbank.org/handle/10986/36248

Descent of Man: Charles Darwin, *The Descent of Man* (New York: American Home Library, 1902).

The Theory of Moral Sentiments: Adam Smith, *The Theory of Moral Sentiments* (London: Printed for A. Millar, A. Kincaid, and J. Bell in Edinburgh, 1759).

The Age of Empathy: Nature's Lessons for a Kinder Society: Frans de Waal, *The Age of Empathy: Nature's Lessons for a Kinder Society* (New York: Crown Publishing Group, 2010).

DNA in common: de Waal, *The Age of Empathy*.

According to Stanford research psychologist Jamil Zaki: Jamil Zaki, *The War for Kindness. Building Empathy in a Fractured World* (New York: Penguin Random House, 2019).

Nearly a third of US households: US Census Bureau, "Census Bureau Releases New Estimates on America's Families and Living Arrangements," November 29, 2021, https://www.census.gov/newsroom/press-releases/2021/families-and-living-arrangements.html#:~:text=There%20were%2037%20million%20one,over%20the%20last%20two%20decades

long periods of loneliness: Centers for Disease Control and Prevention, "Loneliness and Social Isolation Linked to Serious Health Conditions," April 29, 2021, https://www.cdc.gov/aging/publications/features/lonely-older-adults.html#:~:text=Health%20Risks%20of%20Loneliness&text=1-,Social%20isolation%20was%20associated%20with%20about%20a,percent%20increased%20risk%20of%20dementia.&text=Poor%20social%20relationships%20(characterized%20by,32%25%20increased%20risk%20of%20stroke

John F. Schumaker: John Schumaker, "The Demoralized Mind," *Films for Action*, May 10, 2016, https://www.filmsforaction.org/articles/the-demoralized-mind/

top hundred global economic entities: Joe Myers, "How Do the World's Biggest Companies Compare to the Biggest Economies?," *World Economic Forum*, October 19, 2016, https://www.weforum.org/agenda/2016/10/corporations-not-countries-dominate-the-list-of-the-world-s-biggest-economic-entities/

world's first minister of loneliness: "The World's First Minister of Loneliness: Feargus O'Sullivan," *Bloomberg*, January 18, 2018, https://www.bloomberg.com/news/articles/2018-01-18/u-k-appoints-world-s-first-minister-of-loneliness

Neuroscience has revealed: "Mengfei Han, Gaofang Jiang, Haoshuang Luo and Wongcong Shao, "Neurobiological Bases of Social Networks," *Frontiers in Psychology* 12 (April 30, 2021): 626337, https://www.frontiersin.org/articles/10.3389/fpsyg.2021.626337/full

CHAPTER 1

"Empathy is a quality of character": Barack Obama, University of Massachusetts at Boston Commencement Address, June 2, 2006.

Confucian scholar Mengzi: Whalen Lai, "Of One Mind or Two? Query on the Innate Good in Mencius," *Religious Studies* 26, no. 2 (1990): 247–255, http://www.jstor.org/stable/20019406

Italian theologian Thomas Aquinas: Thomas Aquinas, *Summa Theologica* (New York: Benziger Bros., 1947–1948).

German word einfühlung: "From 'Einfühlung' to Empathy: Exploring the Relationship Between Aesthetic and Interpersonal Experience," *Cognitive Processing* 19, no. 4 (May 2018): 141–145, https://www.researchgate.net/publication/325152875_From_Einfuhlung_to_empathy_exploring_the_relationship_between_aesthetic_and_interpersonal_experience

Against Empathy: Paul Bloom, *Against Empathy* (New York: Ecco Books, 2016), 43.

The War for Kindness: Jamil Zaki, *The War for Kindness: Building Empathy in a Fractured World* (New York: Crown Publishing Group, 2019).

our brain has tripled in size: Andrew Du et al., "Pattern and Process in Hominin Brain Size Evolution Are Scale-Dependent," The Royal Society Publishing, February 21, 2018, https://royalsocietypublishing.org/doi/10.1098/rspb.2017.2738

babies engage in "proto-conversations": S. Bråten and C. Trevarthen, "Prologue: From Infant Subjectivity and Participant Movements to Simulation and Conversation in Cultural

Common Sense," in *On Being Moved: From Mirror Neurons to Empathy*, ed. S. Bråten (Amsterdam: John Benjamin Publishing, 2007), 21–34.

cognitive maturation and environmental influences: Jean Decety and Meghan Meyer, "From Emotion Resonance to Empathic Understanding: A Social Developmental Neuroscience Account," *Development and Psychopathology* 20 (2008): 1053–1080.

Healthy neurotypical babies: Lise Eliot, *What's Going On in There? How the Brain and Mind Develop in the First Five Years of Life* (New York: Bantam Books, 1999).

According to psychoanalyst Heinz Kahut: Heinz Kohut, *How Does Analysis Cure?* (Chicago: University of Chicago Press, 1984).

behavioral change researcher Rick van Baaren: R. B. Van Baaren, J. Decety, A. Dijksterhuis, A. Van der Leij, and M. L. Van Leeuwen, "Being Imitated: Consequences of Nonconsciously Showing Empathy," in *The Social Neuroscience of Empathy*, ed. J. Decety and W. Ickes (Cambridge: MIT Press, 2009), 31–42.

The Empathic Civilization: Jeremy Rifkin, *The Empathic Civilization: The Race to Global Consciousness in a World in Crisis* (New York: TarcherPerigee, 2006), 160.

Empathy: A History: Susan Lanzoni, *Empathy: A History* (New Haven: Yale University Press, 2018) 17.

regulate each other's physiology: Daniel Goleman, *Social Intelligence: The Revolutionary New Science of Human Relationships* (New York: Bantam Books, 2006).

according to science reporter Brian Resnick: Brian Resnick, "9 Essential Lessons from Psychology to Understand the Trump Era," January 10, 2019, https://www.vox.com/science-and-health/2018/4/11/16897062/political-psychology-trump-explain-studies-research-science-motivated-reasoning-bias-fake-news

our capacity to empathize decreases: Paul Slovic, "If I Look at the Mass I Will Never Act," *Judgment and Decision Making* 2, no. 2 (April, 2007): 79–95.

pre-COVID cost of compassion fatigue: Centerstone Solutions, "Compassion Fatigue: What Is It? How Does It Relate to Stress and Burnout?," June 25, 2018, https://centerstonesolutions.org/compassion-fatigue/

people from wealthy backgrounds: Roman Krznaric, *The Empathy Effect: How Empathy Drives Common Values, Social Justice and Environmental Action*, March 2015, Friends of the Earth, https://dokumen.tips/documents/the-empathy-effect-by-roman-krznaric.html?page=1

respond to the distress signals of others: Yasmin Anwar, "Low-Income People Quicker to Show Compassion," *Greater Good*, December 20, 2011, https://greatergood.berkeley.edu/article/item/lower_income_people_quicker_to_show_compassion *according to Elizabeth Segal:* Elizabeth Segal, *Assessing Empathy* (New York City: Columbia University Press, 2017), 88.

CHAPTER 2

interpersonal suffering lasted nearly two years: Personal interview, 2021.

American Psychological Association: E. R. Edwards, "Posttraumatic Stress and Alexithymia: A Meta-Analysis of Presentation and Severity," *Psychological Trauma: Theory, Research, Practice, and Policy* (2019), Advance online publication, https://doi.apa.org/doiLanding?doi=10.1037%2Ftra0000539

The human brain: Christian Keysers, *The Empathic Brain: How the Discovery of Mirror Neurons Changes Our Understanding of Human Nature* (La Vergne: Lightning Source, 2011).

According to Allan Young: Suparna Choudhury and Jan Slaby, eds., *Critical Neuroscience: A Handbook of the Social and Cultural Contexts of Neuroscience* (Hoboken: Wiley, 2011).

Neuroscientist Vilayanur Ramachandran: Vilayanur Ramachandran, "Mirror Neurons and Imitation Learning as the Driving Force Behind the Great Leap Forward in Human Evolution," Edge.org, May 31, 2000, https://www.edge.org/conversation/vilayanur_ramachandran-mirror-neurons-and-imitation-learning-as-the-driving-force

overlapping neuronal networks: Philipp Kanske and Tania Singer, "Dissecting the Social Brain: Introducing the EmpaToM to Reveal Distinct Neural Networks and Brain–Behavior Relations for Empathy and Theory of Mind," *NeuroImage* 122 (November 15, 2015): 6–19, https://www.sciencedirect.com/science/article/pii/S1053811915007028

when only paralinguistic cues are available: Nicole Ann Ethier, "Paralinguistic and Nonverbal Behaviour in Social Interactions: A Lens Model Perspective" (PhD thesis, University of Waterloo, 2010).

The Empathic Brain: Keysers, *The Empathic Brain.*

research on "shared circuits": Personal interview, 2021.

our facial muscles are affected: Keysers, *The Empathic Brain.*

The Altruistic Brain: Donald Pfaff, *The Altruistic Brain: How We Are Naturally Good* (Oxford: Oxford University Press, 2014), 3.

The Brain That Changes Itself: Norman Doidge, *The Brain That Changes Itself: Stories of Personal Triumph from the Frontiers of Brain Science* (New York: Penguin Random House, 2007).

"motivated account of empathy": Jamil Zaki, "Empathy: A Motivated Account," *Psychological Bulletin* 140, no. 6 (2014): 1608–1647, https://psycnet.apa.org/record/2014-44494-001

NOTES

Americans sent to prison for drug offenses: "Criminal Justice Facts," The Sentencing Project, https://www.sentencingproject.org/criminal-justice-facts/

state inmates incarcerated: Tara O'Neill Hayes and Margaret Barnhorst, "Incarceration and Poverty in the United States," American Action Forum, June 30, 2020, https://www.americanactionforum.org/research/incarceration-and-poverty-in-the-united-states/

According to Ralph Metzner: Ralph Metzner, "MDMA Recognized as Most Promising Treatment of PTSD," Multidisciplinary Association for Psychedelic Studies, June 29, 2011, https://maps.org/news/media/mdma-recognized-as-most-promising-treatment-of-ptsd/

aggressive marketing campaign: Marsha Rosenbaum and Rick Doblin, "Why MDMA Should Not Have Been Made Illegal," The Psychedelic Library, 1991, http://www.psychedelic-library.org/rosenbaum.htm

Multidisciplinary Association for Psychedelic Studies: "Phase 3: MDMA-Assisted Therapy for PTSD," *MAPS*, https://maps.org/mdma/ptsd/phase3/

executive director, Rick Doblin: Andrew Jacobs, "The Psychedelic Revolution Is Coming. Psychiatry May Never Be the Same," *The New York Times*, 2018, https://www.nytimes.com/2021/05/09/health/psychedelics-mdma-psilocybin-molly-mental-health.html

venture capitalists invest in startups: Tim Ferriss, "Here's a Very Unusual $10M Bet . . .," June 16, 2020, https://tim.blog/2020/06/16/maps-capstone-challenge-mdma-ptsd/

psychedelic drugs market: "Psychedelic Drugs Market Size Is Projected to Reach $10.75 Billion by 2027," https://www.prnewswire.com/news-releases/psychedelic-drugs-market-size-is-projected-to-reach-10-75-billion-by-2027--301273405.html

Users of MDMA: Molly Carlyle et al., "Greater Empathy in MDMA Users," *Journal of Psychopharmacology (Oxford, England)* 33, no. 3 (2019): 295–304, https://pubmed.ncbi.nlm.nih.gov/30717615/

long-term prosocial processes: Cédric M. Hysek et al., "MDMA Enhances Emotional Empathy and Prosocial Behavior," *Social Cognitive and Affective Neuroscience* 9, no. 11 (2014): 1645–1652, https://www.ncbi.nlm.nih.gov/pmc/articles/PMC4221206/#:~:text=MDMA%20increased%20prosociality.,%3D%200.008)%20but%20not%20women

Boris Heifets and Robert Malenka: Boris D. Heifets and Robert C. Malenka, "MDMA as a Probe and Treatment for Social Behaviors," *Cell* 166, no. 2 (2016): 269–272, https://pubmed.ncbi.nlm.nih.gov/27419864/

hormone needed for breastfeeding: Ralph Metzner, *Mind Space and Time Stream* (Berkeley, CA: Regent Press, 2009), 134.

225

CHAPTER 3

give up millions in stock options: Personal interview, 2010.

Bangladesh to Zambia: "Impact & Reach," https://www.roomtoread.org/impact-and-reach/

Post-pandemic data shows: Beth Braverman, "The Coronavirus Is Taking a Huge Toll on Workers' Mental Health Across America," CNBC, April 6, 2020, https://www.cnbc.com/2020/04/06/coronavirus-is-taking-a-toll-on-workers-mental-health-across-america.html

According to a 2021 WorkLab study: Microsoft Worklab, "The Next Great Disruption Is Hybrid Work—Are We Ready?," March 22, 2021, https://www.microsoft.com/en-us/worklab/work-trend-index/hybrid-work

US Bureau of Labor Statistics: "TED: The Economics Daily," US Bureau of Labor Statistics, October 18, 2021, https://www.bls.gov/opub/ted/2021/quits-rate-of-2-9-percent-in-august-2021-an-all-time-high.htm#:~:text=In%20August%202021%2C%20the%20total,by%202042%2C000%20to%204.3%20million

Millennials and Gen Zers: Adobe Document Cloud, *The Future of Time* (San Jose: Adobe, 2021), 8, https://www.adobe.com/content/dam/dx-dc/us/en/pdfs//the-future-of-time.pdf

according to Deloitte: Roxana Corduneanu, Abha Kulkarni, Steve Hatfield, and Susan K. Hogan, "Millennials and the 'Staying Power' of Pay," *Deloitte,* January 5, 2022, https://www2.deloitte.com/xe/en/insights/topics/talent/motivating-millennials-at-work.html

more important than professional recognition: Gloria Cordes Larson Center for Women and Business, "Multigenerational Impacts on the Workplace," Bentley University, 2017, https://www.generations.com/insights/meaning-keeping-millennials-fired-up#:~:text=Bentley%20University%20found%20that%2084,their%20eight%20hours%20a%20day

Global Talent Trends report by Mercer: Mercer, *Global Talent Trends 2022* (New York: Mercer, 2022), https://www.mercer.com/our-thinking/career/global-talent-hr-trends.html

Gallup has been measuring employee satisfaction: TeamStage, "Employee Engagement Statistics: Does It Increase Productivity in 2022?," 2021, https://teamstage.io/employee-engagement-statistics/

37 percent higher absenteeism: TeamStage, "Employee Engagement Statistics."

$350 billion in lost productivity: Evert Akkerman, "The Cost of Disengagement," *HR Professional Now,* April 2019, http://hrprofessionalnow.ca/top-stories/748-the-cost-of-disengagement

NOTES

Tony Schwartz and Jerry Porath: Tony Schwartz and Christine Porath, "Why You Hate Work," *The New York Times*, May 30, 2014, https://www.nytimes.com/2014/06/01 /opinion/sunday/why-you-hate-work.html

John Templeton Foundation: "Psychology of Purpose," John Templeton Foundation, February 2018, https://www.templeton.org/wp-content/uploads/2020/02/Psychology-of -Purpose.pdf

executive director of Artistri Sud: Artistri Sud, https://www.artistrisud.org/

biggest blessing of my life: Personal interview, 2019.

"Limitations are ninety percent mental": Personal interview, 2009.

Originating from the island of Okinawa: "'Ikigai': The Japanese Secret to Finding Your Purpose," *Wellnest*, February 16, 2021, https://www.wellnest.ca/post/ikigai-the-japanese -secret-to-finding-your-purpose

The Little Book of Ikigai: Ken Mogi, *The Little Book of Ikigai* (London: Quercus Publishing, 2017).

Transcend: The New Science of Self-Actualization: Scott Barry Kaufman, *Transcend: The New Science of Self-Actualization* (New York: TarcherPerigee, 2020).

notion of self-transcendence: Abraham Maslow, *Farther Reaches of Human Nature* (New York: Viking Press, 1971), 269.

Man's Search for Meaning: Victor Frankl, *Man's Search for Meaning: An Introduction to Logotherapy* (Vienna: Verlag für Jugend und Volk, 1946).

livestock production: Dominic Moran and Eileen Wall, "Livestock Production and Greenhouse Gas Emissions: Defining the Problem and Specifying Solutions," *Animal Frontiers* 1, no. 1 (July, 2011): 19–25, https://academic.oup.com/af/article/1/1/19/4638592

United Nations Sustainable Development Goals: United Nations, "Sustainable Development Goals," https://www.un.org/sustainabledevelopment/sustainable-development-goals/

The SDGs are: United Nations, Department of Economic and Social Affairs, "The 17 Goals," https://sdgs.un.org/goals

Jyoti Singh: "What Is Nirbhaya Case?," December 18, 2019, https://timesofindia.indiatimes .com/india/what-is-nirbhaya-case/articleshow/72868430.cms

According to the National Crime Records Bureau of India: PTI, "Average 80 Murders, 91 Rapes Daily in 2018: NCRB Data," *The Hindu*, January 9, 2020, https://www .thehindu.com/news/national/average-80-murders-91-rapes-daily-in-2018-ncrb-data /article61646721.ece

every fifteen minutes: "Annual Crime Report 2018–2019," Ministry of Home Affairs, 2018, https://www.mha.gov.in/documents/annual-reports

one million beneficiaries: Red Dot Foundation Global, https://reddotfoundation.org/

"a spiritual journey": Personal interview, 2020.

"brave enough to be it": "Amanda Gorman Inspires the Country with an Empowering Inaugural Poem," *Harper's BAZAAR*, January 20, 2021, https://www.harpersbazaar.com/culture/art-books-music/a35268879/amanda-gorman-inauguration-poem-full/

CHAPTER 4

outperform their peers by 40 percent: Development Dimensions International, "Leadership Skills Research Report," 2016, https://www.ddiworld.com/research/leadership-skills-research

empathy in the workplace positively affects: Tara Van Bommel, *The Power of Empathy in Times of Crisis and Beyond,* Catalyst Inc., 2021, https://www.catalyst.org/reports/empathy-work-strategy-crisis/

Global Empathy Index: Belinda Parmar, "The Most (and Least) Empathetic Companies," *Harvard Business Review,* November 7, 2015, https://hbr.org/2015/11/2015-empathy-index

Society for Human Resource Management: Society for Human Resource Management, "SHRM Reports Toxic Workplace Cultures Cost Billions," press release, September 25, 2019, https://www.shrm.org/about-shrm/press-room/press-releases/pages/shrm-reports-toxic-workplace-cultures-cost-billions.aspx

considered leaving their job: Society for Human Resource Management, "Culture Refresh Report," 2021, https://www.shrm.org/hr-today/trends-and-forecasting/research-and-surveys/documents/2021%20culture%20refresh%20report.pdf

According to a Deloitte study: Deloitte, "Market Growth, Talent and Climate Change: What's Top of Mind for CEOs," press release, October 28, 2021, https://www2.deloitte.com/us/en/pages/about-deloitte/articles/press-releases/market-growth-talent-and-climate-change-whats-top-of-mind-for-ceos.html

recruitment and marketing materials: "The Survey Is In: Gen Z Demands Diversity and Inclusion Strategy," *Tallo,* October 21, 2020, https://tallo.com/blog/genz-demands-diversity-inclusion-strategy/

ask about gender pronouns: "The Survey Is In."

Power, for All: Julie Battilana and Tiziana Casciaro, "Why Leaders Aren't Powerful Without This 1 Thing," *Fast Company,* September 27, 2021, https://www.fastcompany.com/90679955/why-leaders-arent-powerful-without-this-1-thing?utm_source=pos

tup&utm_medium=email&utm_campaign=emotionalintelligence&position=1&partner
=newsletter&campaign_date=10232021

The Empathy Edge: Maria Ross, *The Empathy Edge: Harnessing the Value of Compassion as an Engine for Success: A Playbook for Brands, Leaders and Teams* (Vancouver: Page Two Books, 2019), 95.

kids develop "emotional literacy": Mary Gordon, *Roots of Empathy: Changing the World Child by Child* (Toronto, ON: Thomas Allen Publishers, 2005), 227.

Dialogue in the Dark: Dialogue Social Enterprise, https://www.dialogue-se.com/

In Your Shoes: In Your Shoes Project, https://www.inyourshoesproject.org/

Radical Empathy: Terri Givens, *Radical Empathy: Finding a Path to Bridging Racial Divides* (Bristol: Policy Press, 2020), 1.

The Empathetic Workplace: Katharine Manning, *The Empathetic Workplace: 5 Steps to a Compassionate, Calm, and Confident Response to Trauma on the Job* (New York: Harper-Collins, 2021), 9.

symptoms of anxiety and/or depression: Centers for Disease Control and Prevention, "Anxiety and Depression: Household Pulse Survey," 2020–2022, https://www.cdc.gov/nchs/covid19/pulse/mental-health.htm

women and racialized people: "From Risk to Resilience: An Equity Approach to COVID-19," Annual Report on the State of Public Health in Canada, 2020, https://www.canada.ca/content/dam/phac-aspc/documents/corporate/publications/chief-public-health-officer-reports-state-public-health-canada/from-risk-resilience-equity-approach-covid-19/cpho-covid-report-eng.pdf

Marriages have suffered: W. Bradford Wilcox, Lyman Stone, and Wendy Wang, "The Good and Bad News About Marriage in the Time of COVID," *Institute for Family Studies*, September 2020, https://ifstudies.org/blog/the-good-and-bad-news-about-marriage-in-the-time-of-covid

substance abuse skyrocketed: Centers for Disease Control and Prevention, "Mental Health, Substance Use, and Suicidal Ideation During the COVID-19 Pandemic—United States," August 14, 2020, https://www.cdc.gov/mmwr/volumes/69/wr/mm6932a1.htm

burnout rates shot to all-time highs: Ashley Abramson, "Burnout and Stress Are Everywhere," *American Psychological Association 2022 Trends Report*, January 1, 2022, https://www.apa.org/monitor/2022/01/special-burnout-stress

multilayered empathy approach: Personal interview, 2020.

Applied Empathy: Michael Ventura, *Applied Empathy: The New Language of Leadership* (New York: Atria, 2019).

Dare to Lead: Brené Brown, *Dare to Lead: Brave Work. Tough Conversations. Whole Hearts* (New York: Random House Publishing Group, 2018), 43 and 143.

Reinventing Organizations: Frederic Laloux, *Reinventing Organizations: A Guide to Creating Organizations Inspired by the Next Stage of Human Consciousness* (Brussels, Belgium: Nelson Parker, 2014), 3030.

CHAPTER 5

"how we spend our lives": Annie Dillard, *The Writing Life* (New York: Harper Perennial, Harper Collins, 2013).

ninety thousand hours over our lifetime: Jessica Pryce-Jones, *Happiness at Work* (Hoboken: Wiley, 2010).

"not been successfully managed": World Health Organization, "Burn-Out an 'Occupational Phenomenon'," *International Classification of Diseases,* May 28, 2019, https://www.who .int/news/item/28-05-2019-burn-out-an-occupational-phenomenon-international -classification-of-diseases#:~:text=%E2%80%9CBurn%2Dout%20is%20a%20 syndrome,related%20to%20one's%20job%3B%20and

42 percent refuse to buy: BusinessSolver, "Employees Believe Organizations," June 2016, https://www.businessolver.com/hubfs/Empathy_at_Work_Study_Presentation.pdf

"a must-have business strategy": World Economic Forum, "Why Empathy Is a Must-have Business Strategy," October 18, 2021, https://www.weforum.org/agenda/2021/10 /empathy-business-future-of-work/#:~:text=Empathy%20helps%20create%20a%20 sense,belief%20that%20employees'%20perspectives%20matter.&text=The%20 COVID%2D19%20pandemic%20has,and%20fears%20about%20job%20security

CEO Alan Jope: Unilever, "Unilever Celebrates 10 Years of the Sustainable Living Plan," press release, May 12, 2020, https://www.unilever.ca/news/press-releases/2020/unile ver-celebrates-10-years-of-the-sustainable-living-plan/

environmental targets they announced: Unilever, "How We Will Improve the Health of Our Planet," press release, June 14, 2020, https://www.unilever.ca/news/2020/climate -and-nature/

company's track record: "Unilever Celebrates 10 Years," https://www.unilever.com/news /press-and-media/press-releases/2020/unilever-celebrates-10-years-of-the-sustainable -living-plan/

divide between rich and poor: Leena Nair, "Unilever's Ambitious Commitment to Social Equality," *Gallup*, June 28, 2021, https://www.gallup.com/workplace/351587/unilever-ambitious-commitment-social-equality.aspx

stereotyped by advertising: Janice Tan, "Unilever Cracks Down On Ad Stereotypes with 'Real Structural Changes,'" *Marketing-Interactive*, June 16, 2021, https://www.marketing-interactive.com/unilever-cracks-down-on-ad-stereotypes-with-real-structural-changes

Develop Your Purpose: Rasmus Hougaard, "How Unilever Develops Leaders to Be a Force for Good," *Forbes*, June 2021, https://www.forbes.com/sites/rasmushougaard/2021/06/08/how-unilever-develops-leaders-to-be-a-force-for-good/?sh=74fb56fd2c71

engagement metrics: Unilever, "Annual Report and Accounts," 2021, https://www.unilever.com/files/33321193-0d9a-44dd-93f8-02209fc6bd54/annual-report-and-accounts-2021.pdf#page=35

third most searched-for company: "Former Unilever CEO Paul Polman Says Aiming for Sustainability Isn't Good Enough—The Goal Is Much Higher," *Harvard Business Review*, November 2021, https://hbr.org/2021/11/former-unilever-ceo-paul-polman-says-aiming-for-sustainability-isnt-good-enough-the-goal-is-much-higher

Goalcast is a digital media company: Goalcast, "About Us," https://www.goalcast.com/about-goalcast/

personal growth is encouraged: Personal conversation, 2022.

continuously learn, grow, innovate: Indeed, "Goalcast Management Reviews," January 26, 2021, https://ca.indeed.com/cmp/Goalcast/reviews?fcountry=ALL&ftopic=mgmt

a global creative powerhouse: Frog, https://www.frog.co/

opening sentence of its manifesto: Frog, "Culture," https://www.frog.co/culture?redirectbrand=frogdesign

recognizing team members: Erin Greenawald, "The Founder of $5 Billion Healthy Snack Company Kind on How to Build a Culture of Empathy Without Losing Your Competitive Edge," *Business Insider*, May 6, 2021, https://www.businessinsider.com/kind-founder-how-build-culture-empathy-stay-competitive-2021-5

Empatico, a free video-conferencing tool: Empatico, https://empatico.org/

"survival of the human race": Twenty One Toys, "3 CEOs Using Empathy to Unlock Innovation," https://twentyonetoys.com/blogs/future-of-work/3-ceos-using-empathy-to-unlock-innovation

Bill Drayton founded: "Ashoka Envisions a World in Which Everyone Is a Changemaker," https://www.ashoka.org/en-ca/about-ashoka

"empathy-based society": "Ashoka Is . . .," October 21, 2013, https://www.youtube.com /watch?v=ycslk2K6S-8&t=158s

CEO David Linde: Kristin Toussaint, "How Participant Gave 'Roma' a Fourth Act That's Still Benefiting Domestic Workers," *Fast Company*, April 28, 2020, https://www .fastcompany.com/90489392/how-participant-gave-roma-a-fourth-act-thats-still -benefiting-domestic-workers

According to the International Labour Organization: International Labour Organization, "Beyond Contagion or Starvation: Giving Domestic Workers Another Way Forward," 2020, https://www.ilo.org/wcmsp5/groups/public/---ed_protect/---protrav/---travail /documents/publication/wcms_743542.pdf

human rights activist Bonnie Abaunza: "Roma," https://abaunzagroup.com/project/roma -film/

start by being a billionaire: Eric Nee, "Jeff Skoll," *Stanford Social Innovation Review* 10, no. 2 (2012): 27–29, https://ssir.org/articles/entry/jeff_skoll

Declaration of Interdependence: BCorporation, "About B Corp Certification," https://www .bcorporation.net/en-us/certification/

B the Change Weekly: B the Change, "How Empathy Can Inform the New Capitalism," *B The Change Weekly*, May 15, 2020, https://bthechange.com/how-empathy-can-inform -the-new-capitalism-2ab1eb3e2d5

fewer mental health problems: Emma Seppala and Kim Cameron, "Proof That Positive Work Cultures Are More Productive," *Harvard Business Review*, December 1, 2015, https:// hbr.org/2015/12/proof-that-positive-work-cultures-are-more-productive

CHAPTER 6

Stephen Hawking believed: Stephen Hawking, Stuart Russell, Max Tegmark, and Frank Wilczek, "Stephen Hawking: 'Transcendence Looks at the Implications of Artificial Intelligence—But Are We Taking AI Seriously Enough?'" *The Independent*, May 1, 2014, https://www.independent.co.uk/news/science/stephen-hawking-transcendence -looks-at-the-implications-of-artificial-intelligence-but-are-we-taking-ai-seriously -enough-9313474.html

Chris Milk said: Chris Milk, "How Virtual Reality Can Create the Ultimate Empathy Machine," TED, April 22, 2015, https://www.youtube.com/watch?v=iXHil1TPxvA

Shelly Turkle: Sherry Turkle, "Connected, But Alone?," TED, April 2012, https://www.ted .com/talks/sherry_turkle_connected_but_alone?language=en

NOTES

Franklin Foer of The Atlantic: Franklin Foer, *World Without Mind: The Existential Threat of Big Tech* (New York: Penguin Press, 2017).

researchers at Kyoto University: Toyoshi University of Technology, "Humans Can Empathize with Robots" *EurekAlert!*, November 3, 2015, https://www.eurekalert.org/news-re leases/840810#:~:text=Now%2C%20researchers%20at%20the%20Department, in%20perceived%20pain%20and%20highlighted

taboos will surely shatter: "AI Is Revolutionizing Sex Robots with Machines That Can Do 50 Automated Positions," *Newsweek*, May 7, 2017, https://www.newsweek.com/sex -robots-ai-sextech-631882

sex with an android: "From Robots to Role Play: Study Reveals German Attitudes to Sex," *The Local*, October 6, 2017, https://www.thelocal.de/20171006/from-robots-to-role -play-study-reveals-german-attitudes-to-sex/

happily date a robot: "NESTA FutureFest, ComRes, UK," April 2016, http://comresglobal .com/wp-content/uploads/2016/04/NESTA_FutureFest-Survey_Data-tables_UK .pdf#_LINK_110

techpreneur Elon Musk: Catherine Clifford, "Elon Musk: 'Mark My Words—A.I. Is Far More Dangerous Than Nukes,'" CNBC, March 13, 2018, https://www.cnbc .com/2018/03/13/elon-musk-at-sxsw-a-i-is-more-dangerous-than-nuclear-weapons .html

bestselling book by 2049: Grace Katja et al., "When Will AI Exceed Human Performance? Evidence from AI Experts," Cornell University, May 3, 2018, https://arxiv.org /abs/1705.08807

Google's longtime director of engineering Ray Kurzweil: Society for Science, "Conversations with Maya: Ray Kurzweil," September 1, 2020, https://www.societyforscience.org /blog/conversations-with-maya-ray-kurzweil/

86 percent accuracy rate: Dominic Basulto, "Why Ray Kurzweil's Predictions Are Right 86% of the Time," *Big Think*, December 13, 2012, https://bigthink.com/articles/why -ray-kurzweils-predictions-are-right-86-of-the-time/

Emoshape patents an emotional processing unit: "New Patent Recognizes Emoshape Founder Patrick Levy-Rosenthal as the Inventor of the First Emotion Chip," Emoshape, September 24, 2019, https://emoshape.com/new-patent-recognizes-emoshape-founder -patrick-levy-rosenthal-as-the-inventor-of-the-first-emotion-chip/

Jeremy Bailenson: Jeremy Bailenson, *Experience on Demand: What Virtual Reality Is, How It Works, and What It Can Do* (New York: W. W. Norton, 2018).

NOTES

BeAnotherLab: BeAnotherLab, "The Gender Swap," http://beanotherlab.org/home/work/tmtba/body-swap/

Robert Yang, assistant arts professor at NYU Game Center: Robert Yang, "'If You Walk in Someone Else's Shoes, Then You've Taken Their Shoes': Empathy Machines as Appropriation Machines," *Radiator Blog*, April 5, 2017, https://www.blog.radiator.debacle.us/2017/04/if-you-walk-in-someone-elses-shoes-then.html?m=1

Anna Anthropy, creator of Dys4ia: Joseph Dussault, "Empathy Games Tread Thin Line Between 'Edutainment' and Virtual Voyeurism," *Christian Science Monitor*, September 20, 2017, https://www.csmonitor.com/Technology/2017/0920/Empathy-games-tread-thin-line-between-edutainment-and-virtual-voyeurism#:~:text=%E2%80%9CEmpathy%20games%20rarely%20address%20how,that%20leads%20into%20actionable%20behavior.%E2%80%9D

heartfelt TED Talk: Amy Noel Green, "A Video Game to Cope with Grief," TED, February 2017, https://www.ted.com/talks/amy_green_a_video_game_to_cope_with_grief

two-hour gameplay led by Markiplier: Markiplier, "That Dragon, Cancer," July 16, 2016, 1:57:03, https://www.youtube.com/watch?v=5sWTD6vmH_U

Jane McGonigal: "You Found Me," https://janemcgonigal.com/meet-me/

three billion active players worldwide: Microsoft News Center, "Microsoft to Acquire Activision Blizzard to Bring the Joy and Community of Gaming to Everyone, Across Every Device," Microsoft, January 18, 2022, https://news.microsoft.com/2022/01/18/microsoft-to-acquire-activision-blizzard-to-bring-the-joy-and-community-of-gaming-to-everyone-across-every-device/

CEO Satya Nadella: Microsoft News Center, "Microsoft to Acquire Activision Blizzard."

sexually assaulted by three or four male avatars: Nina Jane Patel, "Reality or Fiction?," *Kabuni*, December 21, 2021, https://medium.com/kabuni/fiction-vs-non-fiction-98aa0098f3b0

Invisible Women: Caroline Criado Perez, *Invisible Women: Data Bias in a World Designed for Men* (New York: Abrams Books, 2019).

Marlynn Wei, Harvard- and Yale-trained psychiatrist: Marlynn Wei, "Can Empathy Exist in the Metaverse and Virtual Reality?," *Psychology Today*, December 12, 2021, https://www.psychologytoday.com/ca/blog/urban-survival/202112/can-empathy-exist-in-the-metaverse-and-virtual-reality

According to Statista: Statista, "Number of Global Social Network Users 2017–2025," January 28, 2022, https://www.statista.com/statistics/278414/number-of-worldwide-social-network-users/#:~:text=Social%20media%20usage%20is%20one,almost%204.41%20billion%20in%202025

NOTES

Pew Research Center study: Lee Rainie and Kathryn Zickuhr, "Chapter 4: Phone Use in Social Gatherings," *Pew Research Center*, August 26, 2015, https://www.pewresearch.org/internet/2015/08/26/chapter-4-phone-use-in-social-gatherings/

reverse engineered to keep us hooked: Asurion, "Americans Check Their Phones 96 Times a Day," November 21, 2019, https://www.asurion.com/press-releases/americans-check-their-phones-96-times-a-day/

worse about their life: Monica Anderson and Jingjing Jiang, "Teens and Their Experiences on Social Media," *Pew Research Center*, November 28, 2018, https://www.pewresearch.org/internet/2018/11/28/teens-and-their-experiences-on-social-media/

"We have seen over and over": Paul Sandle and Kate Holton, "Facebook Will Fuel Further Unrest, Whistleblower Says," Reuters, October 25, 2021, https://www.reuters.com/technology/facebook-sees-safety-cost-whistleblower-says-2021-10-25/

nonprofit organization called Bridge Builders: Personal interview, 2021.

most subversive thing you can do: Dylan Maron, "Empathy Is Not Endorsement," TED, April 2018, https://www.ted.com/talks/dylan_marron_empathy_is_not_endorsement?language=en

technologist Harper Reed: Personal interview, 2022.

Klaus Schwab: Klaus Schwab, "The Fourth Industrial Revolution: What It Means, How to Respond," World Economic Forum, January 14, 2016, https://www.weforum.org/agenda/2016/01/the-fourth-industrial-revolution-what-it-means-and-how-to-respond/

Silicon architect Sebastien Ahmed: Sebastian Ahmed, "The Empathy of Maintainable Code," Linkedin, December 23, 2020, https://www.linkedin.com/pulse/empathy-maintainable-code-sebastien-ahmed/

Empathy-Driven Software Development: Andrea Goulet, *Empathy-Driven Software-Development* (Boston: Addison-Wesley, 2013).

psychological safety and a sense of belonging: Personal interview, 2021.

April Wensel founded Compassionate Coding: April Wensel, "What Does Compassion Have to Do with Coding?" *Compassionate Coding*, August 15, 2016, https://compassionatecoding.com/blog/2016/8/15/what-does-compassion-have-to-do-with-coding

hostility and isolation in the workplace: Nadya Fouad et al., "Women's Reasons for Leaving the Engineering Field," *Frontiers in Psychology; Organizational Psychology* 8, no. 875 (June 30, 2017), https://www.frontiersin.org/articles/10.3389/fpsyg.2017.00875/full

major factor impeding success: Cindy Heath, "Empathy Allows Better Software Creation," April 21, 2021, https://medium.com/digital-diplomacy/empathy-allows-better-software-creation-dca8ffce37d7

Industry veteran Luke Heath: Luke Heath, "Empathy in Engineering," Heath Software, September 12, 2018, https://heath.software/articles/empathy-in-engineering

half of the total US workforce: Adeva, "The State of Women in Tech," 2021, https://adevait .com/state-of-women-in-tech

2019 survey conducted by Wired: "Five Years of Tech Diversity Reports—And Little Progress," *Wired*, October 1, 2019, https://www.wired.com/story/five-years-tech-diversity -reports-little-progress/

McKinsey also reported: Michael Conway, Kweilin Ellingrud, Tracy Nowski, and Renee Wittemye, "Closing the Tech Gender Gap through Philanthropy and Corporate Social Responsibility," *McKinsey and Company*, September 12, 2018, https://www.mckinsey .com/industries/technology-media-and-telecommunications/our-insights/closing -the-tech-gender-gap-through-philanthropy-and-corporate-social-responsibility

so-called "pipeline problem": Lauren Feiner, "Tech Companies Made Big Pledges to Fight Racism Last Year—Here's How They're Doing So Far," CNBC, June 6, 2021, https:// www.cnbc.com/2021/06/06/tech-industry-2020-anti-racism-commitments-progress -check.html

racially and ethnically diverse women: "Women in the Tech Industry: Gaining Ground, but Facing New Headwinds," https://www2.deloitte.com/us/en/insights/industry /technology/technology-media-and-telecom-predictions/2022/statistics-show-women -in-technology-are-facing-new-headwinds.html

Some adjustments that she suggests: Personal interview, 2022.

Amar Peterman, director of the Center for Empathy in Christian and Public Life: Amar D. Peterman, "How the Metaverse Will Pull Us Further Apart," *Sojourners*, November 18, 2021, https://sojo.net/articles/how-metaverse-will-pull-us-further-apart

CHAPTER 7

Brené Brown defines spirituality: Brené Brown, *The Gifts of Imperfection* (Center City, MN: Hazelden Publishing, 2010), 64.

The Circle from East to West: Jean-Francois Charnier, "The Circle from East to West," in *The Louvre Abu Dhabi: A World Vision of Art* (Paris: Skira, 2019).

complex geometric patterns: Department of Islamic Art, "Geometric Patterns in Islamic Art," in *Helibrunn Timeline of Art History* (New York: The Metropolitan Museum of Art, 2001), https://www.metmuseum.org/toah/hd/geom/hd_geom.htm

Sufi concept called "unity in diversity": Personal interview, 2021.

Steve Taylor, a British transpersonal psychologist: Steve Taylor, "Empathy: The Power of Connection," 2012, https://www.stevenmtaylor.com/essays/empathy-power-connection/

The Perfume of Silence: Francis Lucille, *Perfume of Silence* (Temecula, CA: Truespeech Prod., 2006).

exile in Plum Village: Helen Tworkov, "Interbeing with Thich Nhat Hanh: An Interview," *Tricycle Magazine,* 1995, https://tricycle.org/magazine/interbeing-thich-nhat-hanh -interview/

We do not exist independently: Thich Nhat Hanh, "The Insight of Interbeing," Garrison Institute, August 2, 2017, https://www.garrisoninstitute.org/blog/insight-of-interbeing/

simile called clouds in each paper: Thich Nhat Hanh, "Clouds in Each Paper," Awakin, 2002, https://www.awakin.org/v2/read/view.php?tid=222

everything in the universe is inseparable and interconnected: "What Is Nonduality?" *Science and Nonduality,* https://www.scienceandnonduality.com/article/what-is-nonduality

Psychoanalyst Sigmund Freud: Sigmund Freud, *The Ego and the Id* (New York: W. W. Norton, 1961), 13.

One Mind: Larry Dossey, *One Mind: How Our Individual Mind Is Part of a Great Consciousness and Why It Matters* (Carlsbad, CA: Hay House Inc., 2013).

Australian Aborigine writer Mudrooroo: Mudrooroo, *Us Mob: History, Culture, Struggle: An Introduction to Indigenous Australia* (New York: Angus and Robertson, 1995), 33.

The Empathy Effect: Roman Krznaric, "The Empathy Effect: How Empathy Drives Common Values, Social Justice and Environmental Action," March 2015, Friends of the Earth, https://dokumen.tips/documents/the-empathy-effect-by-roman-krznaric.html?page=1

As Dr. King wrote: Martin Luther King Jr., *Strength to Love* (New York: Harper and Row, 1963), 77.

Social psychologist Kenneth B. Clark: K. B. Clark, "Empathy: A Neglected Topic in Psychological Research," *American Psychologist* 35, no. 2 (1980): 187–190, https://doi.org/10.1037/0003-066X.35.2.187

New Forms of Transformative Education: Ann Curry-Stevens, "New Forms of Transformative Education: Pedagogy for the Privileged," *Journal of Transformative Education* 5, no. 1 (January 1, 2007): 33–58, https://journals.sagepub.com/doi/abs/10.1177/1541344607299394

"the action and reflection of men and women": Paulo Freire, *Pedagogy of the Oppressed: 30th Anniversary Edition* (The Continuum International Publishing Group: New York, 2000), 79.

Why Empathy Matters: J. D. Trout, *Why Empathy Matters: The Science and Psychology of Better Judgment* (New York: Penguin Books, 2010), 26.

Revolutionary Love Project: Valerie Kaur, "The Revolutionary Love Project," https://valariekaur.com/revolutionary-love-project/

See No Stranger: Valeria Kaur, *See No Stranger* (New York: Penguin Random House, 2018).

Revolutionary Love: Michael Lerner, *Revolutionary Love: A Political Manifesto to Heal and Transform the World* (Oakland, CA: University of California Press, 2019), 25.

The Time Is Now: Joan Chittister, *Time Is Now: A Call to Uncommon Courage* (New York: Convergent Books, 2019), 15.

Race Matters: Cornel West, *Race Matters, 25th Anniversary* (Boston: Beacon Press, 2017), XV.

massive open online course: "Projects," https://ottoscharmer.com/projects

"transformation of the human heart": Peter Senge, Otto Scharmer, Joseph Jaworski, and Betty Sue Flowers, *Presence: Human Purpose and the Field of the Future* (New York: Doubleday, 2004).

Tibetan Buddhist scholar Jinpa Thupten: Personal interview, 2020.

According to Thich Nhat Hanh: Thich Nhat Hanh, "The Fourteen Precepts of Engaged Buddhism," *Dharma Refuge*, 2017, https://www.dharmarefuge.com/14-precepts-engaged-buddhism.html

"interrelated structure of reality": Martin Luther King Jr., "Remaining Awake through a Great Revolution," Oberlin College Commencement Address, June 1965, https://www2.oberlin.edu/external/EOG/BlackHistoryMonth/MLK/CommAddress.html

"I am more blessed": Personal interview, 2013.

CHAPTER 8

"One Year Road Trip": One Year Road Trip, http://oneyearroadtrip.com/

Matt and Eva wrote in a blog: Conscious Magazine, https://consciousmagazine.co/author/matt-webb/

"we're really not all that different": Personal interview, 2020.

likely to bully their peers: Effrosyni Mitsopoulou and Theodoros Giovazolias, "Personality Traits, Empathy and Bullying Behavior: A Meta-Analytic Approach," *Aggression and Violent Behavior* 21 (2016): 61.

likely to drop out of school: Taylor and Francis Group, "Empathy Helps Explain How Parental Support Can Prevent Teen Delinquency," *Science Daily*, February 22, 2021, https://www.sciencedaily.com/releases/2021/02/210222192833.htm

correlation between empathy and creativity: Helen Demetriou and Bill Nicholl, "Empathy Is the Mother of Invention: Emotion and Cognition for Creativity in the Classroom," *Improving Schools: Sage Journals* 25, no. 1 (January 25, 2021): 4–21, https://journals.sagepub.com/doi/full/10.1177/1365480221989500

Unselfie: Michele Borba, *Unselfie: Why Empathetic Kids Succeed in Our All-About-Me World* (New York: Touchstone, 2016).

Harvard's Making Caring Common Project: Making Caring Common Project, *The Children We Mean to Raise* (Boston: Making Caring Common Project, 2014), https://mcc.gse.harvard.edu/reports/children-mean-raise

parents are more concerned with achievement: Making Caring Common Project, *The Children We Mean to Raise.*

codirector, Richard Weissbourd: Making Caring Common Project, *The Children We Mean to Raise.*

Tomorrow's Change Makers: Marilyn Price-Mitchell, *Tomorrow's Changemakers: Reclaiming the Power of Citizenship for a New Generation* (Bainbridge, WA: Eagle Harbor Publishing, 2015).

bell hooks famously said: bell hooks, *All About Love: New Visions* (New York: Harper, 1999).

Brooke Dodson-Lavalle: Brooke Dodson Lavelle, "Courage of Care. The CourageRISE Model for Building Relational Cultures of Practice," *Arrow Journal* 8, no. 1 (2021): 130–152, https://courageofcare.org/wp-content/uploads/2021/11/RelationSHIFT-The-CourageRISE-Model-for-Building-Relational-Cultures-of-Practice_The-Arrow-Journal-2021.pdf

Communing with people from all walks of life: Personal interview, 2012.

"positive solutions to our common problems": "Our Mission," https://www.empathytent.com/our-mission

Abrahamic religions of Judaism and Islam: Karen Armstrong, *A History of God* (New York: Penguin Random House, 1993).

"compassionate actions of its members": L.A. Times Archives, "King's Widow Urges Acts of Compassion," January 17, 2000, https://www.latimes.com/archives/la-xpm-2000-jan-17-mn-54832-story.html

"It was so painful": Personal interview, 2018.

Harvard Business Review: Cassie Mogilner, "You'll Feel Less Rushed If You Give Time Away," *Harvard Business Review,* September 2012, https://hbr.org/2012/09/youll-feel-less-rushed-if-you-give-time-away

improves physical and mental fitness: Office of Disease Prevention and Health Promotion, "Civic Participation. The Healthy People, 2020: Social Determinants of Health

Topic Area," 2020, https://www.healthypeople.gov/2020/topics-objectives/topic/social-determinants-health/interventions-resources/civic-participation

social connectedness: "The Importance of Human Connection," Canadian Mental Health Association, October 17, 2019, https://cmha.ca/the-importance-of-human-connection/#:~:text=Social%20connection%20can%20lower%20anxiety,put%20our%20health%20at%20risk

people with more social group memberships: Kathryn Doyle, "Social Groups after Retirement May Be Good for Longevity," Reuters, February 16, 2016, https://www.reuters.com/article/us-health-retirement-socializing-idUSKCN0VP2KL

Americans' Changing Lives: "Americans' Changing Lives," Institute for Social Research, University of Michigan, https://acl.isr.umich.edu/

those who volunteered were happier: "Americans' Changing Lives."

researchers at Boston College: Boston College, "Community Involvement Study," 2021, https://ccc.bc.edu/content/ccc/research/reports/community-involvement-study.html

fewer risk factors for cardiovascular disease: Meredith Maran, "The Activism Cure," *Greater Good Magazine*, June 1, 2009, https://greatergood.berkeley.edu/article/item/the_activism_cure

lower risk of cognitive impairment: "Civic Participation," *Healthy People*, Office of Disease Prevention and Health Promotion, 2022, https://www.healthypeople.gov/2020/topics-objectives/topic/social-determinants-health/interventions-resources/civic-participation

Why Good Things Happen to Good People: Maran, "The Activism Cure."

CHAPTER 9

major problems or is in a state of crisis: Sigal Samuel, "This Doctor Is Taking Aim at Our Broken Medical System, One Story at a Time," *Vox*, March 5, 2020, https://www.vox.com/the-highlight/2020/2/27/21152916/rita-charon-narrative-medicine-health-care

primary care physicians think: Samuel, "This Doctor Is Taking Aim."

half of patients and doctors: Jill Suttie, "Should We Train Doctors for Empathy?," *Greater Good Magazine*, July 8, 2015, https://greatergood.berkeley.edu/article/item/should_we_train_doctors_for_empathy?_scpsug=crawled,5589,en_89z4H2MBqkjN0pTcheUp#_scpsug=crawled,5589,en_89z4H2MBqkjN0pTcheUp

doctors regularly miss or dismiss signs of patient distress: Suttie, "Should We Train Doctors for Empathy?"

240

NOTES

strong empathic connections between physicians and patients: Ezequiel Gleichgerrcht and Jean Decety, "Empathy in Clinical Practice: How Individual Dispositions, Gender, and Experience Moderate Empathic Concern, Burnout, and Emotional Distress in Physicians," *PLoS ONE* 8, no. 4 (April 19, 2013): e61526, https://www.ncbi.nlm.nih.gov/pmc/articles/PMC3631218/

Doctors with higher levels of empathy: Gleichgerrcht and Decety, "Empathy in Clinical Practice."

stronger immune system and better health: Gleichgerrcht and Decety, "Empathy in Clinical Practice."

patients perceive their caregiver as empathic: David Rakel, Bruce Barrett, Zhengjun Zhang, Theresa Hoeft, Betty Chewning, Lucille Marchand, and Jo Scheder, "Perception of Empathy in the Therapeutic Encounter: Effects on the Common Cold," *Patient Education and Counseling* 85, no. 3 (2011): 390.

In one pre-COVID-19 study: Crystal Hooper et al., "Compassion Satisfaction, Burnout, and Compassion Fatigue among Emergency Nurses Compared with Nurses in Other Selected Inpatient Specialties," *Journal of Emergency Nursing* 36, no. 5 (May 18, 2020): 420–427. https://pubmed.ncbi.nlm.nih.gov/20837210/

greater risk for compassion fatigue: Alex M. Wagaman et al., "The Role of Empathy in Burnout, Compassion Satisfaction, and Secondary Traumatic Stress among Social Workers," *Oxford Journals* 60, no. 3 (July 2015): 201–209, https://www.jstor.org/stable/24881483?seq=1

introducing the concept of a residency program: Robert M. Centor, "To Be a Great Physician, You Must Understand the Whole Story," *MedGenMed: Medscape General Medicine* 9, no. 1 (March 26, 2007): 59, https://www.ncbi.nlm.nih.gov/pmc/articles/PMC1924990/

empathy dwindles in year three: Eleonora Leopardi and Conor Gillian, "Doctors Are Trained to Be Kind and Empathetic—But a 'Hidden Curriculum' Makes Them Forget on the Job," *The Conversation,* December 12, 2021, https://theconversation.com/doctors-are-trained-to-be-kind-and-empathetic-but-a-hidden-curriculum-makes-them-forget-on-the-job-171942

suicidal ideation during their training: Canadian Medical Association, "One in Four Canadian Physicians Report Burnout," October 10, 2018, https://www.cma.ca/one-four-canadian-physicians-report-burnout

According to Harvard Medical School: Jake Miller, "Paying for Healthcare with Time," *Harvard Medical School,* October 5, 2018, https://hms.harvard.edu/news/paying-health-care-time

NOTES

physicians listen to their patients: N. Singh Ospina et al., "Eliciting the Patient's Agenda— Secondary Analysis of Recorded Clinical Encounters," *Journal of General Internal Medicine* 34, no. 1 (2018): 36–40.

Narrative Medicine: Rita Charon, "Narrative Medicine: A Model for Empathy, Reflection, Profession, and Trust," *Journal of the American Medical Association* 286, no. 15 (2001): 1892–1902, https://jamanetwork.com/journals/jama/fullarticle/194300

Developed and taught at Columbia University: Charon, "Narrative Medicine."

"patient might not tell the whole story": Charon, "Narrative Medicine."

"a powerful instrument for decreasing pain": Charon, "Narrative Medicine."

"doctors who receive narrative training": Sigal Samuel, "This Doctor Is Taking Aim at Our Broken Medical System, One Story at a Time," *Vox*, March 5, 2020, https://www.vox.com/the-highlight/2020/2/27/21152916/rita-charon-narrative-medicine-health-care

structural inequality and social justice in healthcare: "Narrative Medicine," https://sps.columbia.edu/academics/masters/narrative-medicine

"better understanding between physicians and patients": Helen Riess, *The Empathy Effect: 7 Neuroscience-based Keys for Transforming the Way We Live, Love, Work, and Connect Across Differences* (Louisville, CO: Sounds True Publishing, 2018), 44.

"on a personal level": Helen Riess, *The Empathy Effect*, 51.

"disconnected from each other": Brené Brown, *Atlas of the Heart: Mapping Meaningful Connection and the Language of Human Experience* (New York: Random House, 2021).

"seen as aggressive": "Improve Your Tone of Voice in Communication," https://www.tonyrobbins.com/love-relationships/watching-your-tone/

two separate studies investigating the E.M.P.A.T.H.Y approach: Helen Riess, John M. Kelley, Robert W. Bailey, Emily J. Dunn, and Margot Phillips, "Empathy Training for Resident Physicians: A Randomized Controlled Trial of a Neuroscience-Informed Curriculum," *Journal of General Internal Medicine* 27 (2012): 1280–1286, https://www.ncbi.nlm.nih.gov/pmc/articles/PMC3445669/

how to handle a scalpel: VitalTalk, "About Us," https://www.vitaltalk.org/about-us/

balloon to $560 billion: "How Telehealth Maturity Can Keep Pace with Its Growth," https://www.consultancy.eu/news/6647/how-telehealth-maturity-can-keep-pace-with-its-growth

American teachers burn out: David Rakel et al., "Perception of Empathy in the Therapeutic Encounter: Effects on the Common Cold," *Patient Education and Counseling* 85, no. 3 (2011): 390.

242

NOTES

according to a National Education Association poll: Tim Walker, "Survey: Alarming Number of Educators May Soon Leave the Profession," *NEAToday*, February 1, 2022, https://www.nea.org/advocating-for-change/new-from-nea/survey-alarming-number
-educators-may-soon-leave-profession

teachers polled by the American Psychological Association: American Psychological Association, "Teachers, Other School Personnel, Experience Violence, Threats, Harassment During Pandemic," March 17, 2022, https://www.apa.org/news/press/releases
/2022/03/school-staff-violence-pandemic

two decades with Doctors without Borders: Rachel Kiddell-Monroe, "The Power of Choice . . . Choosing Humanity and Solidarity," TEDxMontrealWomend, 2017, https://www
.ted.com/talks/rachel_kiddell_monroe_the_power_of_choice_choosing_humanity
_and_solidarity

according to the CHS Alliance: The Core Humanitarian Standard Alliance and International Council of Voluntary Agencies, *Leading Well: Aid Leaders' Perspectives on Staff Well-Being And Organisational Culture* (Geneva: The Core Humanitarian Standard Alliance and International Council of Voluntary Agencies, 2021), https://d1h79zlghft2zs
.cloudfront.net/uploads/2021/04/Leading-well-report-CHS-Alliance.pdf

disproportionately affected: The Core Humanitarian Standard Alliance and International Council of Voluntary Agencies, *Leading Well.*

mental health of human rights advocates: Amy Joscelyne et al., "Mental Health Functioning in the Human Rights Field: Findings From an International Internet-Based Survey," *PLoS ONE* 10, no. 12 (December 2015): e0145188, https://journals.plos.org/plosone
/article?id=10.1371/journal.pone.0145188

staff wellbeing review at Amnesty International: "Staff Wellbeing Review," Amnesty International, 2019, https://www.amnesty.org/en/wp-content/uploads/2021/05/ORG
6097632019ENGLISH.pdf

felt disillusioned or hopeless: Bert Klandermans, "Disengaging from Movements," in *The Social Movements Reader: Cases and Concepts*, ed. J. Goodwin and J. M. Jasper (Malden, MA: Blackwell, 2003), 116–127.

most prevalent among activists of color: Paul C. Gorski, "Fighting Racism, Battling Burnout: Causes of Activist Burnout in U.S. Racial Justice Activists," *Ethnic and Racial Studies* (2018), advance online publication.

research conducted by the Social Impact Award: Social Impact Award, "New Generation of Social Innovators, Well-Being of Social Entrepreneurs," 2019, https://socialimpactaward
.net/article/wellbeing-social-entrepreneurs-game-changer/

"Wellbeing inspires welldoing": The Wellbeing Project, "Wellbeing Inspires Welldo-ing. How Changemakers' Inner Wellbeing Influences Their Work," 2020, https://wellbeing-project.org/wellbeingreport/

According to Mark Brennan: Mark Brennan, Dana Winters, and Pat Dolan, "We're All First Responders amid Coronavirus, Armed with Kindness, Compassion, and Empathy," March 24, 2020, https://www.usatoday.com/story/opinion/2020/03/24/coronavirus-pandemic-demands-kindness-compassion-empathy-column/2898413001/

the result of secondhand trauma: "Understanding and Coping with Compassion Fatigue in Social Work," Ohio University, September 13, 2021, https://onlinemasters.ohio.edu/blog/what-is-compassion-fatigue/

Compassion satisfaction: Cynthia Rae Harr, Tanya S. Brice, Kelly Riley, and Brenda Moore, "The Impact of Compassion Fatigue and Compassion Satisfaction on Social Work Students," *University of Chicago Press Journals* 5, no. 2 (2014), https://www.journals.uchicago.edu/doi/full/10.1086/676518

protective factor for mental health: Harr et al., "The Impact of Compassion Fatigue."

CHAPTER 10

Neff describes self-compassion: Kristin Neff, "The Five Myths of Self-Compassion," *Greater Good Magazine*, 2015, https://greatergood.berkeley.edu/article/item/the_five_myths_of_self_compassion

three elements of self-compassion: Kristin Neff and Christopher Germer, "Mindful Communications and Such," PBC, January 29, 2019, https://www.mindful.org/the-transformative-effects-of-mindful-self-compassion/

members of racialized groups: Shuyi Lui et al., "Self-Compassion and Social Connected-ness Buffering Racial Discrimination on Depression among Asian Americans," *Mindfulness* 11 (2020): 672–682, https://link.springer.com/article/10.1007/s12671-019-01275-8

the LGBTQ+ community: Abra J. Vigna et al., "Does Self-Compassion Facilitate Resilience to Stigma? A School-Based Study of Sexual and Gender Minority Youth," *Mindfulness* 9 (2018): 914–924, https://link.springer.com/article/10.1007/s12671-017-0831-x

According to Salzberg: Sharon Salzberg, "What Is Loving-Kindness? And How to Prac-tice It in an Era of Intolerance," February 28, 2018, https://medium.com/s/redefining-real-love/what-is-loving-kindness-cec0490de6c7

The Force of Kindness: Sharon Salzberg, *The Force of Kindness: Change Your Life with Love and Compassion* (Louisville, KY: Sounds True, 2005).

reciting mettā phrases: Makenzie E. Tonelli and Amy B. Wachholtz, "Meditation-Based Treatment Yielding Immediate Relief for Meditation-Naïve Migraineurs," *National Library of Medicine* 15, no. 1 (June 20, 2012): 36–40, https://pubmed.ncbi.nlm.nih.gov/24602422/

Exposure to natural environments: Richard M. Ryan et al., "Vitalizing Effects of Being Outdoors and in Nature," *Journal of Environmental Psychology* 30, no. 2 (June 2010): 159–168, https://www.sciencedirect.com/science/article/abs/pii/S0272494409000838

average American spends 93 percent of their time inside: US Environmental Protection Agency, *Report to Congress on Indoor Air Quality: Volume 2* (Washington, DC: US Environmental Protection Agency, 1989), EPA/400/1-89/001C.

the United Nations predicts: "2018 Revision of the World Urbanization Prospects," United Nations, 2018, https://population.un.org/wup/

This does not bode well: Jenny Roe, "Cities, Green Space, and Mental Well-Being," *Environmental Science,* November 22, 2016.

shinrin-yoku as a form of ecotherapy: Bum Jin Park et al., "The Physiological Effects of Shinrin-yoku (Taking in the Forest Atmosphere or Forest Bathing): Evidence from Field Experiments in 24 Forests Across Japan," *Environmental Health and Preventative Medicine* 15, no. 18 (2010), https://environhealthprevmed.biomedcentral.com/articles/10.1007/s12199-009-0086-9#:~:text=The%20term%20Shinrin%2Dyoku%20was,in%2024%20forests%20across%20Japan

Dr. Qing Li: Harriet Sherwood, "Getting Back to Nature: How Forest Bathing Can Make Us Feel Better," *The Guardian,* June 8, 2019, https://www.theguardian.com/environment/2019/jun/08/forest-bathing-japanese-practice-in-west-wellbeing

According to the World Health Organization: World Health Organization, "What Do We Mean by Self-Care?," June 15, 2018, https://www.who.int/news-room/feature-stories/detail/what-do-we-mean-by-self-care#:~:text=WHO%20defines%20self%2Dcare%20as,support%20of%20a%20healthcare%20provider%E2%80%9D

Not only is today's global: "The Global Wellness Economy: Looking Beyond COVID," Global Wellness Institute, 2021, https://globalwellnessinstitute.org/industry-research/the-global-wellness-economy-looking-beyond-covid/

The Empathy Effect: Roman Krznaric, *The Empathy Effect: How Empathy Drives Common Values, Social Justice and Environmental Action,* March 2015, Friends of the Earth, https://dokumen.tips/documents/the-empathy-effect-by-roman-krznaric.html?page=1

two-thirds of African-American women: Delores C. S. James et al., "Barriers and Motivators to Physical Activity among African American Women," *The Health Educator* 46, no. 2 (2014), https://files.eric.ed.gov/fulltext/EJ1153589.pdf

59 percent are obese: Harvard, "Adult Obesity. Obesity Prevention Source," Harvard School of Public Health, 2020, https://www.hsph.harvard.edu/obesity-prevention-source/obesity-trends/obesity-rates-worldwide/

higher rates of hypertension: "Life Expectancy in the United States," *Every CRS Report*, August 16, 2006, https://www.everycrsreport.com/reports/RL32792.html

GirlTrek was created: GirlTrek, https://www.girltrek.org/

"radical act of self-love": GirlTrek.

public response to the crisis: Maria Fernandes-Jesus et al., "More Than a COVID-19 Response: Sustaining Mutual Aid Groups During and Beyond the Pandemic," *Frontiers in Psychology; Cultural Psychology* 12 (October 20, 2021): 716202, https://www.frontiersin.org/articles/10.3389/fpsyg.2021.716202/full

Out in the Open: Out in the Open, "About Us," https://www.weareoutintheopen.org/about-us

Mutual Aid Disaster Relief: Mutual Aid Disaster Relief, "About," https://mutualaiddisasterrelief.org/about/

"adverse experiences" in childhood: Thomas Hübl and Jordan Julie Avritt, *Healing Collective Trauma: A Process for Integrating Our Intergenerational and Cultural Wounds* (Louisville, KY: Sounds True, 2020), 20.

Holocaust survivors: "Transgenerational Trauma," https://en.wikipedia.org/wiki/Transgenerational_trauma

collective trauma: "Transgenerational Trauma."

Symptoms include substance abuse: Hübl and Avritt, *Healing Collective Trauma.*

Thomas Hübl is a spiritual teacher: Hübl and Avritt, *Healing Collective Trauma.*

Using a five-part model: Courage of Care, https://courageofcare.org/

Weave: The Social Fabric Project: "Weave: The Social Fabric Project," https://www.aspeninstitute.org/programs/weave-the-social-fabric-initiative/

The Second Mountain: David Brooks, *The Second Mountain: The Quest for a Moral Life* (New York: Random House, 2019).

The Relationalist Manifesto: "The Relationalist Manifesto," https://www.aspeninstitute.org/blog-posts/the-relationalist-manifesto/

CONCLUSION

The Empathic Civilization: Jeremy Rifkin, *The Empathic Civilization: The Race to Global Consciousness in a World in Crisis* (New York: TarcherPerigee, 2006), 160.

NOTES

UN SDGs could be achieved by 2050: Robert David Steele, "Beyond Data Monitoring," UN Paper, Public Intelligence Blog, 2014.

Designing Regenerative Cultures: Daniel Christian Wahl, *Designing Regenerative Cultures* (Axminster, England: Triarchy Press), 191.

"Quantum physicists posit": Kathryn Pavlovich, "Quantum Empathy: An Alternative Narrative for Global Transcendence," *Journal of Management, Spirituality and Religion* 17 (2020): 333.

John Helliwell, a professor at the University of British Columbia: Shirley Cardenas, "Amid War and Disease, World Happiness Report Shows Bright Spot," McGill Newsroom, March 18, 2022, https://www.mcgill.ca/newsroom/channels/news/amid-war-and-disease-world-happiness-report-shows-bright-spot-338506

LAND ACKNOWLEDGMENT

This book was written on the traditional land of Kanien'kehá:ka, which has long served as a site of meeting and exchange among First Nations. I am grateful to the many generations of stewardship, and I support all efforts to nurture a relationship with Indigenous peoples based on respect, trust, empathy, and cooperation that advance truth, reconciliation, and justice.

PERSONAL
ACKNOWLEDGMENTS

I have discovered that the sweetest part of writing a book is acknowledging everyone who helped me bring it to fruition. It's also bittersweet since it means my book really is done!

Along the way, many friends suggested that I self-publish. Instead, I stubbornly trusted my instincts that I would write a better book with a traditional publisher. And I was right. Everything good about *Purposeful Empathy* can be traced back to my incredible literary agent, Tom Miller, and fabulous editor, Lisa Kloskin.

I value Tom's brilliance, integrity, work ethic, expertise, sound counsel, and good judgment. He deserves credit for the book's title and helping me overcome my addiction to numbered lists. I love that he calls me "a force of nature" and I'll never forget his words, "It sounds like they want to publish the book that you want to write." He went above and beyond for me. As an author, I really have no words.

A huge thanks to Lisa who understood and respected my vision from the very start and gave me the perfect blend of "light touch" and substantive editorial feedback along the way. I felt completely supported by her and fully expressed. Our collaboration was an absolute delight and I congratulate her on the birth of her second child, who arrived just days before my manuscript was submitted.

Working with the entire Broadleaf team has been a pleasure. In particular, I want to thank James Kegley for designing my gorgeous book cover, Adrienne Ingrum, and Pete Feely, as well as the whole sales and marketing group.

I'm also grateful for the magical way *Purposeful Empathy* came to be. Thank you, John Wood, Bonnie Solow, Len Blum, Laura Corrales, Michael Ventura, and David Moldawer for being my "book angels." A special shout-out to Mitch Joel who not only welcomed me into his "Write and Rant" community, but gave me confidence and encouragement by suggesting that I use this line in my proposal: "What Brené Brown did for vulnerability, Anita Nowak will do for empathy."

I will always appreciate the incredible advising, coaching, mentoring, and healing that I received from the following professionals and friends: Simone Hanchet, Adam Halpert, Saman Nasir, Bianca Huot, Milla Craig, Gail Golden, Brett House, and Brenda Keesal (you were right, "It's already written.").

I would be remiss not to thank the many amazing women who have supported me on my professional journey and helped me grow my platform and impact. This includes all my IWF sisters and the members of Lynn's Jelly Bean mastermind group. In particular, I want to acknowledge Cathy Rowe, Colette Vanasse, Marna Pennell, Grace Yang, Elissa Bernstein, Kathy Fazel, Sylvie Mercier, Francoise Lyon, Mirella De Civita, Katherine Wilkinson, Desirée McGraw, and Maka Topuridze.

I'm deeply indebted to the dedicated group of alumni who became part of "Team Purposeful Empathy," especially Lina Dieudonné, Heela Khan Achakzai, Chloe Aboud, Sinthura Chandramohan, Kayla Lafreniere, Cat Carkner, Sashka Avanyan, and David Tsvariani. Thanks also to Dimitri Yang, Brandon Pellegrini, Morgan Davis, Mahaut Armand, Corentin Jeanrot, Jessica Xiao, and Boyan Francuz.

I owe an ongoing debt of gratitude to all the original interviewees of my PhD, as well as everyone who accepted my invitation for an interview for this book or my podcast and YouTube series.

Thank you to the Somers family, the Fortin family, the Shorefast Foundation, the Jeanne Sauvé Foundation, the Governor General Leadership Conference, the International Women's Forum, my PVM Studio partners Caren Yanis and Michael Colson, my personal board of advisors, and all my

McGill students and alumni who have given me so much encouragement over the years.

Thanks also to three inspiring authors who helped me become a member of that special tribe: Steven Pressfield, who helped me "slay resistance" and turn pro. Elizabeth Gilbert, who imbued me with "fierce trust" in my capacity to create. And Brené Brown, who reminded me that vulnerability, like empathy, is a superpower.

A heaping dose of bless you's to my best friend, Julie Kavanagh, who helped me spiritually and psychologically throughout this decade-long journey. And Tullio Cedraschi, who has been an unwavering friend and mentor, despite how long it's taken me to get here.

Finally, I want to thank my family in Tbilisi, Montreal and Toronto. I'm especially grateful to my beautiful daughter, Annika, who cheered me on throughout kindergarten. But most of all, to the amazing man who is my husband. Giorgi, you were my anchor, my sounding board, my soft place to land, and my partner. You listened to every single word I read aloud (time and again) and held down the fort for our family, giving me the time and space I needed to make this dream come true. I lu lu. *Me sheni zalian madlieri var!*